Study Guide

BUSINESS TODAY

Study Guide

Douglas W. Copeland

Johnson County Community College

BUSINESS TODAY

NINTH EDITION

MICHAEL H.
MESCON

COURTLAND L.
BOVÉE

JOHN V.
THILL

PRENTICE HALL, UPPER SADDLE RIVER, NEW JERSEY 07458

Acquisitions editor: *Donald J. Hull*
Associate editor: *Kristen R. Imperatore*
Project editor: *Joan Waxman*
Manufacturer: *Quebecor Printing Group*

Printed in the United States of America

10 9 8 7 6 5 4

ISBN 0-13-096229-5

PRENTICE-HALL INTERNATIONAL (UK) LIMITED, *LONDON*
PRENTICE-HALL OF AUSTRALIA PTY. LIMITED, *SYDNEY*
PRENTICE-HALL CANADA INC., *TORONTO*
PRENTICE-HALL HISPANOAMERICANA, S.A., *MEXICO*
PRENTICE-HALL OF INDIA PRIVATE LIMITED, *NEW DELHI*
PRENTICE-HALL OF JAPAN, INC., *TOKYO*
PEARSON EDUCATION ASIA PTE. LTD., *SINGAPORE*
EDITORA PRENTICE-HALL DO BRASIL, LTDA., *RIO DE JANEIRO*

CONTENTS

...continued on next page...

PREFACE

From the beginning I have tried to create a *Study Guide* that I would want as a student. Therefore, this *Study Guide* is designed to serve two major goals. First, by complimenting the material presented in *Business Today*, Ninth Edition, I hope to increase your understanding and appreciation of business. If I am successful, you will be better equipped to respond intelligently to real-world business-related issues that you read and hear about every day. After all, many international business affairs have far reaching implications for your personal life. Furthermore, a firm grasp of business is invaluable to those of you pursuing careers in business.

Second, and possibly of more immediate and practical concern to you, this *Study Guide* has been designed to prepare you for your examinations--to help you maximize your grade from this class given your limited studying time. I am confident that if you work through each chapter of the *Study Guide* in its entirety after you have studied the chapter in the textbook, you will enter your tests with confidence and will score accordingly. I hope you come to view this *Study Guide* as a close and helpful companion--a much appreciated tutor.

It should be kept in mind that this *Study Guide* is not a substitute for the textbook. Instead, it is a supplement. You should work through each chapter in the *Study Guide* only after you have studied the assigned chapter in the textbook.

The format of each chapter of this book has been designed to maximize your mastery of the material and therefore your ability to perform well on the exams. The order in which you tackle each of these sections is up to you. But you are strongly encouraged to work through *all* of the sections for each of the chapters you are assigned. This is because some sections focus more intently on some concepts introduced in the textbook than do other sections. The specific sections of each chapter are outlined below.

LEARNING OBJECTIVES
You should be able to accomplish these learning objectives after studying the chapter and working through the *Study Guide*. Page references to the text are added for your convenience.

TRUE-FALSE
These true-false questions will be very similar to the types of true-false questions found on your exams (if your professor gives these types of questions--ask your teacher whether or not that is the case). Even if your professor does not ask these types of questions on the exams, you are still strongly encouraged to work through this section anyway. To increase your learning, you are asked to correct any false statements by making them true statements. The answers for this section, as well as all others, are provided at the end of the chapter.

MULTIPLE CHOICE
These multiple-choice questions will be very similar to those you find on your exams--especially considering that most professors give multiple-choice type exams. Choose the one best answer from the options provided. You are strongly encouraged to correct the incorrect responses to make them correct. By doing so, you will come to recognize the subtle differences between potential answers. This is a skill required to be successful in performing well on multiple-choice type exams.

JEOPARDY
The "Jeopardy" games are intended to be a fun way to learn some of the key points and concepts introduced in the textbook. For added "fun," you are asked to provide the "question" tot he answer provided within approximately 5 seconds. If you are unable to do so, you may want to review that concept or topic. Page references are also provided.

MATCH THE TERMS AND CONCEPTS TO THEIR DEFINITIONS

This section is important because many test questions will ask you to define a term or a concept. Moreover, learning the language of business is half the task to understanding business. Page references are provided for your convenience.

WORD SCRAMBLE

This has been added for the fun of it. Many people enjoy these.

LEARNING OBJECTIVES--POTENTIAL SHORT ANSWER OR ESSAY QUESTIONS

Many of you will have professors that will give you "Short Answer" and/or "Essay" type questions. If so, then this section will be particularly useful to you. However, even if you do not expect these types of questions on exams, you are still strongly encouraged to work through this section. It will help you accomplish the learning objectives of this chapter. Page references are provided.

CRITICAL THINKING QUESTIONS

These questions are designed to illicit a higher level of thinking by requiring you to pull together various concepts introduced in the chapter.

BRAIN TEASER

This section consists of one question that is generally one step up in the level of difficulty from the "Critical Thinking Questions." Do not be distraught if you have some difficulty with this question. Remember, "no pain, no gain." You can always consult with your teacher if you are distressed. But, as always, an answer is provided at the end of the chapter.

ANSWERS

This final section of each chapter provides the answers to all of the exercises.

It should not take you too long to work through the material for each chapter in this *Study Guide*. Considering the payoffs, I strongly urge you to do so!

I hope you find this *Study Guide* useful and your course fulfilling.

People to Thank

I wish to thank Kristen Imperatore, editor, for providing me the opportunity to write this book. A very special thanks also goes to Peggy Bray for all her typing help. She was very professional and conscientious. Finally, my very deep thanks go to my wife, Mette.

Douglas W. Copeland
Johnson County Community College

To My Children...

Katrine Mette, Nina Elisabeth, and Paul Nord Copeland

Chapter 1

Foundations and Challenges of Business

LEARNING OBJECTIVES

After studying this chapter, you should be able to:

1. Explain what an economic system is. (2)
2. Name the three major types of economic systems. (2-3)
3. Identify the four major economic roles of the U.S. government. (5-9)
4. List three ways companies compete. (9-11)
5. Explain how supply and demand interact to influence price. (11-13)
6. Name the four factors of production, and discuss why they are becoming less of a competitive advantage in the global marketplace. (14-16)
7. Define the gross domestic product, and explain what it is used for. (16-17)
8. Identify five trends that will influence the economy in years ahead. (20-22)

TRUE-FALSE

Indicate whether the statement is generally true or false by placing a "T" or "F" in the space provided. If it is a false statement, correct it so that it becomes a true statement.

___T___ 1. Capitalism is an economic system characterized by public ownership and operation of key industries combined with private ownership and operation of less vital industries.

___T___ 2. A free market system is an economic system in which the way people spend their money determines which products will be produced and what those products will cost.

___F___ 3. Privatization has, in part, been occurring in many countries because of the difficulty many governments have had in running state-run enterprises.

___F___ 4. Historically, government has played no role in capitalism.

___T___ 5. In order to foster competition, sometimes it is useful for government to regulate more, while, at other times, it is appropriate to deregulate businesses.

___F___ 6. Monopolistic competition exists when a market is dominated by a few producers.

___F___ 7. Government uses fiscal and monetary policies to try to stabilize the business cycle.

___T___ 8. Companies compete with rivals on the basis of price, quality, and innovation.

___F___   9. Macroeconomics is an investigation of a particular segment of the economy, whereas microeconomics is interested in the national economic scene.

___F___   10. One of the challenges facing businesses in the United States today is the need to ignore global economic trends and focus solely on the needs of consumers at home.

MULTIPLE CHOICE
Circle the one best answer for each of the following questions.

1. Globalization implies
   a. opportunities as well as challenges and threats for businesses.
   b. a more integrated global economic system.
   c. a more competitive global marketplace in which only the most efficient firms will survive.
   d. all of the above.

2. In a free market system,
   a. businesses are almost guaranteed to earn a profit.
   b. the way people spend their money determines which products will be produced and what those products will cost.
   c. business owners have little control over pricing, quality, and innovation.
   d. there is little economic freedom and choice.

3. Capitalism is characterized by
   a. economic freedom and competition.
   b. public ownership over all productive resources.
   c. public ownership and operation of key industries combined with private ownership and operation of less vital industries.
   d. government control over prices and what gets produced.

4. Which of the following is *not* one of the roles of government in a capitalist economy?
   a. Enforcing laws and regulation
   b. Contributing to economic stability
   c. Reducing competition
   d. Spending for the public good

5. Pure competition is a situation in which
   a. there are so many buyers and sellers that no single buyer or seller has the ability to influence market price.
   b. many sellers differentiate their products from their competitors in at least some small way.
   c. the market is dominated by a few producers.
   d. the market is dominated by a single producer.

6. Which of the following is statements is true?
   a. Deregulation is the removal or relaxation of rules and restrictions affecting businesses.
   b. Competition is the situation in which two or more suppliers of a product are rivals in the pursuit of the same customers.
   c. Most of the competition in advanced free-market economies is monopolistic competition.
   d. All of the above are true.

7. Which of the following statements is *false*?
    a. True monopolies are prohibited by federal antitrust laws.
    b. The government has the power to prevent combinations of firms that would reduce competition.
    c. Recessions and inflation are a result of government fiscal and monetary policies.
    d. Examples of transfer payments include Social Security, food stamps, welfare and unemployment compensation.

8. Companies may compete on the basis of
    a. price.
    b. quality.
    c. innovation.
    d. all of the above.

9. Which of the following is true?
    a. When markets become filled with competitors and products start to look alike, price often becomes a company's key competitive weapon.
    b. Companies that compete on the basis of quality and service may well end up with a total profit that is equal to or greater than the profit of a business that competes on price.
    c. Innovation can be a key to success for a firm that is able to develop a new product that rivals are unable to duplicate.
    d. All of the above are true.

10. Which of the following is true concerning a market?
    a. Demand indicates that as the price goes up, sales increase.
    b. An equilibrium price exists when the quantity demanded equals the quantity supplied.
    c. Supply shows how much people will buy at various prices.
    d. If demand increases in a market, then the price of the product will likely fall.

11. Which of the following is *not* one of the factors of production?
    a. Natural resources
    b. Money
    c. Capital
    d. Entrepreneurs

12. Which of the following statements is true?
    a. Macroeconomics is concerned with some particular segment of the economic system.
    b. Microeconomics is concerned with the overall national economy.
    c. Gross national product excludes receipts from foreign-owned businesses within a nation's borders.
    d. Gross domestic product includes receipts from overseas operations of domestic producers.

13. Which of the following is *false*?
    a. The United States dominates the global economy more now than ever before.
    b. Technology is becoming increasingly important in determining not only a company's competitive advantage, but a nation's competitive advantage as well.
    c. Doing business in the twenty-first century means working in a world of increasing uncertainty as the very nature of work, organizations, and economics is changing.
    d. The United States has experienced periods of recession and inflation and will likely continue to do so in the future.

14. Which of the following is true concerning the challenges facing American businesses in the future?
   a. Businesses will need to compete more aggressively on the basis of time, quality, and customer satisfaction.
   b. Businesses will have to keep pace with rapidly changing technology and an increasingly competitive global marketplace.
   c. Businesses must cope with the rising public scrutiny of their social, ethical, and environmental performance.
   d. All of the above are true.

JEOPARDY

You have 5 seconds to complete the question to each of the following answers.

	Economic Systems	**The Ways Companies Compete**	**Economic Trends and Business Challenges**
$100	The means by which a society distributes its resources to satisfy its people's wants. (2) What is *an economic system*?	A company has this if it does something which sets itself apart from rivals. (10) What is *competitive advantage*?	This challenge pertains to speed and quality. (20-21) What is_____?
$200	An economic system in which the way people spend their money determines which products will be produced and what products will cost. (2) What is *a free market system*?	Three general ways in which companies compete. (10-11) What is *quality, price, innovation*?	This challenge pertains to powerful new forces reshaping the world. (21-22) What is_____?
$300	Economic system characterized by public ownership and operation of key industries combined with private ownership and operation of less vital industries. (3) What is *socialism*?	A market dominated by a few producers. (6) What is *oligology*?	This challenge requires creativity and a willingness to exploit new opportunities. (22) What is_____?
$400	Economic system based on economic freedom and competition. (2) What is *capitalism*?	The savings from manufacturing, marketing, or buying large quantities. (5) What is *economies of scale*?	This challenge pertains to business behavior. (22) What is_____?
$500	The economic system most conducive to rising incomes and higher standards of living. (2) What is *capitalism*?	The form of competition most prevalent in real-world markets where firms try to differentiate their products from rivals'. (5) What is *monopolistic competition*?	This challenge pertains to "acting locally but thinking globally." (22) What is_____?

MATCH THE TERMS AND CONCEPTS TO THEIR DEFINITIONS

a. business (2)
b. business cycle (7)
c. capital (14)
d. capitalism (2)
e. communism (3)
f. competition (5)
g. competitive advantage (10)
h. demand (11)
i. demand curve (12)
j. deregulation (5)
k. disinflation (7)
l. economic system (2)
m. economies of scale (5)

n. entrepreneurs (14)
o. equilibrium price (13)
p. factors of production (13)
q. fiscal policy (7)
r. free-market system (2)
s. gross domestic product (GDP) (16)
t. gross national product (GNP) (16)
u. human resources (14)
v. inflation (7)
w. macroeconomics (16)
x. monetary policy (7)
y. monopolistic competition (5)
z. monopoly (6)

aa. natural resources (14)
bb. not-for-profit organization (3)
cc. oligopoly (6)
dd. privatization (4)
ee. profit (2)
ff. pure competition (5)
gg. recession (7)
hh. socialism (3)
ii. supply (7)
jj. supply curve (13)
kk. technology (18)
ll. transfer payments (8)

___w___   1. Study of the economy as a whole.

___a___   2. Activity and enterprise that provides goods and services that an economic system needs.

___l___   3. Means by which a society distributes its resources to satisfy its people's needs.

___z___   4. Market in which there are no direct competitors so that one company dominates.

___h___   5. Buyer's willingness and ability to purchase products.

___ii___   6. Specific quantity of a product that the seller is able and willing to provide.

___aa___   7. Land, forests, minerals, water, and other tangible assets usable in their natural state.

___n___   8. People who accept the risk of failure in the private enterprise system.

___p___   9. Knowledge, tolls, techniques, and activities used in the production of goods and services.

___t___   10. Dollar value of all the final goods and services produced by businesses located within a nation's borders: excludes receipts from overseas operations of domestic companies.

___s___   11. Dollar value of all the final goods and services produced by domestic businesses including receipts from overseas operations: excludes receipts from foreign-owned businesses within a nation's borders.

___jj___   12. Graph of relationship between various prices and the quantity demanded at each price.

___ee___   13. Money left over after expenses and taxes have been deducted from revenue generated by selling goods and services.

___r___   14. Economic system in which the way people spend their money determines which products will be produced and what those products will cost.

___d___   15. Economic system based on economic freedom and competition.

_kh_ 16. Economic system characterized by public ownership and operation of key industries combined with private ownership and operation of less vital industries.

_dd_ 17. Trend to substitute private ownership for public ownership.

_f_ 18. Rivalry among businesses for the same customer.

_j_ 19. Removal or relaxation of rules and restrictions affecting businesses.

_cc_ 20. Market dominated by a few producers.

_b_ 21. Fluctuations in the rate of growth that an economy experiences over a period of several years.

_v_ 22. Economic condition in which prices rise steadily throughout the economy.

_k_ 23. Economic condition in which the rate of inflation declines.

_ll_ 24. Payments by government to individuals that are not made in return for goods and services.

_g_ 25. Ability to perform in one or more ways that competitors cannot match.

_p_ 26. Basic inputs that a society uses to produce goods and services, including natural resources, labor, capital, and entrepreneurship.

_ii_ 27. Graph of relationship between various prices and the quantity supplied at each price.

_c_ 28. The physical, human-made elements used to produce goods and services, such as factories and computers; can also refer to the funds that finance the operations of a business.

_h_ 29. Organization's employees.

_o_ 30. Point at which quantity supplied equals quantity demanded.

_e_ 31. Economic system in which all productive resources are owned and operated by the government, to the elimination of private property.

_bb_ 32. Firm whose primary objective is something other than returning a profit to its owners.

_dd_ 33. Situation in which many sellers differentiate their products from those of competitors in at least some small way.

_m_ 34. Savings from manufacturing, marketing, or buying large quantities.

_ff_ 35. Situation in which so many sellers exist that no single buyer or seller individually influences market prices.

_x_ 36. Government policy and actions taken by the Federal Reserve Board to regulate the nation's money supply.

_q_ 37. Use of government revenue collection and spending to influence the business cycle.

_gg_   38. Period during which national income, employment, and production all fall.

WORD SCRAMBLE

1. _business_   2. _demand_   3. _supply_
   sibnuses   namded   plysup

LEARNING OBJECTIVES--POTENTIAL SHORT ANSWER OR ESSAY QUESTIONS

Learning Objective #1: "Explain what an economic system is." (2)

a system which determine how resources will be used to benifit citizens needs.

Learning Objective #2: "Name the three major types of economic systems." (2-3)

capitalism
communism
socialism

Learning Objective #3: "Identify the four major economic roles of the U.S. government." (5-9)

Learning Objective #4: "List three ways companies compete." (9-11)

price
quality
service

<u>Learning Objective #5:</u> "Explain how supply and demand interact to influence price." (11-13)

<u>Learning Objective #6:</u> "Name the four factors of production, and discuss why they are becoming less of a competitive advantage in the global marketplace." (14-16)

natural resources
human   "
capital
entrepreneurs

<u>Learning Objective #7:</u> "Define the gross domestic product, and explain what it is used for." (16-17)

<u>Learning Objective #8:</u> "Identify five trends that will influence the economy in years ahead." (20-22)

CRITICAL THINKING QUESTIONS

1.   Why is the United States economy described as a *mixed* capitalist system?

2.   Which type of market environment do most businesses operate within: pure competition, monopolistic competition, oligopoly, or monopoly? How do you know?

Pure compeition

BRAIN TEASER

1.   Using demand and supply concepts, explain how a market would respond to an increase in demand.

Depending on the market, they may raise their price on an item if the demand is strong enough.

ANSWERS

True-False--*Answers*

1. False: *Socialism* is an economic system characterized by public ownership and operation of key industries combined with private ownership and operation of less vital industries.
2. True
3. True
4. False: Historically, government has played *an important* role in capitalism *by enforcing laws and regulations, fostering competition, contributing to economic stability, and spending for the public good.*
5. True
6. False: *An oligopoly* exists when a market is dominated by a few producers.
7. True
8. True
9. False: *Microeconomics* is an investigation of a particular segment of the economy, whereas *macroeconomics* is interested in the national economic scene.
10. False: One of the challenges facing businesses in the United States today is the need to *become more aware of* global economic trends and *to meet the needs of a diverse work force.*

Multiple Choice--*Answers*

1. d	5. a	9. d	13. a
2. b	6. d	10. b	14. d
3. a	7. c	11. b	
4. c	8. d	12. c	

Jeopardy--*Answers*

	Economic Systems	The Ways Companies Compete	Economic Trends
$100	an economic system	competitive advantage	the need to support quality initiatives and achieving customer satisfaction
$200	a free market system	on the basis of price, quality, and innovation	the need to keep pace with technology and the internet while embracing innovation
$300	socialism	an oligopoly	the need to start and manage a small business in today's competitive environment
$400	capitalism	economies of scale	the need to behave in an ethically and socially responsible manner
$500	capitalism	monopolistic competition	the need to think globally and commit to a culturally diverse work force

Match the Terms and Concepts to Their Definitions--*Answers*

1. w	6. ii	11. t	16. hh	21. b	26. p	31. e	36. x
2. a	7. aa	12. i	17. dd	22. v	27. jj	32. bb	37. q
3. l	8. n	13. ee	18. f	23. k	28. c	33. y	38. gg
4. z	9. kk	14. r	19. j	24. ll	29. u	34. m	
5. h	10. s	15. d	20. cc	25. g	30. o	35. ff	

Word Scramble--*Answers*

1. business   2. demand   3. supply

Learning Objectives--Potential Short Answer or Essay Questions--*Answers*

Learning Objective #1:
   An economic system is a society's way of producing, distributing, and marketing the goods and services desired by its population.

Learning Objective #2:
   Under capitalism, the factors of production are owned by individuals, who make the business decisions. Citizens have a high degree of economic freedom but also face considerable economic risk. Under communism, the government owns all factors of production and makes all the business decisions. Distinctions between rich and poor are minimized. Under socialism, the state owns and operates key industries but allows private ownership of many businesses. Relatively high taxes permit the government to provide many social services.

Learning Objective #3:
   The U.S. government enforces rules and regulations, fosters competition, contributes to economic stability, and provides goods and transfer payments.

Learning Objective #4:
   Companies compete on the basis of price, quality and service, and innovation.

Learning Objective #5:
   In the simplest sense, supply and demand affect price in the following manner: When price goes up, the quantity demanded goes down, but the supplier's incentive to produce more goes up. When price goes down, the quantity demanded increases, whereas the quantity supplied may (or may not) decline. When the interest of buyers and sellers are in balance, an equilibrium price is established. However, price is more than simple notions of supply and demand, as the examples of medicine and gasoline illustrate.

Learning Objective #6:
   The four historical factors of production are natural resources, human resources, capital, and entrepreneurship. Technology and modern transportation have made it possible for countries to shop around the world for these factors. The key industries of the future will place a greater emphasis on having knowledgeable workers than on these traditional factors.

Learning Objective #7:
   The gross domestic product (GDP) is the sum of all goods and services produced by both domestic and foreign companies as long as they are located within a nation's boundaries. The GDP is used to measure the productivity of a nation and to evaluate the effectiveness of a government's policies and economic systems.

Learning Objective #8:
   The five trends identified in the chapter are (1) the need to compete on the basis of time, quality, and customer satisfaction; (2) the accelerating pace of technological change and the resulting emergence of a new information-based economy; (3) the competition small business faces from industry giants and the global economy; (4) the continued public and governmental scrutiny of business's social, ethical, and environmental performance; and (5) the increasingly global nature of the economy and the challenges of meeting the needs of a diverse work force.

Critical Thinking Questions--*Answers*

1. The United States economy is described as a mixed capitalist system because it combines the elements of pure capitalism (private ownership of resources; economic activity is coordinated through a system of markets and prices) with some government involvement (to correct for the shortcomings associated with an unbridled capitalist system by enforcing laws and regulations, fostering competition, contributing to economic stability, and spending for the public good.)

2. Most companies operate within a monopolistically competitive market environment because most firms compete by differentiating (distinguishing) their product from their rivals in some way or another (in terms of quality, service, packaging, hours of operation, etc.)

Brain Teaser--*Answer*

1. An increase in demand means buyers are willing and able to purchase more at any price (this is reflected graphically as a rightward shift of the demand curve). This creates a temporary shortage at the original equilibrium price (shown graphically as the extent to which the new demand curve lies beyond the supply curve). Buyers will then competitively bid up the price (or sellers realize they can charge a higher price). Over time, as the price rises, the quantity demanded falls, and the quantity supplied rises. As a consequence, the shortage gets smaller. The price continues to rise until the quantity demanded once again equals the quantity supplied. At this point, the new market equilibrium price will be established. Note that, with the help of a graph, it can be seen that because the point of intersection between the demand and supply curves illustrates the equilibrium price and the amount bought and sold, then an increase in demand (an outward or rightward shift of the demand curve) will result in a new point of intersection where the equilibrium price and the amount bought and sold are both greater than before.

Chapter 2

Global Business

LEARNING OBJECTIVES

After studying this chapter, you should be able to:

1. Differentiate between absolute, comparative, and national competitive advantage. (33-34)
2. Distinguish between the balance of trade and the balance of payments. (39-41)
3. Identify four techniques that countries use to protect their domestic industries. (41-44)
4. Outline the arguments for and against protectionism. (44-45)
5. Explain how trading blocs, the GATT, and the WTO affect trade. (44-50)
6. Define foreign exchange, and discuss the effect of a weaker U.S. dollar on U.S. companies that do business abroad. (52-53)
7. Discuss five forms of international business activity. (35-37)
8. Identify six ways to improve communication in an international business relationship. (53-55)

TRUE-FALSE

Indicate whether the statement is generally true or false by placing a "T" or "F" in the space provided. If it is a false statement, correct it so that it becomes a true statement.

F 1. If a nation has a comparative advantage in the production of a good, this means that the nation is relatively more efficient at producing that good than any other nation.

T 2. If a nation has an absolute advantage in the production of a product, then this means the nation possess the ability to be more innovative and to move to a higher level of technology and productivity.

T 3. Licensing is a cooperative partnership in which organizations share investment costs, risks, management, and profits in the development, production, or selling of products.

T 4. A strategic alliance is a long-term relationship in which two or more companies share ideas, resources, and technologies in order to establish competitive advantages.

F 5. Importing is the investment of money by foreign companies in domestic business enterprises.

F 6. The balance of payments is the relationship between the value of the products a nation exports and those it imports.

F 7. A trade deficit exists if a nation exports more than it imports.

F   8. A tariff is a tax on an imported product, whereas a quota is a limit on the quantity allowed to enter the country.

T   9. Countries have created trading blocs as a means of cooperatively trying to reap the benefits associated with free trade among members.

T   10. In addition to promoting free trade by supporting international organizations like the World Trade Organization (WTO), the United States has established domestic agencies and policies that help U.S. companies compete abroad.

T   11. A fixed exchange rate system is a world exchange rate system in which the values of all currencies are determined by supply and demand.

T   12. A weaker U.S. dollar will increase American exports and decrease American imports.

T   13. An international business needs to learn as much as possible about the culture of the foreign countries it does business with.

MULTIPLE CHOICE
Circle the one best answer for each of the following questions.

1. Which of the following statements is true?
    a. Globalization is becoming increasingly more prevalent.
    b. Even if a nation does not have an absolute advantage, it is still beneficial for that nation to participate in international trade if it has a comparative advantage.
    c. Nations trade with each because they are better off by doing so.
    d. All of the above are true.

2. Licensing is
    a. purchasing goods or services form another country and bringing them into one's own country.
    b. an agreement to produce and market another company's product in exchange for a royalty or fee.
    c. a cooperative partnership in which organizations share investment costs, risks, management, and profits in the development, production, or selling of products.
    d. a long-term relationship in which two or more companies share ideas, resources, and technologies in order to establish competitive advantages.

3. Investment of money by foreign companies in domestic business enterprises is
    a. exporting.
    b. licensing.
    c. foreign direct investment (FDI).
    d. franchising.

4. Which of the following statements is true?
   a. The United States still accounts for the largest percentage of total world production even though the U.S. share of total world production has been declining in the last decade or so.
   b. The United States has been expanding its world market share in the last few years.
   c. Foreign direct investment in the United States has been increasing in the last decade or so.
   d. All of the above are true.

5. Which of the following statements is true?
   a. A trade deficit means a nation is importing more than it is exporting.
   b. The United States has been experiencing a trade surplus for the last decade.
   c. Intrafirm trade is a term describing the total ban on trade with a particular nation or in a particular market.
   d. The balance of trade is a broader measure of a nation's international accounts than the balance of payments.

6. Which of the following statements is true?
   a. Protectionism typically increases the jobs within a nation.
   b. Dumping is charging less than the actual cost or less than the home-country price for goods sold in other countries.
   c. A quota is a tax on an imported good, while a tariff is a limit on the quantity allowed to enter the country.
   d. Rarely are trade barriers politically popular.

7. Which of the following is *not* a trade barrier (a form of protectionism)?
   a. Voluntary export restraints (VERs)
   b. Restrictive standards
   c. Foreign direct investment (FDI)
   d. Subsidies

8. Which of the following is *not* an argument in favor of protectionism?
   a. Protectionism raises the prices of both domestic and foreign goods.
   b. Protectionism preserves domestic jobs.
   c. Protectionism helps weak domestic industries stay afloat.
   d. Protectionism allows a nation to retaliate against unfair foreign competition.

9. A permanent negotiating forum for implementing and monitoring international trade procedures and for mediating trade disputes between its member countries is the
   a. World Trade Organization (WTO).
   b. The Asian Pacific Economic Cooperation Council (APEC).
   c. The European Union (EU).
   d. The North American Free Trade Agreement (NAFTA).

10. Which of the following statements is true?
    a. The General Agreement on Tariffs and Trade (GATT) was very successful in reducing tariff barriers among countries.
    b. Trading blocs are organizations of nations that remove barriers to trade among their members and that establish uniform barriers to trade with nonmembers.
    c. Critics of trade blocs fear that overall world trade could decline as members become more protective of their own regions.
    d. All of the above are true.

11. American companies interested in conducting business abroad
    a. are affected by a number of U.S. laws passed to encourage participation in international trade.
    b. must comply with the Foreign Corrupt Practices Act.
    c. are encouraged to do so by the U.S. government's allowing these companies to set up foreign sales corporations (FSCs).
    d. All of the above are true.

12. An increase in the value of the U.S. dollar in foreign exchange markets will cause
    a. a decrease in the relative price of American imports, but an increase in the relative price of American exports.
    b. Americans to import more while America's exports fall.
    c. America to experience a trade deficit.
    d. all of the above.

13. Which of the following statements is *false*?
    a. Countertrade is a trading practice in which local products are offered instead of cash in exchange for imported products.
    b. Stereotypes are very useful when doing international business.
    c. A multidomestic management approach in a global corporation allows local units to act independently whereas a transnational approach is one in which management coordinates the activities of all its units to achieve world-wide goals.
    d. Managing a multinational corporation is more complicated than managing a strictly domestic company.

14. To improve international communications, firms need to
    a. learn as much as possible about the cultures of people they work with.
    b. keep an open mind, avoid stereotyping, and learn how to show respect in another culture.
    c. anticipate misunderstandings and guard against them.
    d. do all of the above.

JEOPARDY

You have 5 seconds to complete the question to each of the following answers.

	Trade Barriers	Arguments For and Against Protectionism	Forms of International Business Activity
$100	Taxes levied on imports. (42) What is _a tariff_ ?	A major argument against protectionism pertaining to prices. (45) What is _____ ?	Selling a product outside the country. (35) What is _____ ?
$200	Fixed limits on the quantity of imports a nation will allow for a specific product. (42) What is _a quota_ ?	A major argument in favor of protectionism pertaining to the effect on domestic economies. (45) What is _____ ?	When an operation is run in another country, without local participation. (37) What is _____ ?
$300	Self-imposed limits on the amount of certain goods a country exports. (42) What is _VER_ ?	A major argument in favor of protectionism pertaining to jobs. (45) What is _____ ?	An agreement to produce and market another company's product in exchange for a royalty or fee. (36) What is _____ ?

$400	A total ban on trade with a particular nation or in a particular market. (42) What is _a. embargo_ ?	A major argument against protectionism pertaining to jobs. (42) What is_____ ?	A cooperative partnerships in which firms share investment, costs, risks management, and profits in the development, production, or selling of products. (36-37) What is_____ ?
$500	The effect of trade barriers on the price of both domestic and foreign goods. (45) What is_____ ?	A major argument in favor of protectionism pertaining to unfair competition. (42) What is_____ ?	This is a particularly good way for smaller companies to enter the global marketplace. (36) What is_____ ?

MATCH THE TERMS AND CONCEPTS TO THEIR DEFINITIONS

a. absolute advantage (33)
b. balance of payments (39)
c. balance of trade (40)
d. comparative advantage (33)
e. countertrade (53)
f. dumping (44)
g. embargo (42)
h. exchange rate (52)
i. exporting (35)
j. floating exchange rate system (52)

k. foreign direct investment (14)
l. foreign exchange (52)
m. foreign sales corporation (51)
n. free trade (44)
o. importing (35)
p. intrafirm trade (39)
q. licensing (36)
r. joint venture (36)
s. most favored nation (MFN) trading status (49)
t. multinational corporation (MNC) (34)
u. national competitive advantage (33)

v. protectionism (42)
w. quotas (42)
x. strategic alliances (37)
y. tariffs (42)
z. trade deficit (39)
aa. trade surplus (39)
bb. trading blocs (46)
cc. voluntary export restraints (VERS) (42)

_____ u 1. Ability of a nation's industries to be innovative and move to a higher level of technology and productivity.

_____ d/a 2. Nation's ability to produce certain items more efficiently and at a lower cost than other items, relative to other nations.

_____ o 3. Purchasing goods or services from another country and bringing them into one's own country.

_____ q 4. Agreement to produce and market another company's product in exchange for a royalty of fee.

_____ a/d 5. Nation's ability to produce a particular product with fewer resources per unit of output than any other nation.

_____ x 6. Long-term relationships in which two or more companies share ideas, resources, and technologies in order to establish competitive advantages.

_____ p 7. Trade between global units of a multinational corporation.

___t___ 8. Companies with operations in more than one country.

___i___ 9. Selling and shipping goods or services to another country.

___r___ 10. Cooperative partnership in which organizations share investment costs, risks, management, and profits in the development, production, or selling of products.

___m___ 11. Tax-sheltered subsidiaries of U.S.-based corporations that engage in exporting.

___h___ 12. Rate at which the money of one country is traded for the money of another.

e ___p___ 13. Trading practice in which local products are offered instead of cash in exchange for imported products.

___k___ 14. Investment of money by foreign companies in domestic business enterprises (sometimes abbreviated as FDI).

___c___ 15. Relationship between the value of the products a nation exports and those it imports.

___aa___ 16. Positive trade balance created when a country exports more than it imports.

___z___ 17. Negative trade balance created when a country imports more than it exports.

b ___w___ 18. Sum of all payments one nation has made to other nations minus the payments it has received from other nations during a specified period of time.

g ___bb___ 19. Total ban on trade with a particular nation or in a particular product.

___cc___ 20. Self-imposed limits on the amount of certain goods a country exports.

w ___g___ 21. Fixed limits on the quantity of imports a nation will allow for a specific product.

___y___ 22. Taxes levied on imports.

v ___bb___ 23. Government policies aimed at shielding a country's industries from foreign competition.

bb ___x___ 24. Organizations of nations that remove barriers to trade among their members and that establish uniform barriers to trade with nonmember nations.

___s___ 25. A privilege granted by the United States that greatly simplifies and reduces import duties levied on goods from certain countries.

___f___ 26. Charging less than the actual cost or less than the home-country price for goods sold in other countries.

___n___ 27. International trade unencumbered by restrictive measures.

___u___ 28. Trading one currency for the equivalent value of another currency.

_____ 29. World economic system in which the values of all currencies are determined by supply and demand.

WORD SCRAMBLE

1. ___tariffs___
   riftafs

2. ___quotas___
   toquas

3. ___comparative advantage___
   tarcompaive   ageadvant

LEARNING OBJECTIVES--POTENTIAL SHORT ANSWER OR ESSAY QUESTIONS

Learning Objective #1: "Differentiate between absolute, comparative, and national competitive advantage." (33-34)

Learning Objective #2: "Distinguish between the balance of trade and the balance of payments." (39-41)

Learning Objective #3: "Identify four techniques that countries use to protect their domestic industries." (41-44)

<u>Learning Objective #4</u>: "Outline the arguments for and against protectionism." (44-45)

<u>Learning Objective #5</u>: "Explain how trading blocs, the GATT, and the WTO affect trade." (44-50)

<u>Learning Objective #6</u>: "Define foreign exchange, and discuss the effect of a weaker U.S. dollar on U.S. companies that do business abroad." (52-53)

<u>Learning Objective #7</u>: "Discuss five forms of international business activity." (35-37)

Learning Objective #8: **"Identify six ways to improve communication in an international business relationship."** (53-55)

learn about customs and culture

CRITICAL THINKING QUESTIONS

1. From a national perspective, do the benefits (pros) of international trade outweigh the costs (cons), or do the costs outweigh the benefits over time? In other words, does protectionism promote the general welfare? If not, then why do some politicians push for protectionist policies (trade barriers)?

2. Why is a weaker dollar good for American business but not necessarily good for the American consumer?

BRAIN TEASER

1. Given that either a tariff or a quota is going to be imposed, which would an international business prefer and why? Which would the imposing government prefer and why?

ANSWERS

True-False--*Answers*

1. True
2. False: If a nation has an absolute advantage in the production of a product, then this means the nation possesses the ability to *produce a particular product with fewer resources per unit of output than any other nation.*
3. False: *A joint venture* is a cooperative partnership in which organizations share investment costs, risks, management, and profits in the development, production, or selling of products.
4. True
5. False: *Foreign direct investment (FDI)* is the investment of money by foreign companies in domestic business enterprises.
6. False: The balance of *trade* is the relationship between the value of the products a nation exports and those it imports.
7. False: A trade deficit exists if a nation *imports* more than it *exports.*.
8. True
9. True
10. True
11. False: A *flexible* exchange rate system is a world exchange rate system in which the values of all currencies are determined by supply and demand.
12. True
13. True

Multiple Choice--*Answers*

1. d	5. a	9. a	13. b
2. b	6. b	10. d	14. d
3. c	7. c	11. d	
4. d	8. a	12. d	

Jeopardy--*Answers*

	Trade Barriers	Arguments For and Against Protectionism	Forms of International Business Activity
$100	tariffs	Protectionism creates higher prices for both domestic and foreign goods.	exporting
$200	quotas	Protectionism boosts domestic economies by restricting foreign competition.	a wholly owned facility
$300	voluntary export restraints	Protectionism boosts domestic jobs.	licensing
$400	embargo	The cost of saving jobs is enormous, and some jobs may be lost due to higher import prices.	a joint venture (or strategic alliance)
$500	higher prices for both domestic and foreign goods	Nations must sometimes retaliate against foreign trade restrictions.	franchising

Match the Terms and Concepts to Their Definitions--*Answers*

1. u	6. x	11. m	16. aa	21. w	26. f
2. d	7. p	12. h	17. z	22. y	27. n
3. o	8. t	13. e	18. b	23. v	28. l
4. q	9. i	14. k	19. g	24. bb	29. j
5. a	10. r	15. c	20. cc	25. s	

Word Scramble--*Answers*

1. tariffs   2. quotas   3. comparative advantage

Learning Objectives--Potential Short Answer or Essay Questions--*Answers*

Learning Objective #1:

A country with an absolute advantage can produce a particular product with fewer resources than any other nation. A country with a comparative advantage produces a particular product more efficiently than other products, relative to other nations. A country with a national competitive advantage has the ability to innovate and upgrade to a higher level of technology and productivity, which makes it more competitive in the world market.

Learning Objective #2:

The balance of trade is the total value of exports minus the value of imports over a specific period. The balance of payments is the total flow of money into the country minus the flow of money out of the country.

Learning Objective #3:

Four of the most common forms of protectionism are tariffs, quotas, subsidies, and restrictive standards.

Learning Objective #4:

People who support protectionism believe that building in a preference for a country's home industries can boost local economies and save local jobs. It can also shield domestic industries from head-to-head competition with overseas rivals. Those who argue against protectionism say that it leads to higher consumer prices, high costs of saving jobs and the possibility of losing jobs in other sectors of the economy, damage to U.S. companies that depend on imports, the stifling of innovation, and the existence of many loopholes.

Learning Objective #5:

Trading blocs are regional groupings of countries within which trade barriers have been removed. These alliances ease trade between bloc members and strengthen barriers for nonmembers. The World Trade Organization (WTO) is a worldwide forum encompassing 138 nations seeking to reduce certain trade barriers and increase world trade. The WTO also provides a legal framework in which to handle trade disputes. The WTO replaces the GATT which is a trade agreement that has greatly reduced tariffs in the past 50 years.

Learning Objective #6:

Foreign exchange is the conversion of one currency into an equivalent amount of another currency. When the dollar falls in value relative to other currencies, U.S. products become cheaper on the world market. Because U.S. products cost less, demand rises, and U.S. companies can export more. At the same time, imports become more expensive, which puts U.S. products at an advantage in the U.S. market.

Learning Objective #7:

Importing and exporting, licensing, franchising joint ventures, strategic alliances, and wholly owned facilities are five of the most common forms of international business activity. Each contains different levels of risk and provides a company with varying degrees of control.

Learning Objective #8:

To improve international communication, learn as much as you can about the cultures of the people you are working with; keep an open mind and avoid stereotyping; be sensitive to other people's customs; anticipate misunderstandings and guard against them; adapt your style to match the style of others; and learn how to show respect in another culture.

Critical Thinking Questions--*Answers*
1. The evidence is clear that the costs (cons) associated with protectionist policies outweigh the benefits (pros) for a *nation*. However, free trade does hurt some specific individuals (those who own or work for domestic businesses which cannot compete internationally). It is these individuals we would expect to make a case for protectionism and to lobby government for trade barriers. Some politicians may succumb to that political pressure or are unaware of the fact that the costs do outweigh the benefits. Nonetheless, it is generally true that the costs for the nation as a whole in the form of higher prices consumers must pay for both domestic and foreign products do outweigh the benefits which accrue to selected protected industries and their workers over time.

2. A weaker dollar reduces the relative price of American exports to foreigners. They would, therefore, buy more of our exports. This is beneficial to American firms which export their products around the globe. However, at the same time, a weaker dollar will hurt many American consumers because imported products will become more expensive.

Brain Teaser--*Answer*
1. An international business would prefer a quota because a tariff implies a tax which must be paid to the imposing government. With a quota, there is no such tax payment. However, the imposing government would prefer a tariff because of the tax revenues it generates.

Chapter 3
Ethical and Social Responsibilities of Business

LEARNING OBJECTIVES
After studying this chapter, you should be able to:

1. Explain the differences between ethical dilemmas and ethical lapses. (64-65)
2. List and explain four philosophical approaches to resolving ethical questions in business. (65-66)
3. Identify four stakeholder groups to which business has a responsibility. (66-71)
4. Name the three kinds of pollution, and outline actions to control them. (71-76)
5. List the four rights of consumers. (76-80)
6. Discuss the problem of discrimination, and explain how government and business are working to end it. (80-86)
7. Discuss two general ways that businesses may cheat investors. (86-89)
8. Identify steps that businesses are taking to encourage socially responsible and ethical behavior. (89)

TRUE-FALSE
Indicate whether the statement is generally true or false by placing a "T" or "F" in the space provided. If it is a false statement, correct it so that it becomes a true statement.

F 1. An ethical dilemma occurs when an individual makes an unethical decision.

F 2. Socially responsible behavior and ethical business practices rarely increase the profits of businesses.

T 3. The "utilitarian" philosophy towards ethical decision making aims to ensure the equal distribution of burdens and benefits.

T 4. The "justice" philosophy towards ethical decision making aims to protect rights guaranteed by a legal system or by moral norms and principles.

T 5. Determining what is right in any given situation can be difficult.

T 6. Balancing the individual needs and interests of a company's stakeholders is one of management's most difficult tasks.

F 7. Four stakeholder groups to which business has a responsibility are investors, employees, consumers, and society.

_____T____   8.   Many businesses are now creating official positions to guide their ethics policies.

_____F____   9.   Air, water, and land pollution are no longer significant social problems.

_____F____   10.   The National Environmental Policy Act of 1969 set up the Environmental Protection Agency to regulate the disposal of hazardous wastes and to clean up polluted areas.

_____T____   11.   Very few companies have acted on their own to reduce the pollution they produce, to recycle waste materials, or to safely dispose of hazardous wastes.

_____T____   12.   Consumers have the right to fair prices, good service, the right to complain, and the right to return products unused for a full refund.

_____T____   13.   Consumerism was a movement that began in the 1960s which put pressure on businesses to consider consumer needs and interests.

_____T____   14.   Discrimination is the practice of restricting an individual's right to opportunity.

_____T____   15.   The Civil Rights Act of 1964 established the Equal Employment Opportunity Commission (EEOC)--the regulatory agency that battles job discrimination.

_____T____   16.   "Affirmative action" programs are designed to recruit and promote members of minority groups.

_____F____   17.   Today, many companies are implementing diversity initiatives designed to encourage understanding of the cultures and talents of all individuals.

_____T____   18.   Investors can be cheated in many ways, but most scams fall into two categories: (1) misrepresenting the potential of the investment and (2) diverting earnings or assets so that the investor's rightful return is reduced.

_____T____   19.   Only a handful of large companies have adopted a code of ethics, which defines the values and principles that should be used to guide decisions.

_____T____   20.   One way businesses are trying to encourage socially responsible and ethical behavior is by establishing ethics hot lines to encourage whistle-blowing.

MULTIPLE CHOICE
Circle the one best answer for each of the following questions.

1. A situation in which both sides of an issue can be supported with valid arguments is
   a. very rare.
   b. an ethical lapse.
   c. an ethical dilemma.
   d. all of the above.

2. Which of the following is a philosophical approach to resolving ethical questions in business?
   a. The application of religious principles
   b. To uphold the importance of individual rights
   c. The application of the concept of utilitarianism
   d. All of the above

3. The philosophical approach to resolving ethical questions in business that aims to ensure the equal distribution of burdens and benefits is the
   a. utilitarian approach.
   b. individual rights approach.
   c. justice approach
   d. religious approach.

4. Which of the following is a stakeholder group to which business has a responsibility?
   a. Consumers, and society in general
   b. Investors
   c. Employees
   d. All of the above are.

5. Which of the following statements is true?
   a. One way companies can evaluate their ethical standards is by conducting a social audit.
   b. The only real stakeholder to a company is investors.
   c. The idea that business has certain obligations to society beyond the pursuit of profits faded in the1960s.
   d. Rarely do businesses profit from socially responsible behavior.

6. Which of the following statements is *false*?
   a. Socially responsible business behavior is a concept that dates back to at least the latter 1800s.
   b. Government laws and regulations designed to prevent pollution have in practice only made pollution worse.
   c. Sometimes costs of production, and therefore, prices are higher when businesses take the steps necessary to pollute less.
   d. The three major kinds of pollution are air, water, and land pollution.

7. Consumerism
   a. began in the 1960s.
   b. is a movement that pressures businesses to consider consumer needs and interests.
   c. prompted many businesses to create consumer-affairs departments to handle customer complaints and many state and local agencies to set up bureaus to offer consumer information and assistance.
   d. did all of the above.

8.   Which of the following is *not* one of President John F. Kennedy's "bills of rights" for consumers?
     a.   The right to a fair price
     b.   The right to be informed
     c.   The right to safety
     d.   The right to choose

9.   Government product labeling requirements, on canned goods, for example, is a response to which of the following consumer rights?
     a.   The right to be heard
     b.   The right to be informed
     c.   The right to choose
     d.   The right to complain

10.   Which of the following statements is true?
      a.   Job discrimination is no longer considered to be a social problem in the United States.
      b.   The Civil Rights Act of 1964 significantly reduced the powers of the Equal Employment Opportunity Commission (EEOC).
      c.   The EEOC is responsible for monitoring the hiring practices of companies and for investigating complaints of job-related discrimination.
      d.   Job discrimination based on race or gender has not had any significant impact on the distribution of income in the United States.

11.   Affirmative action
      a.   programs were developed to encourage organizations to recruit and promote members of minority groups, and any company that does business with the federal government must have an affirmative action program.
      b.   proponents argue that minorities deserve and require preferential treatment to boost opportunities and to make up for years of discrimination.
      c.   opponents argue that creating special opportunities for women and minorities creates a double standard that infringes on the rights of other workers and forces companies to hire, promote, and retain people who are not necessarily the best choice from a business standpoint.
      d.   All of the above.

12.   Which of the following statements is *false*?
      a.   Affirmative action efforts have not been entirely successful in ensuring that more minorities are hired because negative attitudes about differences among individuals persist.
      b.   U.S. companies have abolished diversity initiatives because of the widespread criticism that they perpetuate stereotypes and myths about minorities.
      c.   The glass ceiling has resulted in women making more money than they otherwise would have.
      d.   Today, women's earnings are equal to that of men.

13.   Investors
      a.   can be cheated if they are not provided the rate of return on their funds that they expected.
      b.   can be cheated if companies or individuals misrepresent the value of an investment, or if company funds are diverted by managers for their personal use.
      c.   are rarely ever cheated.
      d.   All of the above.

14. Questionable business practices include
    a. insider trading.
    b. corporate spying.
    c. gift giving.
    (d.) all of the above.

15. Which of the following are ways companies encourage ethically and socially responsible behavior?
    a. They have adopted social codes of behavior.
    b. They have appointed ethics officers and provide ethics training.
    c. They have developed systems to help employees deal with ethical dilemmas and have established ethics hot lines to encourage whistle blowing.
    (d.) All of the above.

JEOPARDY

You have 5 seconds to complete the question to each of the following answers.

	Ethical Dilemmas, Lapses, and Philosophical Approaches	Stakeholder Groups; Pollution; and Consumerism	Discrimination; Business Ethics Initiatives
$100	A situation in which an individual makes an unethical decision. (65) What is _an ethical lapse_ ?	Four stakeholder groups to which business has a responsibility. (66-67) What is _employees, stockholders, society, customers_ ?	EEOC (80) _Equal Employment Opportunity Comm_ What is _____ ?
$200	A situation when it is not clear what is the ethically correct thing to do. (64) What is _an ethical dilemma_ ?	Three types of pollution. (71-72) What is _air, water, land_ ?	Discriminating against a person on the basis of gender. (82) What is _sexual discrimination_ ?
$300	Philosophy used in making ethical decisions that aims to achieve the greatest good for the greatest number of people. (65) What is _utilitarianism philosophy_ _ethics_ ?	The National Environmental Policy Act of 1969 created this agency which regulates pollution and the cleaning up of polluted sites. (72) _EPA_ What is _Environmental Protection Agency_ ?	Activities undertaken by business to recruit and promote women and minorities. (80) What is _affirmative action_ ?
$400	Philosophy used in making ethical decisions that aims to protect rights guaranteed by a legal system or by moral norms and principles. (65) What is _individual rights phil_ ?	The four consumer "bill of rights." (76-80) _right to choose_ _" " be informed_ _" " safety_ _" " be heard_ What is _____ ?	Unwelcome sexual advances, request for sexual favors, or other verbal or physical conduct of a sexual nature within the workplace. (83) What is _sexual harassmen_ ?
$500	Philosophy used in making ethical decisions that aims to ensure the equal distribution of burdens and benefits. (65) What is _justice philosophy_ ?	The controversy surrounding the banning of liquor ads on TV is most associated with which consumer right? (79) What is _right to choose_ ?	One way businesses are encouraging socially responsible and ethical behavior. (90) What is _adopting code of ethics_ ?

MATCH THE TERMS AND CONCEPTS TO THEIR DEFINITIONS

a. affirmative action (80)   h. ethical lapse (65)   o. pollution (71)
b. code of ethics (89)   i. ethics (64)   p. sexism (82)
c. consumerism (76)   j. glass ceiling (82)   q. sexual harassment (83)
d. discrimination (80)   k. individual rights (65)   r. social audit (67)
e. diversity initiatives (82)   l. insider trading (87)   s. social responsibility(64)
f. ecology (72)   m. justice (65)   t. stakeholders (66)
g. ethical dilemma (64)   n. minorities (80)   u. utilitarianism (65)

_b_   1. Written statement setting forth the principles that should guide an organization's decisions.

_l_   2. Employee's or manager's use of unpublicized information gained in the course of his or her job to benefit from fluctuations in the stock market.

_q_   3. Unwelcome sexual advance, request for sexual favors, or other verbal or physical conduct of a sexual nature within the workplace.

_s_   4. The idea that business has certain obligations to society beyond the pursuit of profits.

_g_   5. Situation in which both sides of an issue can be supported with valid arguments.

_u_   6. Philosophy used in making ethical decisions that aims to achieve the greatest good for the greatest number.

_t_   7. Individual or groups for whom business has a responsibility.

_r_   8. Assessment of a company's performance in the area of social responsibility.

_o_   9. Damage or destruction to the natural environment caused by human action.

_i_   10. Study of standards of conduct and individual choices based on rules, values, and moral beliefs.

_k_   11. Philosophy used in making ethical decisions that aim to protect rights guaranteed by a legal system or by moral norms and principles.

_m_   12. Philosophy used in making ethical decisions that aims to ensure the equal distribution of burdens and benefits.

_j_   13. Invisible barrier of subtle discrimination that keeps women out of the top positions in business.

_f_   14. Study of the relationship between living things in the water, air, and soil, their environments, and the nutrients that support them.

_d_   15. In a social and economic sense, denial of opportunities to individuals on the basis of some characteristic that has no bearing on their ability to perform in a job.

_p_   16. Discriminating against a person on the basis of gender.

e *d* 17. Company   policies designed to enhance opportunities for minorities and promote understanding of diverse cultures, customs, and talents.

a *e* 18. Activities undertaken by business to recruit and promote women and minorities based on an analysis of the work force and the available labor pool.

_n_ 19. In a social and economic sense, categories of people that society at large singles out for discriminatory, selective, or unfavorable treatment.

_h_ 20. Situation in which an individual makes an unethical decision.

_c_ 21. Movement that pressures businesses to consider consumer needs and interests.

WORD SCRAMBLE

1. ___ethics___
thesic

2. ___pollution___
liolotpun

3. ___discrimination___
criationmindis

LEARNING OBJECTIVES--POTENTIAL SHORT ANSWER OR ESSAY QUESTIONS
Learning Objective #1: **"Explain the differences between ethical dilemmas and ethical lapses."** (64-65)

Learning Objective #2: **"List and explain four philosophical approaches to resolving ethical questions in business."** (65-66)

Learning Objective #3: **"Identify four stakeholder groups to which business has a responsibility."** (66-71)

Learning Objective #4: "Name the three kinds of pollution, and outline actions to control them." (71-76)

Learning Objective #5: "List the four rights of consumers." (76-80)

Learning Objective #6: "Discuss the problem of discrimination, and explain how government and business are working to end it." (80-86)

Learning Objective #7: "Discuss two general ways that businesses may cheat investors." (86-89)

Learning Objective #8: "Identify steps that businesses are taking to encourage socially responsible and ethical behavior." (89)

CRITICAL THINKING QUESTIONS

1. Why might a business experience an increase in its profits even though it voluntarily undertakes a costly antipollution effort or undertakes some other kind of costly but socially responsible behavior?

2. What role must top management play in promoting socially and ethically responsible behavior by its employees?

BRAIN TEASER

1. Is the fact that men as a group are paid more than women as a group sufficient to prove that gender discrimination exists? If not, then when do we know when gender discrimination exists?

ANSWERS

True-False--*Answers*

1. False: An ethical *lapse* occurs when an individual makes an unethical decision.
2. False: Socially responsible behavior and ethical business practices *usually* increase the profits of businesses *over time.*
3. False: The *"justice"* philosophy towards ethical decision making aims to ensure the equal distribution of burdens and benefits.
4. False: The *"individual rights"* philosophy towards ethical decision making aims to protect rights guaranteed by a legal system or by moral norms and principles.
5. True
6. True
7. True
8. True
9. False: Air, water, and land pollution are *still* significant social problems.
10. True
11. False: *Many* companies have acted on their own to reduce the pollution they produce, to recycle waste materials, *and* to safely dispose of hazardous wastes.
12. False: Consumers have the right to *safety, the right to be informed, the right to choose, and the right to be heard.*
13. True
14. True
15. True
16. True
17. True
18. True
19. False: *More than 80%* of large companies have adopted a code of ethics, which defines the values and principles that should be used to guide decisions.
20. True

Multiple Choice--*Answers*

1. c	5. a	9. b	13. b
2. d	6. b	10. c	14. e
3. c	7. d	11. d	15. d
4. d	8. a	12. a	

Jeopardy---*Answers*

	Ethical Dilemma, Lapses and Philosophical Approaches	Stakeholder Groups; Pollution; and Consumerism	Discrimination; Business Ethics Initiatives
$100	an ethical lapse	society, consumers, employees, and investors	the abbreviation for the Equal Employment Opportunity Commission
$200	an ethical dilemma	air, water, and land	sexual discrimination
$300	the utilitarian philosophy	the Environmental Protection Agency (EPA)	affirmative action

$400	the individual rights philosophy	the right to safety, to be informed, to choose, and to be heard	sexual harassment
$500	the justice philosophy	the right to choose	(any of the following:) adopting codes of ethics, appointing ethics officers, providing ethics training, developing systems to help employees deal with ethical dilemmas, and establishing ethics hot lines to encourage whistle-blowing

Match the Terms and Concepts to Their Definitions--*Answers*

1. b	4. s	7. t	10. i	13. j	16. p	19. n
2. l	5. g	8. r	11. k	14. f	17. e	20. h
3. q	6. u	9. o	12. m	15. d	18. a	21. c

Word Scramble--*Answers*

1. ethics
2. pollution
3. discrimination

Learning Objectives---Potential Short Answer or Essay Questions--*Answers*

Learning Objective #1:

An ethical dilemma is an issue with two conflicting but arguably valid sides. An ethical lapse occurs when an individual makes an unethical decision.

Learning Objective #2:

When resolving ethical questions, companies may apply standards based on religious teachings, the principles of utilitarianism (the greatest good for the greatest number of people), individual rights (respect for rights guaranteed by legal systems or moral norms and principles), and justice (fair distribution of society's benefits and burdens).

Learning Objective #3:

Companies have a responsibility to society, to consumers, to employees, and to investors.

Learning Objective #4:

Air, water, and land pollution are all significant problems. The government passed the National Environmental Policy Act of 1969 and set up the Environmental Protection Agency to regulate the disposal of hazardous wastes and to clean up polluted areas. Also, many companies have acted to reduce the pollution they produce, to recycle waste materials, and to safely dispose of hazardous wastes.

Learning Objective #5:

Consumers have the right to safety, the right to be informed, the right to choose, and the right to be heard.

Learning Objective #6:

Discrimination is the practice of restricting an individual's right to pursue opportunity. People are often discriminated against because of their ethnic backgrounds, race, gender, age, religion, or physical ability. Government and business has encouraged affirmative action to combat discrimination since the 1960s. Today, many companies are implementing diversity initiatives designed to encourage understanding of the cultures and talents of all individuals.

Learning Objective #7:

Investors are cheated (1) when companies or individuals misrepresent the value of an investment and (2) when companies divert earnings or assets for their personal use, thus reducing the amount available to investors.

Learning Objective #8:

Business are adopting codes of ethics, appointing ethics officers, providing ethics training, developing systems to help employees deal with ethical dilemmas, and establishing ethics hot lines to encourage whistle-blowing.

Critical Thinking Questions--*Answers*

1. Because, over time, the business will likely earn the reputation of being a very socially responsible business and experience a rather dramatic increase in its sales for that reason alone. Most people prefer to buy products produced by socially responsible companies--even if they cost a little more.

2. Top management must make an uncompromising commitment to ethical behavior and lead by example. If top management does not take it seriously, then no one else will either.

Brain Teaser--*Answer*

1. The simple fact that men as a group are paid more than women as a group is not sufficient to prove that gender discrimination exists. This is because discrimination exists whenever equals are treated unequally or whenever unequals are treated equally. Men and women, as groups, are not equal in their education, training, and skill levels, and therefore their pay is different. But, gender discrimination does exist when men and women are equally productive and are paid unequally. Unfortunately, too often equally productive women are paid less than their male counterparts. (In addition, note that by this definition---which may be debatable—"reverse discrimination" exists whenever unequals are treated equally.)

Chapter 4
Forms of Business Ownership

LEARNING OBJECTIVES
After studying this chapter, you should be able to:

1. Identify the two broad sectors of the U.S. economy and its eight subsectors. (100-104)
2. Name five factors that have contributed to the growth of the service sector. (101-102)
3. Discuss the three basic forms of business ownership. (104-116)
4. List five advantages and four disadvantages of forming a sole proprietorship. (105)
5. Explain the difference between a general and limited partnership. (106-107)
6. Delineate the three groups that govern a corporation, and describe the role of each. (109)
7. Cite four advantages of corporations. (109-110)
8. Describe the five waves of merger activity. (116-121)

TRUE-FALSE

Indicate whether the statement is generally true or false by placing a "T" or "F" in the space provided. If it is a false statement, correct it so that it becomes a true statement.

___T___ 1. All things considered, most business analysts argue that the corporation is the most advantageous form of business.

___T___ 2. Most production is accounted for by corporations.

___T___ 3. The goods-producing sector of our economy comprises most of the revenues produced in the United States.

___F___ 4. The service sector includes wholesale and retail trade, finance and insurance, transportation and utilities, and other services.

___F___ 5. The corporation has the disadvantage of having unlimited liability.

___F___ 6. Corporations have the disadvantage of having their income taxed twice.

___F___ 7. The dominant form of business is the partnership.

_F___   8. A general partnership is owned by at least one general partner who runs the business and limited partners who are passive investors and generally liable for no more than the amount of their investment.

_T___   9. The three major groups which govern a corporation are the shareholders, the board of directors, and the officers of the corporation.

_T___   10. Corporations have the power to raise large sums of capital, they offer the shareholders protection from liability, they provide liquidity for investors, and they have an unlimited life span.

_F___   11. Partnerships provide the same tax advantages as sole proprietorships, because profits are taxed at personal income tax rates rather than corporate rates.

_T___   12. In a partnership, partners are legally responsible for paying off the debts of the group.

_F___   13. No other form of business can match the success of the partnership in bringing together money, resources, and talent; in accumulating assets; and in creating wealth.

_F___   14. Publicly traded corporations withhold their stock from public sale.

_F___   15. A merger is the combination of two companies in which one company purchases the other and assumes control of its property and liabilities.

_F___   16. A horizontal merger combines companies that participate in different phases of the same industry.

_T___   17. A hostile takeover is a situation in which an outside party buys enough stock in a corporation to take control against the wishes of the board of directors and corporate officers.

_T___   18. A proxy fight is an attempt to gain control of a takeover target by urging shareholders to vote for directors favored by the acquiring party.

_T___   19. A poison pill is a defense against hostile takeovers that makes the company less attractive in some way to the potential raider.

_T___   20. A generous compensation package guaranteed executives in the event they would lose their jobs after a takeover is called a golden parachute.

MULTIPLE CHOICE

Circle the one best answer for each of the following questions.

1. Which of the following is a reason for the large growth of the service sector?
    a. Economic prosperity has increased the demand for services.
    b. The number and complexity of goods needing service are increasing.
    c. Businesses need help in a complex global economy.
    d. All of the above are.

2. Which of the following is *not* part of the service sector?
    a. Construction and mining
    b. Retailing and wholesaling
    c. Finance and insurance
    d. Transportation and utilities

3. The sole proprietorship
    a. is the easiest and least expensive form of business to start.
    b. is the most common type of business in the United States.
    c. has the disadvantage of facing unlimited liability.
    d. is all of the above.

4. Which of the following is *not* an advantage of sole proprietorships?
    a. They provide the owner with control and independence.
    b. The business may cease when the owner dies.
    c. The owner reaps all the profits.
    d. Income is taxed at personal rates.

5. Which of the following is *not* a disadvantage of sole proprietorships?
    a. The company's financial resources are usually limited.
    b. Management talent may be thin.
    c. The company's plans and financial performance remain private.
    d. The owner is liable for the debts and damages incurred by the business.

6. Which of the following statements is true?
    a. A limited partnership is owned by at least one general partner who runs the business and limited partners who are passive investors and generally liable for no more than the amount of their investment.
    b. A general partnership is owned by general partners who are equally liable for the business's debts.
    c. Cooperatives are associations of people or small companies with similar interests, formed to obtain greater bargaining power or other economies of scale.
    d. All of the above are true.

7. A corporation
    a. has a legal status and obligations independent of its owners.
    b. is characterized by a separation of ownership and management.
    c. can be a small company, and most small corporations are privately held, which means that the company's stock is not traded publicly.
    d. is all of the above.

8. Which of the following is *not* an advantage of corporations?
    a. They have the power to raise large sums of money.
    b. They have to disclose financial information.
    c. They offer shareholders protection from liability.
    d. They provide liquidity for investors.

9. Which of the following statements is *false*?
    a. Government-owned corporations are formed by government for a specific public purpose.
    b. A closed corporation is a corporation that actively sells stock on the open market.
    c. An S corporation is a corporation with no more than 75 shareholders that may be taxed as a partnership.
    d. A holding company is a company that owns most, if not all, of another company's stock but does not actively manage that other company.

10. Which of the following statements is true?
    a. A subsidiary corporation is a corporation whose stock is owned entirely or almost entirely by another corporation.
    b. A proxy is a document authorizing another person to vote on behalf of a shareholder in a corporation.
    c. The chief executive officer (CEO) is a person appointed by a corporation's board of directors to carry out the board's policies and supervise the activities of the corporation.
    d. All of the above are true.

11. Which of the following statements is *false*?
    a. A labor-intensive business is a business in which labor costs are more significant than capital costs
    b. Barriers to entry are factors that make it difficult to launch a business in a particular industry.
    c. Partnerships are superior to sole proprietorships in that partnerships offer protection against unlimited liability to general partners.
    d. Partnerships are superior to sole proprietorships in that partnerships offer a diversity of skills which can lead to innovation and greater chances at success.

12. Which of the following statements is *false*?
    a. A vertical merger is the combination of companies that are direct competitors in the same industry.
    b. A divestiture is the sale of part of a company.
    c. An acquisition is a combination of two companies in which one company purchases the other and assumes control of its property and liabilities.
    d. A merger is a combination of two or more companies in which the old companies cease to exist and the new enterprise is created.

13. Monopolistic arrangements established when one company buys a controlling share of the stock of competing companies in the same industry are referred to as
    a. trusts.
    b. conglomerate mergers.
    c. golden parachutes.
    d. poison pills.

14. Which of the following statements is true?
   a. A hostile takeover is a situation in which an outside party buys enough stock in a corporation to take control against the wishes of the board of directors and corporate officers.
   b. A tender offer is an invitation made directly to shareholders by an outside party who wishes to buy a company's stock at a price above the current market price.
   c. A proxy fight is an attempt to gain control of a takeover target by urging shareholders to vote for directors favored by the acquiring party.
   d. All of the above are true.

15. A defensive move against a hostile takeover that makes the company less attractive in some way to the potential raider is called a
   a. golden parachute.
   b. shark repellent.
   c. poison pill.
   d. white knight.

16. A generous compensation package guaranteed to executives in the event that they lose their jobs after a takeover is called a:
   a. shark repellent.
   b. white knight.
   c. golden parachute.
   d. tender offer.

JEOPARDY

You have 5 seconds to complete the question to each of the following answers..

	Sole Proprietorships and Partnerships	Corporations	Mergers and Acquisitions
$100	One advantage of sole proprietorships. (105) What is _owner gets all profits_?	One advantage of corporations. (109-110) What is _____?	A combination of two or more companies in which the old company ceases to exist and a new enterprise is created. (117) What is _merger_?
$200	One disadvantage of sole proprietorships. (105) What is _unlimited liability_?	One disadvantage of corporations. (110-111) What is _____?	A combination of two companies in which one company purchases the other and assumes control of its property and liabilities. (117) What is _aquistion_?
$300	One advantage partnerships have over sole proprietorships. (107-108) What is _chances of success_?	The three groups that govern a corporation. (112) What is _shareholders board of directors_? _Execs_	A combination of companies that are in unrelated businesses. (118) What is _conglomerate merger_?

$400	One disadvantage of partnerships. (108) What is_____ _____?	Corporations whose stock is owned entirely or almost entirely by another corporation. (112) What is _subsidiary corp._?	A situation in which an outside party buys enough stock in a corporation to take control against the wishes of the board of directors and corporate officers. (119) What is _hostile takeover_?
$500	A partnership composed of one or more general partners and one or more partners whose liability is usually limited to the amount of their capital invested. (107) What is _limited partnership_?	Corporations with no more than 75 shareholders that may be taxed as a partnership. (112) What is _S corporation_?	A friendly buyer who agrees to take over a company to prevent a raider from taking it over. (120) What is _white knight_?

MATCH THE TERMS AND CONCEPTS TO THEIR DEFINITIONS

a. acquisition (116)
b. barriers to entry (103)
c. board of directors (113)
d. capital-intensive businesses (102)
e. chief executive officer (115)
f. commodity business (104)
g. conglomerate mergers (117)
h. consortium (108)
i. cooperatives (100)
j. corporation (109)
k. divestiture (116)
l. general partnership (107)
m. golden parachute (122)
n. goods-producing businesses (100)
o. government-owned corporation (110)
p. holding company (112)
q. horizontal mergers (117)
r. hostile takeovers (118)
s. labor-intensive businesses (103)
t. limited liability companies (LLCs) (112)
u. limited partnership (107)
v. liquidity (110)
w. master limited partnership (MLP) (107)

x. merger (116)
y. not publicly traded corporations (111)
z. parent company (112)
aa. partnership (107)
bb. poison pill (122)
cc. private corporations (113)
dd. proxy (113)
ee. proxy fight (119)
ff. publicly traded corporations (111)
gg. quasi-government corporation (111)
hh. S corporation (111)
ii. service businesses (100)
jj. shareholders (109)
kk. shark repellent (104)
ll. sole proprietorship (104)
oo. stock (109)
pp. subsidiary corporations (112)
qq. tender offer (119)
rr. trusts (117)
ss. unlimited liability (105)
tt. vertical mergers (117)
uu. white knight (122)

_ii_   1.   Businesses that provide intangible products or perform useful labor on behalf of another business.

_n_   2.   Businesses that produce tangible products.

_b_   3.   Factors that make it difficult to launch a business in a particular industry.

___ll___ 4. Business owned by a single individual.

___ss___ 5. Legal condition under which any damages or debts attributable to the business can also be attached to the owner because the two have no separate legal existence.

___bb___ w 6. Business partnership that acts like a corporation, trading partnership units on listed stock exchanges; if 90% of income is passive, MLPs are taxed at individual rates.

___l___ 7. Partnership in which all partners have the right to participate as co-owners and are individually liable for the business's debts.

___u___ 8. Partnership composed of one or more general partners and one or more partners whose liability is usually limited to the amount of their capital investment.

___j___ 9. Legally chartered enterprise having most of the legal rights of a person, including the right to conduct business, to own and sell property, to borrow money, and to sue or be sued; owners of the company enjoy limited liability.

___jj___ 10. Owners of a corporation.

___oo___ 11. Shares of ownership in a corporation.

___v___ 12. The level of ease with which an asset can be converted to cash.

___o___ 13. Corporation formed and owned by a government body for a specific public purpose.

___cc___ hh 14. Companies owned by private individuals or companies.

___gg___ 15. Corporation with no more than 75 shareholders that may be taxed as a partnership; also know as subchapter S corporation.

___z___ 16. Company that owns most, if not all, of another company's stock and that takes an active part in managing that other company.

___p___ 17. Company that owns most, if not all, of another company's stock but does not actively participate in the management of that other company.

___pp___ 18. Corporations whose stock is owned entirely or almost entirely by another corporation.

___dd___ 19. Document authorizing another person to vote on behalf of a shareholder in a corporation.

___e___ 20. Person appointed by a corporation's board of directors to carry out the board's policies and supervise the activities of the corporation.

r r ___g___ 21. Monopolistic arrangements established when one company buys a controlling share of the stock of competing companies in the same industry.

___tt___ 22. Combination of companies that participate in different phases of the same industry (i.e., materials, production, distribution).

___g___ 23. Combination of companies that are direct competitors in the same industry.

___X___ 24. Combination of two or more companies in which the old companies cease to exist and a new enterprise is created.

___a___ 25. Combination of two companies in which one company purchases the other and assumes control of its property and liabilities.

___gg___ 26. Invitation made directly to shareholders by an outside party who wishes to buy a company's stock at a price above the current market price.

___ee___ 27. Attempt to gain control of a takeover target by urging shareholders to vote for directors favored by the acquiring party.

___uu___ 28. Friendly buyer who agrees to take over a company to prevent a raider from taking it over.

___bb___ 29. Defense against hostile takeovers that makes the company less attractive in some way to the potential raider.

___m___ 30. Generous compensation packages guaranteed to executives in the event they lose their jobs after a takeover.

___ll___ 31. Direct takeover defense in which the company's board requires a large majority of voting shares to approve any takeover attempt.

___d___ 32. Businesses that require large investments in capital assets.

___s___ 33. Businesses in which labor costs are more significant than capital costs.

___f___ 34. Businesses in which products are undifferentiated and price becomes the chief competitive weapon; usually applied to basic goods such as minerals and agricultural products.

___aa___ 35. Unincorporated business owned and operated by two or more persons under a voluntary legal association.

___h___ 36. Group of companies working jointly to promote a common objective or engage in a project of benefit to all members.

___i___ 37. Association of people or small companies with similar interests, formed to obtain greater bargaining power and other economies of scale.

___x___ 38. Public utilities having a monopoly to provide basic services.

___ff___ 39. Corporations that actively sell stock on the open market; also called open corporations.

___y___ 40. Corporations that withhold their stock from public sale; also called closed corporations.

___w___ 41. Organizations that combine the benefits of S corporations and limited partnerships without the drawbacks of either.

___c___ 42. Group of people, elected by the shareholders, who have the ultimate authority in guiding the affairs of a corporation.

_____ _K_ 43. Sale of part of a company.

_g_ _____ 44. Combination of companies that are in unrelated businesses, designed to augment a company's growth and diversify risks.

_____ _r_ 45. Situations in which an outside party buys enough stock in a corporation to take control against the wishes of the board of directors and corporate officers.

WORD SCRAMBLE

1. _partnership_   2. _Sole_   _proprietorship_   3. _corporation_
   tarpsnerpih   lose   shipprotorprie   portonaicor

LEARNING OBJECTIVES--POTENTIAL SHORT ANSWER OR ESSAY QUESTIONS

Learning Objective #1: "Identify the two broad sectors of the U.S. economy and its eight subsectors." (100-104)

Learning Objective #2: "Name five factors that have contributed to the growth of the service sector." (101-102)

Learning Objective #3: "Discuss the three basic forms of business ownership." (104-116)

Learning Objective #4: "List five advantages and four disadvantages of forming a sole proprietorship." (105)

Learning Objective #5: "Explain the difference between a general and limited partnership." (106-107)

Learning Objective #6: "Delineate the three groups that govern a corporation, and describe the role of each." (109)

Learning Objective #7: "Cite four advantages of corporations." (109-110)

Learning Objective #8: "Describe the five waves of merger activity." (116-121)

CRITICAL THINKING QUESTION

1. As an up and coming business consultant you advise people, for a small fee, who are interested in starting their own businesses. You provide advice with respect to the legal form which their business ought to take, given their individual circumstances. Which form of business would you recommend to the following clients? Why?

   a. Peggy Bray has been a very dependable manager of a large grocery store's floral shop for years. She has enjoyed working directly with the public and gets along with everyone. She is good at designing floral arrangements but doesn't particularly like doing paper work. Although she enjoys her current position and its security, her desire for a bigger challenge and an opportunity to more fully express her independence has had her thinking about her own floral shop for years. She is very confident that her own floral shop would be very prosperous. However, she lacks some of the financial resources to get started.

   b. Frederick Nord is a talented computer scientist and software designer who has developed a name for himself in Silicon Valley. He has recently become troubled with the apparent lack of willingness on the part of his current employer to take the long-term monetary risks necessary to invest in his latest software development ideas. He claims that the short-sightedness by his employer may result in the company losing out on a vast new market for software technology and huge potential profits. He is willing to put up much of his own money to invest in the creation of a new company but he is not willing to lose all that he has gained over the years. What he can invest in the creation of a new business is still far from the funds necessary to undertake the research and development which will be required to develop this next generation of software capabilities. Moreover, he wants to undertake only the research and development, not the day-to-day management of the firm.

c. Sam Jackson is a highly motivated young man who wants to be his own boss. He has been making his current boss a lot of money as a house painter for quite some time. Because of his reputation in the community of being an excellent and dependable painter, he is convinced he could make even more money for himself running his own house-painting business. He already has the equipment and the funds necessary to get started. His insurance and operating expenses are expected to be relatively very small.

BRAIN TEASER

1. Antitrust laws in the United States grant the federal government the power to prevent mergers and acquisitions if it can be shown they would significantly reduce competition. In recent years, the federal government has been more lenient in its antitrust enforcement, allowing more mergers and acquisitions than in earlier years. Thinking in terms of an increasingly global economy, what reasoning could justify this more lenient approach to antitrust enforcement?

ANSWERS

True-False--*Answers*

1. True
2. True
3. False: The *service* sector of our economy comprises most of the revenues produced in the United States.
4. True
5. False: The *sole proprietorship* has the disadvantage of having unlimited liability.
6. True
7. False: The dominant form of business is the *corporation.*
8. False: A *limited* partnership is owned by at least one general partner who runs the business and limited partners who are passive investors and generally liable for no more than the amount of their investment.
9. True
10. True
11. True
12. True
13. False: No other form of business can match the success of the *corporation* in bringing together money, resources, and talent; in accumulating assets; and in creating wealth.

14. False: *Not p*ublicly traded corporations withhold their stock from public sale.
15. False: *An acquisition* is the combination of two companies in which one company purchases the other and assumes control of its property and liabilities.
16. False: A *vertical* merger combines companies that participate in different phases of the same industry.
17. True
18. True
19. True
20. True

Multiple Choice--*Answers*

1. d	5. c	9. b	13. a
2. a	6. d	10. d	14. d
3. d	7. d	11. c	15. c
4. b	8. b	12. a	16. c

Jeopardy--*Answers*

	Sole Proprietorships and Partnerships	Corporations	Mergers and Acquisitions
$100	they are easy to establish; they provide the owner with control and independence; the owner reaps all the profits; income is taxed as personal rates; or the company's plans and financial performance remain private	have the power to raise large sums of capital, they offer the shareholders protection from liability, they provide liquidity for investors, or they have an unlimited life span.	a merger
$200	the company's financial resources are usually limited; management talent may be thin; the owner is liable for the debts and damages incurred by the business; or the business may cease when the owner dies	they have to disclose financial information or their profits are taxed twice	an acquisition
$300	they increase the diversity of skills; they may have better luck at obtaining financing; or there are greater chances the business will endure because new partners can be drawn into the business to replace those who die or retire	shareholders, the board of directors, and the corporate officers	a conglomerate merger
$400	the active partners face unlimited liability or there is the potential for interpersonal problems	a subsidiary corporation	a hostile takeover
$500	a limited partnership	an S corporation; also known as a subchapter S corporation	a white knight

Match the Terms and Concepts to Their Definitions---*Answers*

1. ii	8. u	15. hh	22. tt	29. bb	36. h	43. k
2. n	9. j	16. z	23. q	30. m	37. I	44. g
3. b	10. jj	17. p	24. x	31. kk	38. gg	45. r
4. ll	11. oo	18. pp	25. a	32. d	39. ff	
5. ss	12. v	19. dd	26. qq	33. s	40. y	
6. w	13. o	20. e	27. ee	34. f	41. t	
7. l	14. cc	21. rr	28. uu	35. aa	42. c	

Word Scramble--*Answers*

1. partnership 2. sole proprietorship 3. corporation

Learning Objectives--Potential Short Answer or Essay Questions--*Answers*

Learning Objective #1:

The economy consists of (1) the service sector, which includes wholesale and retail trade, finance and insurance, transportation and utilities, and other services; and (2) the goods-producing sector, which includes manufacturing, construction, mining, and agriculture.

Learning Objective #2:

In recent years, the service sector has expanded because economic prosperity had increased the demand for services, demographic patterns in the United States continue to change, the number of and complexity of goods needing service are increasing, businesses find themselves needing more services to help them deal with a complex global economy, and technology keeps creating new service opportunities.

Learning Objective #3:

A sole proprietorship is a business owned by a single person. A partnership is an association of two or more people. A partnership is an association of two or more people who share in the ownership of an enterprise. The dominant form of business is the corporation, a legally chartered entity having many of the same rights and duties as a person.

Learning Objective #4:

Sole proprietorships have five advantages: (1) They are easy to establish, (2) they provide the owner with control and independence, (3) the owner reaps the all the profits, (4) income is taxed at personal rates, and (5) the company's plans and financial performance remain private. The four main disadvantages of a sole proprietorship are (1) the company's financial resources are usually limited, (2) management talent may be thin, (3) the owner is liable for the debts and damages incurred by the business, and (4) the business may cease when the owner dies.

Learning Objective #5:

A general partnership is owned by general partners who are equally liable for the business's debts. A limited partnership is owned by at least one general partner who runs the business and limited partners who are passive investors and generally liable for no more than the amount of their investment.

Learning Objective #6:

Shareholders are the basis of the corporate structure. They elect the board of directors, who in turn elect the officers of the corporation. The corporate officers carry out the policies and decisions of the board. In practice, the shareholders and board members have often followed the lead of the chief executive officer. However, board members are becoming increasingly active in corporate governance.

Learning Objective #7:

Corporations have the power to raise large sums of capital, they offer the shareholders protection from liability, they provide liquidity for investors, and they have an unlimited life span.

Learning Objective #8:

The earliest mergers occurring from 1881 to 1911, were horizontal mergers, combining two companies that compete in the same industry. A second wave of mergers occurred in the 1920s and were vertical mergers, combining two companies that participate in different phases of the same industry. The 1960s and 1970s introduced a third wave of mergers known as conglomerate mergers, combining unrelated companies. The mergers of the 1980s focused on the purchase of undervalued companies, which were then dismantled and sold off piece by piece. The most recent wave of mergers, occurring in the 1990s, can be described as strategic, with large corporations acquiring businesses that will enhance their market position.

Critical Thinking Question--*Answers*

1. a. General partnership. A very reliable and very dependable partner (remember there is unlimited liability) who likes to do paperwork and who has the needed funds to get started would be ideal.
   b. Corporation. There is a need for large sums of money, he wants limited liability and doesn't want to run the company on a day-to-day basis although he would want enough control over the stock to influence investment decisions. Moreover, his reputation should help the chances of selling stock in the first place and for the corporation to raise funds later.
   c. Sole proprietorship. Because he wants to be his own boss, there is little need for outside sources of funds and virtually no chance of losing personal property in the event of business failure.

Brain Teaser--*Answer*

1. Because we live in an ever more globally competitive environment, the federal government has allowed more concentration (bigger companies) in American industry. It is argued that this will allow those industries to experience greater economies of scale which should reduce their costs enhancing their price competitiveness in the global economy. That is, it may be necessary to allow more concentration in American industries in order for those industries to compete, or to survive, in the global economy. Moreover, it may now be more necessary to measure the degree of competitiveness in an industry in the context of the global economy as opposed to looking at the size and number of firms that exist in our domestic economy. Moreover, there is less concern today that concentration in an industry will result in higher "monopoly" prices because of the competition from abroad.

Chapter 5
Small Businesses, New Ventures, and Franchises

LEARNING OBJECTIVES
After studying this chapter, you should be able to:

1. Differentiate between lifestyle businesses and high-growth ventures. (130)
2. Identify three characteristics (other than size) that differentiate small companies from larger ones. (130-131)
3. List four important functions of small businesses in the economy. (132)
4. Identify three factors contributing to the increase in the number of small businesses. (133-134)
5. Enumerate three ways of getting into business for yourself. (134-136)
6. Outline the pros and cons of owning a franchise. (137-144)
7. Name twelve topics that should be covered in a formal business plan. (147-148)
8. Explain how small businesses can benefit from using the internet. (149-151)

TRUE-FALSE
Indicate whether the statement is generally true or false by placing a "T" or "F" in the space provided. If it is a false statement, correct it so that it becomes a true statement.

_____ 1. Most small businesses are high-growth ventures, intended to achieve rapid growth and high profits on investment.

_____ 2. One reliable source of information for small businesses is the Small Business Association (SBA), a government agency which serves as a resource and advocate for small firms.

_____ 3. Small companies tend to be innovative, partly because company owners are more accessible and partly because these companies offer more opportunity for individual expression.

_____ 4. Running a small business takes a lot of hard work, and being a successful corporate employee doesn't necessarily translate into being a successful small-business owner.

_____ 5. Small businesses do not provide for very many new jobs.

_____ 6. Many small businesses act as distributors, servicing agents, and suppliers to large corporations.

_____ 7. Small businesses have accounted for a small fraction of the nation's new product developments.

_____ 8. As technology gets cheaper and more advanced, small companies can compete on a level playing field with larger companies.

_____ 9. Women entrepreneurs make up one of the fastest-growing segments in the small-business economy.

_____ 10. You can start a new business from scratch, buy a going concern, or invest in a franchise.

_____ 11. A franchisee is the seller of a franchise, whereas a franchisor is the buyer of the franchise.

_____ 12. One disadvantage of a franchise is wide name recognition and mass advertising.

_____ 13. One advantage of a franchise is the help and support provided by the franchisor.

_____ 14. One disadvantage of a franchise is the monthly royalty payment to the franchisor.

_____ 15. Today, the relationship between franchisor and franchisee is becoming less of a joint venture.

_____ 16. The best way to protect yourself from a poor franchise investment is to study the opportunity very carefully before you commit.

_____ 17. Hoping to boost their economies and create jobs, state and local governments have launched hundreds of programs to help small businesses.

_____ 18. After you have started a new business, you need to develop a business plan.

_____ 19. In a business plan, at a minimum, one should describe the basic concept of the business and outline specific goals, objectives, and resource requirements.

_____ 20. The internet provides small companies with the ability to market and distribute their products globally, seek assistance and find resources to help them do a better job, establish two-way communication with customers, and test to see whether a market exists for their product and service.

MULTIPLE CHOICE
Circle the one best answer for each of the following questions.

1. Which of the following statements is true?
   a. Small businesses are the cornerstone of the U.S. economy.
   b. Lifestyles businesses are intended to grow rapidly and earn large profits on investment.
   c. High-growth businesses are intended to provide the owner with a comfortable livelihood.
   d. All of the above are true.

2. Small businesses are characterized by
   a. being innovative.
   b. having limited resources.
   c. their owners working hard to perform a variety of job functions.
   d. all of the above.

3. Which of the following is *false* of small businesses in the economy?
   a. Small businesses provide almost half of the private U.S. work force.
   b. Small businesses rarely provide specialized goods and services.
   c. Small businesses supply many of the needs of large corporations.
   d. Small businesses provide for many new product developments.

4. Which of the following is a factor contributing to the increase in the number of small businesses?
   a. The affordability and advancement of new technology
   b. There has been a relatively large increase in the number of minority entrepreneurs entering the work force.
   c. Corporate downsizing and outsourcing have fueled the growth in small businesses.
   d. All of the above are factors.

5. Outsourcing
   a. has become less common in the last few decades.
   b. is not very common in the field of information technology.
   c. is subcontracting work to outside companies.
   d. is a business arrangement in which a small business obtains rights to sell the goods or services of the supplier.

6. A way to get into business for yourself is to
   a. start a new company from scratch.
   b. buy a going concern.
   c. invest in a franchise.
   d. do all of the above.

7. Which of the following statements is *false*?
   a. Franchising is very common.
   b. A franchise enables one to use a larger company's trade name and sell its products or services in a specific territory.
   c. If a franchisee pays an initial fee in establishing the franchise, then he/she does not have to pay the franchisor a monthly royalty fee.
   d. A franchise may constrain the franchisee's independence.

8. Which of the following is *false* about a franchise?
   a. Owning a franchise rarely involves any considerable start-up expense.

   b.   A franchisee has the advantage of training and support from the franchisor.

   c.   A franchisee may have the advantage of financial support from the franchisor.

   d.   A franchisee has the advantage of wide name recognition and mass advertising.

9. A franchise agreement
   a.   is a legally binding contract that defines the relationship between the franchisee and the franchisor.
   b.   is drawn up by the franchisor, and the terms and conditions generally favor the franchisor.
   c.   should be viewed by an attorney at the request of the franchisee before purchasing the franchise.
   d.   is all of the above.

10. Which of the following statements is true about the SBA?
   a.   If you apply to several banks for financing and are turned down by all of them, you may be able to qualify for a loan backed by the SBA.
   b.   In addition to operating its loan guarantee program, the SBA provides a limited number of direct loans to minorities, women, and veterans.
   c.   Although SBA-backed loans are especially attractive because they generally have longer terms than conventional bank loans, they are difficult to receive because the demand for them vastly outstrips the agency's supply of capital.
   d.   All of the above are true.

11. Which of the following is true?
   a.   State and local governments have launched hundreds of programs to help small businesses--most now have some sort of small-company financing, and more than half offer venture-capital funds as well as research-and-development grants.
   b.   The SBA (Small Business Association) and SCORE (Service Corps of Retired Executives) are excellent government resources for small businesses.
   c.   Many state and local economic development offices and universities are forming incubator facilities to nurture fledgling businesses.
   d.   All of the above are true.

12. Which of the following statements is *false* about a business plan?
   a.   Bankers and investors prefer lengthy and very detailed business plans.
   b.   A business plan is a written document that provides an orderly statement of a company's goals and how it intends to achieve those goals.
   c.   A business plan can help persuade lenders and investors to back your business.
   d.   A good business plan must present both the company's strengths and anticipated weaknesses.

13. Small businesses can benefit by using the internet to
   a.   market and distribute their products globally.
   b.   establish two-way communication with customers.
   c.   seek assistance and find resources to help them do a better job.
   d.   do all of the above.

14. Which of the following is *false*?
   a.   If an entrepreneur is good at launching a business, then he/she is assured of success in managing the business over the long term.
   b.   One way companies expand their business is by franchising their concepts to others.
   c.   One way to overcome obstacles in expanding a business internationally is to use an export management company.
   d.   By using the internet, smaller firms can compete with bigger firms.

JEOPARDY
You have 5 seconds to complete the question to each of the following answers.

	Terms and Concepts	Small Businesses	Franchising
$100	Company that is independently owned and operated, is not dominant in its field, and meets certain criteria for the number of employees and annual sales. (130) What is_____ _____?	Most small businesses are these kinds of small businesses (130) What is_____ _____?	Someone who buys a franchise is called this. (139) What is_____ _____?
$200	Subcontracting work to outside companies. (134) What is_____ _____?	Three ways of getting into business for yourself. (134-136) What is_____ _____?	The advantages of a franchise. (141) What is_____ _____?
$300	A written document that provides an orderly statement of a company's goals and how it intends to achieve those goals. (147) What is_____ _____?	Three characteristics that differentiate small companies from larger ones. (130-131) What is_____ _____?	The disadvantages of a franchise. (142) What is_____ _____?
$400	Small businesses intended to achieve rapid growth and high profits on investment. (130) What is_____ _____?	Four important functions of small businesses in the economy. (132) What is_____ _____?	The fast-food chains, like McDonalds, are characterized by this term describing a type of franchise. (141) What is_____ _____?
$500	Supplier that grants franchise to an individual or group in exchange for payments. (139) What is_____ _____?	Three factors contributing to the increase in the number of small businesses. (5) What is_____ _____?	Today, the relationship between franchisor and franchisee is becoming more like this. (142) What is_____ _____?

MATCH THE TERMS AND CONCEPTS TO THEIR DEFINITIONS

a. business plan (147)
b. franchise (140)
c. franchisee (140)
d. franchisor (140)

e. high-growth venture (162)
f. incubator (146)
g. lifestyle (132)
h. outsourcing (134)

i. Service Corps of Retired Executives (SCORE) (146)
j. small business (130)
k. start-up companies (136)

_____   1. Supplier that grants franchise to an individual or group in exchange for payments.

_____ 2. Company that is independently owned and operated, is not dominant in its field, and meets certain criteria for the number of employees and annual sales revenues.

_____ 3. Subcontracting work to outside companies.

_____ 4. Small business owner who contracts for the right to sell goods or services of the supplier in exchange for some payment.

_____ 5. New ventures.

_____ 6. Facility that houses small businesses during their early growth phase.

_____ 7. Business arrangement in which a small business obtains rights to sell the good or service of the supplier.

_____ 8. SBA (Small Business Association) program in which retired executives volunteer as consultants to assist small businesses.

_____ 9. A written document that provides an orderly statement of a company's goals and how it intends to achieve those goals.

_____ 10. Small businesses intended to provide the owner with a comfortable livelihood.

_____ 11. Small business intended to achieve rapid growth and high profits on investment.

WORD SCRAMBLE

1. _____   2. _____   3. _____   _____
   sanchfire   toursougnic   subsines   lanp

LEARNING OBJECTIVES--POTENTIAL SHORT ANSWER OR ESSAY QUESTIONS

Learning Objective #1: **"Differentiate between lifestyle businesses and high-growth ventures."** (130)

Learning Objective #2: **"Identify three characteristics (other than size) that differentiate small companies from larger ones."** (130-131)

Learning Objective #3: **"List four important functions of small businesses in the economy."** (132)

Learning Objective #4: **"Identify three factors contributing to the increase in the number of small businesses."** (133-134)

Learning Objective #5: **"Enumerate three ways of getting into business for yourself."** (134-136)

Learning Objective #6: **"Outline the pros and cons of owning a franchise."** (137-144)

Learning Objective #7: **"Name twelve topics that should be covered in a formal business plan."** (147-148)

Learning Objective #8: **"Explain how small businesses can benefit from using the internet."** (149-151)

CRITICAL THINKING QUESTIONS

1. What are some of the things one needs to do when starting up a new business?

2. What are some of the questions which need to be addressed before signing a franchise agreement?

3. Describe the elements of a formal business plan.

BRAIN TEASER

1. State and local governments launch hundreds of programs to help small businesses boost their local economies. These programs help to create jobs for these local economies. However, constituents must pay taxes to fund these programs. Are these programs worth these tax dollars?

ANSWERS

True-False--*Answers*

1. False: Most small businesses are *lifestyle businesses*, intended to *provide the owner with a comfortable livelihood.*
2. True
3. True
4. True
5. False: Small businesses *are a principle source of* new jobs.
6. True
7. False: Small businesses have accounted for a *large* fraction of the nation's new product developments.
8. True
9. True
10. True
11. False: A franchisee is the *buyer* of a franchise , whereas a franchisor is the *seller* of the franchise.
12. False: One *advantage* of a franchise is wide name recognition and mass advertising.
13. True
14. True
15. False: Today, the relationship between franchisor and franchisee is becoming *more* of a joint venture.
16. True
17. True
18. False: *Before* you have started a new business, you need to develop a business plan.
19. True
20. True

Multiple Choice--*Answers*

1. a	5. c	9. d	13. b
2. d	6. d	10. d	14. a
3. b	7. c	11. d	
4. d	8. a	12. a	

Jeopardy---*Answers*

	Terms and Concepts	**Small Businesses**	**Franchising**
$100	a small business	lifestyle businesses	franchisee
$200	outsourcing	starting a new company from scratch, buying a going concern, or investing in a franchise	wide name recognition and mass advertising, financial help, and training and support
$300	a business plan	they tend to be more innovative, have limited resources, and their owners perform a variety of job functions	owning a franchise involves considerable start-up expense, monthly royalty payments to the franchisor, and constraints on the owner's independence
$400	high-growth ventures	they provide jobs, introduce new goods and services, supply the needs of large corporations, and provide specialized services	a *business-format* franchise
$500	a franchisor	the affordability and advancement of technology, an increase in the number of minority entrepreneurs entering the work force, and corporate downsizing and outsourcing	a joint venture

Match the Terms and Concepts to Their Definitions--*Answers*

1. d	4. c	7. b	10. g
2. j	5. k	8. i	11. e
3. h	6. f	9. a	

Word Scramble--*Answers*

1. franchise   2. outsourcing   3. business plan

Learning Objectives---Potential Short Answer or Essay Questions--*Answers*

Learning Objective #1:

Most small businesses are lifestyle businesses, intended to provide the owner with a comfortable living. High-growth ventures, on the other hand, are businesses with ambitious sales, profit, and growth objectives.

Learning Objective #2:

Small companies tend to be innovative, they tend to have limited resources, and their owners perform a variety of job functions.

Learning Objective #3:

Small businesses provide jobs, introduce new goods and services, supply the needs of large corporations, and provide specialized goods and services.

<u>Learning Objective #4:</u>
The affordability and advancement of technology, an increase in the number of minority entrepreneurs entering the work force, and corporate downsizing and outsourcing are three factors contributing to the growth in the number of small businesses today.

<u>Learning Objective #5:</u>
You can start a new company from scratch, buy a going concern, or invest in a franchise.

<u>Learning Objective #6:</u>
A franchise has the advantages of wide name recognition and mass advertising, financial help, and training and support. However, owning a franchise involves considerable start-up expense, monthly royalty payments to the franchisor, and constraints on the franchisee's independence.

<u>Learning Objective #7:</u>
A formal business plan should (1) summarize your business concept, (2) describe the company and its industry, (3) explain the product, (4) analyze the market, (5) summarize the background and qualifications of management, (6) describe your marketing strategy, (7) discuss design and development plans, (8) explain your operations plan, (9) provide your overall schedule, (10) identify risks and potential problems, (11) provide detailed financial information, and (12) explain how investors will cash out on their investment.

<u>Learning Objective #8:</u>
Small companies can market and distribute their products globally, seek assistance and find resources to help them do a better job, establish two-way communication with customers, and test to see whether a market exists for their product or service.

Critical Thinking Questions--*Answers*

1. One needs to undertake market research to make sure there is sufficient demand for one's good or service. Also, establish a business plan. Make sure it is succinct, yet thorough. In addition, create a start-up checklist similar to the one shown in Exhibit 5.6 on page 139 of the textbook.

2. See Exhibit 5.8 on page 143 of the textbook.

3. See the list of pages 147-148 of the textbook.

Brain Teaser--*Answer*

1. Yes. Although taxes must be collected to pay for these programs, these programs typically more than pay for themselves through the additional tax revenues generated from the additional jobs and income these programs create.

Chapter 6
Management Fundamentals

LEARNING OBJECTIVES
After studying this chapter, you should be able to:

1. Explain the role that goals and objectives play in management. (162-163)
2. Describe the three levels of management. (164-165)
3. Identify and explain the three types of managerial skills. (165-167)
4. Clarify how total quality management (TQM) is changing the way organizations are managed. (167-171)
5. Define the four management functions. (167-180)
6. Discuss how strategic, tactical, and operational plans are developed and used. (171)
7. Cite three leadership styles, and explain why no one style is best. (175-177)
8. Describe six measures that companies can take to better manage crises. (181-183)

TRUE-FALSE
Indicate whether the statement is generally true or false by placing a "T" or "F" in the space provided. If it is a false statement, correct it so that it becomes a true statement.

_____ 1. A statement of an organization's purpose is known as a vision.

_____ 2. The best organizational goals are specific, measurable, relevant, challenging, attainable, and time limited.

_____ 3. Objectives are broad, long-range targets or aims, whereas goals are short-term targets or aims.

_____ 4. A company using differentiation develops a level of service, a product image, unique product features (including quality), or new technologies that distinguish its product form competitors' products.

_____ 5. First-line managers are those at the top of the organization's management hierarchy.

_____ 6. Middle managers develop plans to implement the goals of top managers and coordinate the work of first-line managers.

_____ 7. Tactical objectives focus on departmental issues and describe the results necessary to achieve the organization's strategic goals.

_____ 8. In addition to setting goals and assuming various roles, managers also employ skills that fall into three basic categories: interpersonal, technical, and conceptual skills.

_____ 9. Interpersonal skills are the ability to perform the mechanics of a particular job.

_____ 10. The four management functions are: planning, organizing, leading, and controlling.

_____ 11. Total quality management (TQM) is a comprehensive, strategic management approach that builds quality into every organizational process as a way of improving customer satisfaction.

_____ 12. Benchmarking is comparing your company's process and products to the standards of the world's best companies and then working to match or exceed those standards.

_____ 13. Controlling is the primary management function.

_____ 14. Tactical plans are plans that define the actions and the resource allocation necessary to achieve strategic objectives.

_____ 15. Typically, top managers develop strategic plans, middle managers develop tactical plans, and first-line mangers develop operational plans.

_____ 16. When planning, managers working in those organizations that practice TQM must take into account employee involvement, customer focus, benchmarking, and continuous improvement.

_____ 17. Planning is the process of arranging resources to carry out the organization's plans.

_____ 18. Autocratic leaders are leaders who delegate authority and involve employees in decision making.

_____ 19. Management by objectives (MBO) provides a systematic method of setting goals for work groups and individuals so that all their activities are directly linked to achieving organizational goals.

_____ 20. Contingency plans should be created with the company's strategy goals, these plans outline steps that can prevent or counter the most serious threats and help the company recover quickly.

MULTIPLE CHOICE

Circle the one best answer for each of the following questions.

1. Which of the following statements is true?
   a. Quality is a measure of how closely a product conforms to predetermined standards and customer expectations.
   b. A mission statement is a written procedure for coordinating resources to meet organizational goals.
   c. A goal is a specific, short-term target or aim, while an objective is a broad, long-term target or aim.
   d. All of the above are true.

2. Setting appropriate company goals
   a. can give the company a competitive edge by using differentiation, cost leadership, or focus strategies.
   b. is not necessary if management is effective.
   c. is not necessary if a company utilizes a management by objective (MBO) philosophy.
   d. is not necessary if a company utilizes total quality management (TQM).

3. Middle managers
   a. set tactical objectives and coordinate the work of first-line managers.
   b. establish operational objectives and supervise the work of operating employees.
   c. take responsibility for the organization and set strategic goals.
   d. need to have good technical skills to perform their jobs effectively.

4. Which of the following statements is true?
   a. Total quality management (TQM) is both a management philosophy and a management process that focuses on delivering quality to customers.
   b. Managerial roles consist of the interpersonal role, the informational role, and the decisional role.
   c. Conceptual skills are the ability to understand relationships of parts to the whole.
   d. All of the above are true.

5. Decision making involves
   a. conceptual skills.
   b. identifying a decision situation, analyzing the problem, weighing the alternatives, choosing an alternative, and evaluating the results.
   c. some programmed and some nonprogrammed decisions.
   d. all of the above.

6. Which of the following is *not* one of the key elements of the TQM approach?
   a. Undertake employee involvement which involves employees in decision making by building teams and soliciting employee input.
   b. Undertake reverse engineering which involves buying a competitor's product, disassembling it, studying its design and manufacturing, and copying or improving when possible.
   c. Undertake a customer focus, which involves gathering customer feedback and then acting on the feedback to bettor serve customers.
   d. Undertake continuous improvement which requires an ongoing commitment to reducing defects, cutting costs, slashing production and delivery times, and offering customers innovative products.

7. Which of the following statements is true?
    a. Today's flatter organizations use more middle managers.
    b. Tactical planning establishes the actions and the resource allocation required to accomplish strategic goals.
    c. Planning is the primary management function.
    d. All of the above are true.

8. Which type of plans are usually defined for periods of two to five years and are developed by top managers?
    a. Operational plans
    b. Strategic plans
    c. Tactical plans
    d. Forecasting plans

9. The management function that monitors progress toward company goals, resets the course if goals or objectives change, and corrects deviations if goals or objectives are not being attained is called the
    a. planning function of management.
    b. organizing function of management.
    c. controlling function of management.
    d. leading function of management.

10. The order in which plans are undertaken is
    a. tactical, operational, and then strategic.
    b. strategic, tactical, and then operational.
    c. operational, strategic, and then tactical.
    d. operational, tactical, and then strategic.

11. Leaders who lead by leaving the actual decision making up to employees are practicing which leadership style?
    a. Autocratic
    b. Democratic
    c. Laissez-faire
    d. Anarchy

12. Which of the following statements is true?
    a. Not all managers are good leaders, and not every leader can manage effectively.
    b. Strong leadership is a key element in establishing a productive organizational culture.
    c. Managers can provide effective leadership by coaching and by mentoring.
    d. All of the above are true.

13. Which of the following is *not* one of steps in the management by objectives (MBO) process?
    a. Setting goals
    b. Implementing plans
    c. Reviewing performance
    d. Forecasting future performance

14. During a crisis, management should
    a. move quickly to explain the problem to the public and to its employees.
    b. make senior managers available to the media and the public to demonstrate concern.
    c. make every effort to control the situation.
    d. do all of the above.

JEOPARDY

You have 5 seconds to complete the question to each of the following answers.

	Management Goals and Objectives; Levels of Management	Types of Managerial Skills; Management Functions	Strategic, Tactical, and Operational Plans; Leadership Styles
$100	A statement of the organization's purpose. (160) What is_____ _____?	The three types of managerial skills. (165-166) What is_____ _____?	A leadership style which does not involve others in decision making. (175) What is_____ _____?
$200	These managers take responsibility for the organization and set strategic goals. (162) What is_____ _____?	This type of management skill implies the ability to understand the relationship of parts to the whole. (166) What is_____ _____?	A leadership style in which the leader delegates authority and involves employees in decision making. (175) What is_____ _____?
$300	These managers have the task of implementing the broad goals set by top management as well as setting tactical objectives. (163) What is_____ _____?	The four functions of management. (167) What is_____ _____?	These plans cover less than one year and are designed by first-line managers. (171) What is_____ _____?
$400	These managers establish operational objectives and supervise the work of operating employees. (163) What is_____ _____?	This management function entails establishing objectives and goals for an organization and determining the best ways to accomplish them. (171) What is_____ _____?	These plans usually cover one to three years and are designed by middle managers. (171) What is_____ _____?
$500	Goals are often designed to give a company a competitive edge by way of these three methods. (162) What is_____ _____?	TQM redirects management to focus on these four key elements. (168) What is_____ _____?	Plans establishing the actions and the resource allocations required to accomplish long-range goals. (171) What is_____ _____?

MATCH THE TERMS AND CONCEPTS TO THEIR DEFINITIONS

a. administrative skills (166)
b. autocratic leaders (174)
c. coaching (176)
d. conceptual skills (166)
e. contingency leadership (175)
f. contingency plans (182)
g. controlling (178)
h. crisis management (181)
i. decision making (166)
j. democratic leaders (174)

q. management (162)
r. management by objectives (MBO) (180)
s. management pyramid (164)
t. mentor (177)
u. middle managers (165)
v. mission statement (162)
w. motivating (174)
x. objective (163)
y. operational objectives (165)

ff. roles (165)
gg. standards (178)
hh. strategic goals (164)
ii. strategic plans (171)
jj. tactical objectives (165)
kk. tactical plans (171)
ll. technical skills (166)
mm. top managers (164)
nn. total quality management (TQM) (168)

k. first-line managers (165)
l. forecasting (172)
m. goal (163)
n. interpersonal skills (165)
o. laissez-faire leaders (175)
p. leading (174)

z. operational plans (171)
aa. organizational culture (177)
bb. organizing (173)
cc. participative management (168)
dd. planning (171)
ee. quality (162)

oo. transactional
    leaders (175)
pp. transformational
    leaders (175)
qq. vision (162)

_____ 1. A viable view of the future that is rooted in but improves on the present.

_____ 2. Broad, long-range target or aim.

_____ 3. Process of coordinating resources to meet organizational goals.

_____ 4. Organizational structure comprising top, middle, and lower management.

_____ 5. Goals that focus on broad organizational issues and aim to improve performance.

_____ 6. Specific, short-range target or aim.

_____ 7. Behavioral patterns associated with certain positions.

_____ 8. A statement of the organization's purpose.

_____ 9. Those in the middle of the management hierarchy; they develop plans to implement the goals of top managers and coordinate the work of first-time managers.

_____ 10. Those at the highest level of the organization's management hierarchy; they are responsible for setting strategic goals, and they have the most power and responsibility in the organization.

_____ 11. A measure of how closely a product conforms to predetermined standards and customer expectations.

_____ 12. Skills required to understand other people and to interact effectively with them.

_____ 13. Comprehensive, strategic management approach that builds quality into every organizational process as a way of improving customer satisfaction.

_____ 14. Those at the lowest level of the management hierarchy, who supervise the operating employees and implement the plans set at the higher management levels; also called supervisory managers.

_____ 15. Technical skills in information gathering, data analysis, planning, organizing, and other aspects of managerial work.

_____ 16. Ability and knowledge to perform the mechanics of a particular job.

_____ 17. Objectives that focus on departmental issues and describe the results necessary to achieve the organization's strategic goals.

_____ 18. Ability to understand the relationship of parts to the whole.

_____ 19. Sharing information with employees and involving them in decision making.

_____ 20. Establishing objectives and goals for an organization and determining the best ways to accomplish them.

_____ 21. Objectives that focus on short-term issues and describe the results needed to achieve tactical objectives and strategic goals.

_____ 22. Plans that lay out the actions and the resource allocation needed to achieve operational objectives and to support tactical plans; usually defined for less than one year and developed by first-time managers.

_____ 23. Process of identifying a decision situation, analyzing the problem, weighing the alternatives, choosing and implementing an alternative, and evaluating the results.

_____ 24. Making educated assumptions about future trends and events that will have an impact on the organization.

_____ 25. Process of guiding and motivating people to work toward organizational goals.

_____ 26. Plans that define the actions and the resource allocation necessary to achieve tactical objectives and to support strategic plans; usually defined for a period of one to three years and developed by middle managers.

_____ 27. Adapting the leadership style to what is most appropriate, given current business conditions.

_____ 28. Leaders who lead by leaving the actual decision making up to employees.

_____ 29. Plans that establish the actions and the resource allocation required to accomplish strategic goals; usually defined for periods of two to five years and developed by top managers.

_____ 30. Process of arranging resources to carry out the organization's plans.

_____ 31. Helping employees reach their highest potential by meeting with them, discussing problems that hinder their ability to work effectively, and offering suggestions and encouragement to overcome these problems.

_____ 32. Leaders who do not involve others in decision making.

_____ 33. Process of measuring progress against goals and objectives and correcting deviations if results are not as expected.

_____ 34. Instilling employees with a desire to do the job and to perform at their peak.

_____ 35. Leaders who excel at creating an efficient organization and motivating employees to meet expectations.

_____ 36. Criteria against which performance may be measured.

_____ 37. Experienced manager or employee with a wide network of industry colleagues that can explain office politics, serve as a role model for appropriate business behavior, and help other employees negotiate the corporate structure.

_____ 38. Leaders who delegate authority and involve employees in decision making.

_____ 39. A blueprint for actions the company can take to cope with unforeseen events.

_____ 40. A set of shared values and norms that support the management system and that guide management and employee behavior.

_____ 41. System for minimizing the harm that might result from some unusually threatening situations.

_____ 42. Leaders who possess the ability to inspire long-term vision, creativity, and change in their employees.

_____ 43. A motivational tool whereby managers and employees work together to structure personal goals and objectives for every individual, department, and project to mesh with the organization's goals.

WORD SCRAMBLE

1. _____   2. _____   3. _____
   groaniginz   nangplin   trollconing

LEARNING OBJECTIVES--POTENTIAL SHORT ANSWER OR ESSAY QUESTIONS

Learning Objective #1: "Explain the role that goals and objectives play in management." (162-163)

Learning Objective #2: "Describe the three levels of management." (164-165)

Learning Objective #3: **"Identify and explain the three types of managerial skills."** (165-167)

Learning Objective #4: **"Clarify how total quality management (TQM) is changing the way organizations are managed."** (167-171)

Learning Objective #5: **"Define the four management functions."** (167-180)

Learning Objective #6: **"Discuss how strategic, tactical, and operational plans are developed and used."** (171)

Learning Objective #7: **"Cite three leadership styles, and explain why no one style is best."** (175-177)

Learning Objective #8: **"Describe six measures that companies can take to better manage crises."** (181-183)

CRITICAL THINKING QUESTIONS

1. You are applying for a supervisory position in a local company. In preparing for the upcoming interview, what types of managerial skills should you stress that you possess?

2. Holding everything else the same, which type of leadership style do you think would be most appropriate in managing relatively unskilled workers? What about managing professionals?

BRAIN TEASER

1. Why do managers establish "procedures," "policies," and "rules"?

ANSWERS

True-False--*Answers*

1. False: A statement of an organization's purpose is known as a *mission statement*.
2. True
3. False: *Goals* are broad, long-range targets or aims, whereas *objectives* are short-term targets or aims.
4. True
5. False: *Top* managers are those at the top of the organization's management hierarchy.
6. True
7. True
8. True
9. False: *Technical* skills are the ability to perform the mechanics of a particular job.
10. True
11. True
12. True
13. False: *Planning* is the primary management function.
14. False: *Strategic* plans are plans that define the actions and the resource allocation necessary to achieve strategic objectives.
15. True
16. True
17. False: *Organizing* is the process of arranging resources to carry out the organization's plans.
18. False: *Democratic* leaders are leaders who delegate authority and involve employees in decision making.
19. True
20. True

Multiple Choice--*Answers*

1. a	5. d	9. c	13. d
2. a	6. b	10. b	14. d
3. a	7. c	11. c	
4. d	8. b	12. d	

Jeopardy—*Answers*

	Management Goals and Objectives; Levels of Management	Types of Managerial Skills; Management Functions	Strategic, Tactical, and Operational Plans; Leadership Styles
$100	a mission statement	interpersonal, technical, and conceptual skills	an autocratic leadership style
$200	top managers	a conceptual skill	a democratic leadership style
$300	middle managers	planning, organizing, leading, and controlling	operational plans
$400	first-line managers	planning	tactical plans
$500	differentiation, cost leadership, and focus	employee involvement, customer focus, benchmarking, and continuous improvement	strategic plans

Match the Terms and Concepts to Their Definitions--*Answers*

1. qq	7. ff	13. nn	19. cc	25. p	31. c	37. t	43. r
2. m	8. v	14. k	20. dd	26. kk	32. b	38. j	
3. q	9. u	15. a	21. y	27. e	33. g	39. f	
4. s	10. mm	16. ll	22. z	28. o	34. w	40. aa	
5. hh	11. ee	17. jj	23. i	29. ii	35. oo	41. h	
6. x	12. n	18. d	24. l	30. bb	36. gg	42. pp	

Word Scramble---*Answers*

1. organizing   2. planning   3. controlling

Learning Objectives--Potential Short Answer or Essay Questions--*Answers*

Learning Objective #1:

Goals and objectives establish long- and short-range targets that help managers fulfill the company's mission. Setting appropriate goals increases employee motivation, establishes standards by which individual and group performance can be measured, guides employee activity, and clarifies management's expectations. In addition, goals are often designed to give the company a competitive edge by using differentiation, cost leadership, or focus strategies.

Learning Objective #2:

Top managers take overall responsibility for the organization and set strategic goals. Middle managers have the task of implementing the broad goals set by top management as well as setting tactical objectives and coordinating the work of first-line managers. First-line managers establish operational objectives and supervise the work of operating employees.

Learning Objective #3:

Managers use (1) interpersonal skills to communicate with other people, work effectively with them, and lead them, (2) technical skills to perform the mechanics of a particular job, and (3) conceptual skills (including decision making) to see the organization as a whole, to see it in the context of its environment, and to understand how the various parts interrelate.

Learning Objective #4:

Total quality management is both a management philosophy and a management process that focuses on delivering quality to customers. TQM redirects management to focus on four key elements: Employee involvement includes team building and soliciting employee input on decisions. Customer focus involves gathering customer feedback and then acting on that feedback to better serve customers. Benchmarking involves measuring the company's standards against the standards of industry leaders. Continuous improvement requires an ongoing commitment to reducing defects, cutting costs, slashing production and delivery times, and offering customers innovative products.

Learning Objective #5:

The four management functions are (1) planning-establishing objectives and goals for the organization and determining the best ways to achieve them; (2) organizing-arranging resources to carry out the organization's plans; (3) leading-influencing and motivating people to work effectively and willingly toward company goals; and (4) controlling-monitoring progress toward organizational goals, resetting the course if goals or objectives change in response to shifting conditions, and correcting deviations if goals or objectives are not being attained.

Learning Objective #6:

Strategic plans usually cover two to five years and are designed by top managers to achieve strategic goals. Tactical plans are then laid out to achieve tactical objectives and to support strategic plans. They usually cover one to three years and are designed by middle managers who consult with first-line managers before reporting to top management. Operational plans are laid out to achieve operational objectives and to support tactical plans. They cover less than one year and are designed by first-line managers, who consult with middle managers.

Learning Objective #7:

Three leadership styles are autocratic, democratic, and laissez-faire (also called free-rein). Each may work best in a different situation: autocratic when quick decisions are needed, democratic when employee participation in decision making is desirable, and laissez-faire when fostering creativity is a priority. Good leaders are flexible enough to respond with the best approach for the situation.

Learning Objective #8:

During a crisis, an organization can (1) move quickly to explain the problem to the public and to its employees, (2) make senior managers available to the media and the public to demonstrate concern and commitment, and (3) make every effort to control the situation. Before the crisis occurs, an organization may (4) set up a crisis team of people who react well under stress and who can communicate effectively, (5) prepare contingency plans to deal with the most serious threats, and (6) hold drills under simulated crisis conditions.

Critical Thinking Questions--*Answers*

1. Although the three basic managerial skills--interpersonal, technical, and conceptual--necessary for effective management are important at all levels of management, technical skills are relatively more important at the supervisory level because it is a first-line manager position. But because interpersonal skills are equally important at all levels of management, then you should stress your technical *and* interpersonal skills in the interview.

2. Unskilled workers are typically less sophisticated and motivated. A more autocratic style of leadership may prove more fruitful in "getting the job done." However, most professionals don't like being "bossed around." A more democratic or laissez-faire style is usually more appropriate and successful.

Brain Teaser--*Answer*

1. "Procedures," "policies," and "rules" are really programmed decisions. These types of decisions involve simple, frequently occurring problems or opportunities for which solutions have been determined previously. Such decisions are made quickly by making reference to a procedure, rule or company policy, and managers need spend little time in identifying and evaluating alternatives. In sum, rules and procedures allow managers to spend their time more wisely on more important matters. They are a built-in time-management tool for managers.

Chapter 7
Organization, Teamwork, and Communication

LEARNING OBJECTIVES

After studying this chapter, you should be able to:
1. Describe the three ways to design a company's formal organization structure. (191-200)
2. Explain the concepts of authority, accountability, responsibility, delegation, and span of management. (192-195)
3. Define four types of departmentalization. (195-199)
4. Clarify how vertical organization differs from horizontal coordination. (199-200)
5. Describe the four primary types of teams. (200-204)
6. Review the five stages of team development. (205)
7. Explain how companies use internal and external communication networks. (209-214)
8. List some of the barriers to effective communication, and explain how to overcome them. (215-216)

TRUE-FALSE
Indicate whether the statement is generally true or false by placing a "T" or "F" in the space provided. If it is a false statement, correct it so that it becomes a true statement.

_____ 1. An organization chart essentially depicts the official design for accomplishing tasks that lead to achieving the organization's goals.

_____ 2. Three ways to design a formal organization structure include vertical organization, departmentalization, and horizontal coordination.

_____ 3. Horizontal organization refers to the structure which links activities at the top of the organization with those at the middle and lower levels.

_____ 4. Accountability is the obligation to perform the duties and achieve the goals and objectives associated with a particular position.

_____ 5. Regardless of how an organization divides its tasks, it will function more smoothly if employees are clear about two things: who is responsible for each task, and who has the authority to make official decisions.

_____ 6. The simplest and most common chain-of-command system is known as "line-and-staff organizations."

_____ 7. When a large number of people report directly to one person, that person has a wide span of management.

_____ 8. A flat organization has a narrow span of management and many hierarchical levels.

_____ 9. The trend in business today is towards centralization—concentration of decision-making authority at the top of the organization.

_____ 10. Departmentalization by function is grouping departments according to similarities in product, process, customer, or geography.

_____ 11. Departmentalization by matrix is electronically connecting separate companies that perform selected tasks for a small headquarters organization.

_____ 12. Horizontal coordination is coordinating communication and activities across departments.

_____ 13. Formal teams typically fall into three categories: vertical teams, horizontal teams, and special-purpose teams.

_____ 14. The most common type of informal team is the problem-solving team.

_____ 15. Vertical teams are composed of employees from about the same level of the hierarchy but from different functional areas and are often called "cross-functional teams."

_____ 16. A task force is a team of people from several departments who are temporarily brought together to address a specific issue.

_____ 17. The five stages of team development are the forming, storming, norming, performing, and adjourning stages.

_____ 18. In the forming stage of team development, conflict often arises as coalitions and power struggles develop.

_____ 19. Internal communication networks involve both formal and informal communication channels.

_____ 20. Effective communicators overcome the main barriers to communication by crafting their messages carefully, selecting the appropriate communication medium, minimizing noise, and facilitating recipient feedback.

MULTIPLE CHOICE
Circle the one best answer for each of the following questions.

1. Which of the following elements are needed for a company to achieve its goals?
    a. Vertical organization
    b. Departmentalization
    c. Horizontal organization
    d. All of the above are needed.

2. Which of the following statements is true?
    a. Horizontal organization links the activities at the top of the organization with those at the middle and lower levels.
    b. Authority is the power granted by the organization to make decisions, take actions, and allocate resources to accomplish goals.
    c. Delegation is the obligation to report results to supervisors or team members and justify outcomes that fall below expectations.
    d. Accountability is the obligation to perform the duties and achieve the goals and objectives associated with a particular position.

3. Which of the following statements is true?
    a. A flat organization has a narrow span of management and many hierarchical levels.
    b. The line-and-staff organization system has a clear chain of command but also includes functional groups of people who provide advice and specialized services.
    c. If a manager has very few people reporting directly to her, then she has a wide span of management.
    d. All of the above are true.

4. Which of the following statements is true?
    a. No formula exists for determining the ideal span of management.
    b. Organizations that focus decision-making authority near the top of the chain of command are said to be decentralized.
    c. The most complicated chain-of-command is the line organization.
    d. All of the above are true.

5. Departmentalization:
    a. can occur by function, division, matrix, and network.
    b. by function is grouping workers according to their similar skills, resource use, and expertise.
    c. by matrix is permanently assigning employees to both a functional group and a project team.
    d. is all of the above.

6. Which of the following statements is true?
    a. Regardless of whether an organization uses a functional, divisional, matrix, or network structure, it must coordinate activities and communication among its different departments.
    b. Horizontal communication is coordinating communication and activities across departments.
    c. One way to achieve horizontal communication is to use a managerial integrator--someone who coordinates activities of several functional departments but belongs to none
    d. All of the above are true.

7. Which of the following statements about teams is *false*?
    a. The type, structure, and composition of individual teams within an organization all depend on the organization's strategic goals.

b. Problem-solving teams are informal teams of 5 to 12 employees from the same department who meet voluntarily to find ways of improving quality, efficiency, and the work environment.

c. A task force is a team that may become a permanent part of the organization and is designed to deal with regularly recurring tasks.

d. A self-directed team is a team in which members are responsible for an entire process or operation.

8. A temporary team that exists outside the formal organization hierarchy and is created to achieve a specific goal is called a
   a. virtual team.
   b. functional team.
   c. special-purpose team.
   d. committee.

9. Which of the following is *not* a stage of team development?
   a. escalating
   b. storming
   c. norming
   d. performing

10. The stage of team development in which conflicts are resolved and harmony develops is the
    a. forming stage.
    b. norming stage.
    c. adjourning stage.
    d. storming stage.

11. Which of the following is true about teams?
    a. As teams move through the various stages of development, two things happen: they develop a certain level of cohesiveness, and they develop norms.
    b. When team cohesiveness is coupled with strong management support for team objectives, teams tend to be more productive.
    c. Team members can assume one of four roles: a task-specialist role, a nonparticipator role, a socioemotional role, and a dual role of focusing on task and people.
    d. All of the above are true.

12. Which of the following statements is true?
    a. Team members who focus primarily on the task-specialist role typically make effective team leaders.
    b. Team conflicts can arise for a number of reasons and avoidance, defusion, and confrontation are ways of dealing with conflict.
    c. The benefits of teams always outweigh their costs.
    d. All of the above are true.

13. Which of the following is *false* about communication in an organization?
    a. When managers depend too heavily on formal channels for communicating, they risk encountering distortion.
    b. The grapevine is an informal communication network.
    c. Networking is a term describing the communication system that enables computers to transmit and receive messages over telephone lines or other electronic networks.
    d. There are many barriers to effective communication but there are ways of overcoming them.

JEOPARDY

You have 5 seconds to complete the question to each of the following answers.

	Organization	**Teams**	**Communication**
$100	Three ways to design a formal organization structure. (191) What is_____ _____?	The four primary types of teams. (202) What is_____ _____?	The exchange of information and ideas within an organization. (209) What is_____ _____?
$200	Assignment of work and the authority and responsibility required to complete it. (192) What is_____ _____?	Generally, this range is considered the optimal size for teams. (204) What is_____ _____?	The two basic forms of communication. (212) What is_____ _____?
$300	An organization structure having a narrow span of management and many hierarchical levels. (193) What is_____ _____?	The two things a team must accomplish if it is to be successful over time. (204-205) What is_____ _____?	The extent to which listening and observing skills are important in effective communication. (212) What is_____ _____?
$400	Grouping workers according to their similar skills, resource use, and expertise. (195) What is_____ _____?	A team member who doesn't contribute sufficiently to the group's activities because members are not being held individually accountable for their work. (208) What is_____ _____?	Two barriers to effective communication. (215-216) What is_____ _____?
$500	This type of coordination is essential and coordinates communication and activities across departments. (199) What is_____ _____?	The five stages of team development. (205) What is_____ _____?	Two ways to overcome barriers to communication. (216) What is_____ _____?

MATCH THE TERMS AND CONCEPTS TO THEIR DEFINITIONS

a.　accountability (192)

b.　authority (192)

c.　centralization (195)

d.　chain of command (193)

e.　cohesiveness (205)

f.　committee (203)

g.　cross-functional team (202)

h.　customer divisions (197)

i.　decentralization (195)

j.　delegation (192)

k.　departmentalization (195)

l.　departmentalization by division (195)

y.　horizontal coordination (199)

z.　informal organization (193)

aa.　internal communication (209)

bb.　line organization (193)

cc.　line-and-staff organization (19)

dd.　managerial integrator (199)

ee.　networking (212)

ff.　norms (206)

gg.　organization chart (192)

hh.　organization structure (192)

ii.　problem-solving team (202)

jj.　process divisions (196)

m. departmentalization by function (195)
n. departmentalization by matrix (198)
o. departmentalization by network (199)
p. distortion (210)
q. electronic mail (e-mail) (213)
r. external communication network (212)
s. flat organization (193)
t. formal communication network (209)
u. free rider (208)
v. functional team (202)
w. geographic divisions (197)
x. grapevine (211)

kk. product divisions (197)
ll. responsibility (192)
mm. self-directed team (203)
nn. span of management (193)
oo. special-purpose team (204)
pp. tall organization (193)
qq. task force (203)
rr. team (201)
ss. vertical organization (191)
tt. virtual team (204)
uu. work specialization (191)

_____ 1. Structure linking activities at the top of the organization with those at the middle and lower levels.

_____ 2. Obligation to perform the duties and achieve the goals and objectives associated with a particular position.

_____ 3. Network of informal employee interactions that are not defined by the formal structure.

_____ 4. Specialization in or responsibility for some portion of an organization's overall work tasks; also called division of labor.

_____ 5. Power granted by the organization to make decisions, take actions, and allocate resources to accomplish goals.

_____ 6. Pathway for the flow of authority from one management level to the next.

_____ 7. Team that uses communication technology to bring geographically distant employees together to achieve goals.

_____ 8. Organization having a wide span of management and few hierarchical levels.

_____ 9. Divisional structure based on the major steps of a production process.

_____ 10. Manager who coordinates activities of several functional departments but belongs to none.

_____ 11. Divisional structure based on location of operations.

_____ 12. Organization system that has a clear chain of command but that also includes functional groups of people who provide advice and specialized services.

_____ 13. Making and using contacts both inside and outside the organization.

_____ 14. Delegation of decision-making authority to employees in lower-level positions.

_____ 15. A measure of how committed the team members are to their team's goals.

_____ 16. Team member who doesn't contribute sufficiently to the group's activities because members are not being held individually accountable for their work.

_____ 17. Team in which members are responsible for an entire process or operation.

_____ 18. Concentration of decision-making authority at the top of the organization.

_____ 19. Organization structure having a narrow span of management and many hierarchical levels.

_____ 20. Communication network that follows the official structure of the organization.

_____ 21. Framework enabling managers to divide responsibilities, ensure employee accountability, and distribute decision-making authority.

_____ 22. Communication among employees within an organization.

_____ 23. Obligation to report results to supervisors or team members and justify outcomes that fall below expectations.

_____ 24. Communication network of the informal organization.

_____ 25. Chain-of-command system that establishes a clear line of authority flowing from the top down.

_____ 26. Grouping people within an organization according to function, division, matrix, or network.

_____ 27. Diagram showing how employees and tasks are grouped and where the lines of communication and authority flow.

_____ 28. Grouping departments according to similarities in product, process, customer, or geography.

_____ 29. Permanently assigning employees to both a functional group and a project team (thus using functional and divisional patterns simultaneously).

_____ 30. Team of people from several departments who are temporarily brought together to address a specific issue.

_____ 31. Communication system that enables computers to transmit and receive written messages over telephone lines or other electronic networks.

_____ 32. Team that may become a permanent part of the organization and is designed to deal with regularly recurring tasks.

_____ 33. A unit of two or more people who share a mission and collective responsibility as they work together to achieve a goal.

_____ 34. Team that draws together employees from different functional areas.

_____ 35. Informal standards of conduct that guide team behavior.

_____ 36. Team whose members come from a single functional department and which is based on the organization's vertical structure.

_____ 37. Electronically connecting separate companies that perform selected tasks for a small headquarters organization.

_____ 38. Temporary team that exist outside the formal organization hierarchy and is created to achieve a specific goal.

_____ 39. Number of people under one manager's control; also known as span of control.

_____ 40. Communication channels that carry information in and out of the organization.

_____ 41. Divisional structure that focuses on customers or clients.

_____ 42. Coordinating communication and activities across departments.

_____ 43. Divisional structure based on the major steps of a production process.

_____ 44. Assignment of work and the authority and responsibility required to complete it.

_____ 45. Grouping workers according to their similar skills, resource use, and expertise.

_____ 46. Misunderstanding that results from a message passing through too many links in the organization.

_____ 47. Informal team of 5 to 12 employees from the same department who meet voluntarily to find ways of improving quality, efficiency, and the work environment.

WORD SCRAMBLE

1. _____   2. _____   3. _____
   wortmeak   talmentraizdepation   tommunconicia

LEARNING OBJECTIVES--POTENTIAL SHORT ANSWER OR ESSAY QUESTIONS

Learning Objective #1: "Describe the three ways to design a company's formal organization structure." (191-200)

Learning Objective #2: **"Explain the concepts of authority, accountability, responsibility, delegation, and span of management."** (192-195)

Learning Objective #3: **"Define four types of departmentalization."** (195-199)

Learning Objective #4: **"Clarify how vertical organization differs from horizontal coordination."** (199-200)

Learning Objective #5: **"Describe the four primary types of teams."** (200-204)

Learning Objective #6: **"Review the five stages of team development."** (205)

Learning Objective #7: **"Explain how companies use internal and external communication networks."** (209-214)

Learning Objective #8: **"List some of the barriers to effective communication, and explain how to overcome them."** (215-216)

CRITICAL THINKING QUESTIONS

1. Why are the flatter, more horizontal organizational structures observed in corporations today (discussed in this chapter) more often accompanied by more democratic styles of leadership (discussed in the last chapter)?

2. You are at a party and one person comments that the downsizing taking place in corporate America is the result of greed on the part of the corporation. Another person replies that, because of the increasing globalization of markets and production, much of the downsizing is due to the increased competition facing American corporations from abroad. You are asked to respond? How do you reply?

BRAIN TEASER

1. Why might downsizing without restructuring (reengineering) be counterproductive?

ANSWERS

True-False--*Answers*

1. True
2. True
3. False: *Vertical* organization refers to the structure which links activities at the top of the organization with those at the middle and lower levels.
4. False: *Responsibility* is the obligation to perform the duties and achieve the goals and objectives associated with a particular position.
5. True
6. False: The simplest and most common chain-of-command system is known as *"line organizations."*
7. True
8. False: A *tall* organization has a narrow span of management and many hierarchical levels.
9. False: The trend in business today is towards *decentralization—delegation of decision-making authority to employees in lower-level positions.*
10. False: Departmentalization by *division* is grouping departments according to similarities in product, process, customer, or geography.
11. False: Departmentalization by *network* is electronically connecting separate companies that perform selected tasks for a small headquarters organization.

12. True
13. True
14. True
15. False: *Horizontal* teams are composed of employees from about the same level of the hierarchy but from different functional areas and are often called "cross-functional teams."
16. True
17. True
18. False: In the *storming* stage of team development, conflict often arises as coalitions and power struggles develop.
19. True
20. True

Multiple Choice--*Answers*

1. d	5. d	9. a	13. c
2. b	6. d	10. b	
3. b	7. c	11. d	
4. a	8. c	12. b	

Jeopardy—*Answers*

	Organization	**Teams**	**Communication**
$100	vertical organization, departmentalization, and horizontal organization	vertical, horizontal, special-purpose, and self-directed teams	internal communication
$200	delegation	5 - 12	verbal and nonverbal
$300	tall organization	it must accomplish its task and meet its members social well-being	very important
$400	departmentalization by function	a free rider	perceptual differences, filtering, cultural differences, language, lack of attention, information overload, lack of trust, steep hierarchies, physical distractions, or improper medium selection
$500	horizontal coordination	forming, storming, norming, performing, and adjourning	crafting the message carefully, choosing an appropriate communication medium, minimizing noise, or facilitating recipient feedback

Match the Terms and Concepts to Their Definitions--*Answers*

1. ss	7. tt	13. ee	19. pp	25. bb	31. q	37. o	43. kk
2. ll	8. s	14. i	20. t	26. k	32. f	38. oo	44. j
3. z	9. jj	15. e	21. hh	27. gg	33. rr	39. nn	45. m
4. uu	10. dd	16. u	22. aa	28. l	34. g	40. r	46. p
5. b	11. w	17. mm	23. a	29. n	35. ff	41. h	47. ii
6. d	12. cc	18. c	24. x	30. qq	36. v	42. y	

Word Scramble--*Answers*

1. teamwork   2. departmentalization   3. communication

Learning Objectives--Potential Short Answer or Essay Questions--*Answers*

Learning Objective #1:
  Three ways to design a formal organization structure include (1) vertical organization--defining individual jobs to complete the tasks necessary to achieve company goals; (2) departmentalization--grouping jobs into departments and larger units; and (3) horizontal coordination--aligning all tasks across departments and divisions.

Learning Objective #2:
  Authority is the power to make decisions, issue orders, carry out actions, and allocate resources to achieve the organization's goals. Accountability is the obligation to report work results to supervisors or team members and to justify any outcomes that fall below expectations. Responsibility is the employee's obligation to perform the duties and achieve the goals and objectives associated with a job. Delegation is the assignment of work and the transfer of authority and responsibility to complete that work. Span of management refers to the number of employees that a manager directly supervises (a manager who oversees many employees has a wide span of management, and one who oversees relatively few employees has a narrow span of management).

Learning Objective #3:
  Companies may departmentalize in any combination of four ways: (1) by function, which groups employees according to their skills, resource use, and expertise; (2) by division, which establishes self-contained departments formed according to similarities in product, process, customer, or geography; (3) by matrix, which assigns employees from functional departments to interdisciplinary project teams and requires them to report to both a department head and a team leader; and (4) by network, which connects separate companies that perform selected tasks for a headquarters organization.

Learning Objective #4:
  Vertical organization links the activities of top, middle, and lower organizational levels, whereas horizontal coordination links the activities of and facilitates the communication between departments without having to involve the vertical chain of command.

Learning Objective #5:
  The four primary types of teams are (1) vertical teams, which are organized along the lines of the organization's vertical structure and are limited to a single functional area; (2) horizontal teams, which are composed of employees from similar levels of the organization and draw together people with different areas of expertise; (3) special-purpose teams, which are temporary entities created to achieve a specific goal and which stand apart from the normal functions of the organization; and (4) self-directed teams, which are composed of cross-trained employees and are empowered to manage their own activities.

Learning Objective #6:
  Teams typically go through five stages of development. In the forming stage, team members become acquainted with each other and with the group's purpose. In the storming stage, conflict often arises as coalitions and power struggles develop. In the norming stage, conflicts are resolved and harmony

develops. In the performing stage, members focus on achieving the team's goals. In the adjourning stage, the team dissolves upon completion of its task.

Learning Objective #7:

Companies use internal communication networks to exchange information and ideas within the organization. Internal communication involves both formal communication channels (which follow the official organization chart and transmit communication up, down, and across the hierarchical levels) and informal communication channels (which develop from the personal relationships people form within the organization). In contrast, external communication is used to send and receive information between the organization and outside entities such as customers, vendors, suppliers, competitors, and community representatives.

Learning Objective #8:

The barriers to effective communication include perceptual differences, filtering, cultural differences, language, lack of attention, information overload, lack of trust, steep hierarchies, physical distractions, and improper medium selection. Effective communicators overcome these barriers by crafting their messages carefully, thinking about which communication medium is the most appropriate for their message, minimizing noise, and facilitating recipient feedback.

Critical Thinking Questions--*Answers*

1. The flatter, more horizontal organization, where middle management positions are eliminated, requires more direct communication, cooperation, and input from employees. A more democratic style of leadership, and the use of teams, is more fruitful in empowering employees with greater responsibility and input into decision making. Moreover, when employees believe they have had an input into a decision, they will be more apt to see to its success.

2. It may be true (and it may not be true) that some corporations are concentrating too much on short-run profit-maximization and are, therefore, looking for ways to reduce costs by downsizing (even though long-term thinking may question this wisdom. However, it is also true that there is increased competition facing corporate America from abroad. This greater competition has forced many American corporations to look for more effective ways to organize, to reduce costs, to increase their price competitiveness in the global economy. The greater competition from abroad forcing American firms to seek out more cost-effective means of production will not likely go away. Whether downsizing your staff is appropriate to achieve a competitive advantage is debatable.

Brain Teaser--*Answer*

1. Downsizing without restructuring work processes can lead to an organization so nervous about who will be laid off next that employees begin to think only of themselves and become unwilling to take risks that might benefit the firm. In addition, downsizing can cripple a company's long-term ability to meet customer needs. So, if a firm downsizes, it should also restructure.

Chapter 8
Production of Quality Goods and Services

LEARNING OBJECTIVES

After studying this chapter, you should be able to:

1. Explain the strategic importance of production and operations management. (226-227)
2. Describe the evolution of production efficiency. (227-228)
3. Discuss the role of computers and automation technology in production. (228-233)
4. Identify the key issues managers must consider when designing operations. (233-236)
5. Explain the strategic importance of managing inventory, and review the management systems used to control it. (236-241)
6. Describe the advantages and disadvantages of just-in-time (JIT) systems in production planning. (240-241)
7. Discuss the differences between quality control and quality assurance. (241-244)
8. Define the five basic steps in production control. (244-248)

TRUE-FALSE

Indicate whether the statement is generally true or false by placing a "T" or "F" in the space provided. If it is a false statement, correct it so that it becomes a true statement.

_____ 1. An analytic production system combines two or more materials to form a single product; a synthetic production system breaks raw materials into one or more distinct products, which may or may not resemble the original material in form and function.

_____ 2. Production and operations management (POM) is the coordination of an organization's resources for manufacturing goods or producing services.

_____ 3. Like other types of management, production and operation management involves the basic functions of planning, organizing, leading, and controlling.

_____ 4. Production efficiency is maximizing cost by minimizing the level of output from each resource.

_____ 5. Even though mass production has several advantages, the competitive pressures of the global economy often require production techniques that are more flexible, customer focused, and quality-oriented.

_____ 6. Automation is the manufacture of uniform products in great quantities.

_____ 7. Flexible manufacturing systems (FMS) are designed to reduce setup costs.

_____   8. Flexible manufacturing systems (FMS) are particularly desirable for "job shops," which make dissimilar items or produce at so irregular a rate that repetitive operations won't help.

_____   9. Electronic data interchange (EDI) is an information system that transmits documents such as invoices and purchase orders between computers, thereby lowering ordering costs and paperwork.

_____   10. Capacity planning is a long-term strategic decision that determines the level of resources available to an organization to meet customer demand.

_____   11. Managers interested in minimizing costs must first consider capacity, then location, and finally facility layout.

_____   12. A process layout is a method of arranging a facility so that parts with similar shapes or processing requirements are processed together in work centers.

_____   13. The goods and materials kept in stock for production or sale make up inventory, which must be managed to minimize costs and ensure that the right supplies are in the right place at the right time.

_____   14. Material requirements planning (MRP) is a computer-based system that integrates data from all departments to manage inventory and production planning and control.

_____   15. Lead time is the period that elapses between the ordering of materials and their arrival.

_____   16. Just-in-time systems reduce waste and improve quality by trying to eliminate finished-goods inventory, by pulling work through the system as opposed to pushing it, and by ordering supplies only when they are needed.

_____   17. Just-in-time systems are more susceptible to disruptions in the flow of raw materials, and they can place a heavy burden on suppliers.

_____   18. Quality assurance focuses on measuring finished products against a preset standard and weeding out any defects; quality control is a system of company-wide policies, practices, and procedures that build quality into a product and assure that each product meets quality standards.

_____   19. The five steps in production control are planning, routing, scheduling, dispatching, and following up.

MULTIPLE CHOICE

Circle the one best answer for each of the following questions.

1. Production and operations management
   a. is the coordination of an organization's resources for manufacturing goods and producing services.
   b. uses the basic functions of planning, organizing, leading, and controlling.
   c. is becoming the focus of many companies' efforts to improve quality and competitiveness.
   d. is all of the above.

2. Production has become more efficient over the last 200 years by
   a. mechanization.
   b. standardization.
   c. automation.
   d. all of the above.

3. A series of workstations at which each employee performs a specific task in the production process is
   a. mechanization.
   b. standardization.
   c. an assembly line.
   d. automation.

4. Production and operations management
   a. is undergoing rapid change.
   b. involves many activities, from interpreting market research to production planning and control of the production process.
   c. applies to all kinds of companies, regardless of size or product.
   d. is all of the above.

5. Improving production through technology can be accomplished by employing computer-aided design (CAD), which is the use of
   a. computer graphics and mathematical modeling in the development of products.
   b. computers to control production equipment.
   c. information systems that transmit documents such as invoices and purchase orders between computers, thereby lowering costs and paperwork.
   d. a computer-based system that coordinates and controls all the elements of design and production.

6. Which of the following is statements is true?
   a. Flexible manufacturing systems typically increase setup costs.
   b. The highest level of computerization in operations management is computer-integrated manufacturing (CIM).
   c. Electronic data interchange systems (EDI) link the people, machines, databases, and decisons involved in each step of producing a good.
   d. All of the above are true.

7. When designing operations, managers must first consider
   a. capacity--the volume of manufacturing or service capability that an organization possesses.
   b. the least-cost location.
   c. facility layout--the arrangement of production work centers and other facilities.
   d. personal property tax rates.

8. The best location minimizes costs with respect to
   a. regional costs--including the costs of land, construction, labor, local taxes, leasing, and energy.
   b. transportation costs.
   c. raw materials costs.
   d. all of the above.

9. Facility layout does *not* affect which of the following?
   a. the utilization of equipment
   b. the efficiency of materials handling
   c. productive capacity
   d. the productivity and morale of employees

10. A method of arranging a facility so that production proceeds along a line of workstations is a
    a. product layout.
    b. process layout.
    c. cellular layout.
    d. fixed-position layout.

11. A system for determining the right quantity of various items to have on hand and keeping track of their location, use, and condition is called
    a. supply-chain management.
    b. inventory control.
    c. purchasing.
    d. lead time.

12. The method of getting the correct materials where they are needed, on time, and without carrying unnecessary inventory is called
    a. lead time management.
    b. quality control.
    c. material requirements planning (MRP).
    d. quality assurance.

13. Just-in-time (JIT) systems attempt to reduce waste and improve quality by
    a. ordering supplies only when they are needed.
    b. holding a sufficient buffer stock of inventory to handle unforeseen circumstances.
    c. increasing finished-goods inventory to ensure that only non-defects will be shipped to customers.
    d. all of the above.

14. Which of the following is *not* one of the five basic steps in production control?
    a. Planning
    b. Performing
    c. Routing
    d. Following up

15. The step in the production control process of figuring out how production will proceed is
    a. dispatching.
    b. scheduling.
    c. planning.
    d. routing.

JEOPARDY

You have 5 seconds to complete the question to each of the following answers.

	Production	Operations	Quality Control and Assurance
$100	Minimizing cost by maximizing the level of output from each resource. (227) What is_____ _____?	The first key issue managers must consider when designing operations. (233) What is_____ _____?	Routine checking and testing of a finished product for quality against an established standard. (241) What is_____ _____?
$200	Producing customized goods and services through mass production techniques. (228) What is_____ _____?	This key issue in designing operations is concerned with regional, transportation, and raw materials cost.. (234-235) What is_____ _____?	System of policies, practices, and procedures implemented throughout the company to create and produce quality goods and services. (241) What is_____ _____?
$300	Production system using computer-controlled machines that can adapt to various versions of the same operation. (230) What is_____ _____?	This key issue in designing operations is concerned with the arrangement of production work centers and other elements. (235-236) What is_____ _____?	Monitoring all aspects of the production process to see whether the process is operating as it should. (242) What is_____ _____?
$400	This is the highest level of computerization in operations management. (230) What is_____ _____?	Operations management is concerned with these key issues. (236-248) What is_____ _____?	Planning, routing, scheduling, dispatching, and following up on production so as to achieve efficiency and high quality. (245) What is_____ _____?
$500	Two potential problems with the use of technology in production. (232) What is_____ _____?	An inventory-control technique that helps a manufacturer get the correct materials where they are needed, when they are needed, and without unnecessary stockpiling. (5) What is_____ _____?	Planning tool that managers of complex projects use to determine the optimal order of activities, the expected time for project completion, and the best use of resources. (247) What is_____ _____?

MATCH THE TERMS AND CONCEPTS TO THEIR DEFINITIONS

a. analytic system (226)

b. assembly line (227)

c. automation (227)

d. bill of materials (246)

e. capacity planning (233)

f. cellular layout (235)

aa. perpetual inventory (239)

bb. process layout (235)

cc. product layout (235)

dd. production (226)

ee. production and operations management (POM) (227)

g. computer-aided design (CAD) (228)
h. computer-aided engineering (CAE) (228)
i. computer-aided manufacturing (CAM) (229)
j. computer-integrated manufacturing (CIM) (229)
k. critical path (247)
l. dispatching (247)
m. electronic data interchange (EDI) (232)
n. fixed-position layout (235)
o. flexible manufacturing system (FMS) (230)
p. Gantt chart (246)
q. inventory (238)
r. inventory control (238)
s. ISO 9000 (243)
t. just-in-time (JIT) system (240)
u. lead time (238)
v. manufacturing resource planning (MRP II) (239)
w. mass customization (228)
x. mass production (227)
y. material requirements planning (MRP) (239)
z. mechanization (227)

ff. production control (245)
gg. production efficiency (227)
hh. production forecasting (245)
ii. program evaluation and review technique (PERT) (247)
jj. purchasing (236)
kk. quality assurance (241)
ll. quality control (241)
nn. robots (228)
oo. routing (246)
pp. scheduling (246)
qq. setup costs (230)
rr. standardization (227)
ss. statistical process control (SPC) (242)
tt. statistical quality control (SQC) (242)
uu. supply-chain management (238)
vv. synthetic system (226)

_____ 1. A long-term strategic decision that determines the level of resources available to an organization to meet customer demand.

_____ 2. Series of workstations at which each employee performs a specific task in the production process.

_____ 3. Estimating how much of a company's goods and services must be produced in order to meet future demand.

_____ 4. Transformation of resources into goods or services that people need or want.

_____ 5. Method of arranging a facility so that parts with similar shapes or processing requirements are processed together in work centers.

_____ 6. Issuing work orders and schedules to department heads and supervisors.

_____ 7. Computer-based systems that coordinate and control all the elements of design and production, including CAD and CAM.

_____ 8. Integrating all of the facilities, functions, and processes associated with the production of goods and services, from suppliers to customers.

_____ 9. System that uses computers to monitor inventory levels and automatically generate purchase orders when supplies are needed.

_____ 10. Use of computer graphics and mathematical modeling in the development of products.

_____ 11. Use of random sampling and control charts to monitor the production process.

_____ 12. Goods kept in stock for the production process or for sales to final customers.

_____ 13. Method of arranging a facility so that the product is stationary and equipment and personnel come to it.

_____ 14. Production process that breaks incoming materials into various component products.

_____ 15. Routine checking and testing of a finished product for quality against an established standard.

_____ 16. Monitoring all aspects of the production process to see whether the process is operating as it should.

_____ 17. Programmable machines that can complete a variety of tasks by working with tools and materials.

_____ 18. List of all parts and materials in a product that are to be made or purchased.

_____ 19. Acquiring the raw materials, parts, components, supplies, and finished products needed to produce goods and services.

_____ 20. Production process that combines two or more materials or components to create finished products; the reverse of an analytic system.

_____ 21. Expenses incurred each time a producer organizes resources to begin producing goods or services.

_____ 22. Use of computers to control production.

_____ 23. Computer-based system that integrates data from all departments to manage inventory and production planning and control.

_____ 24. Period that elapses between the ordering of materials and their arrival from the supplier.

_____ 25. Coordination of an organization's resources for the manufacture of goods or the delivery of services.

_____ 26. Method of getting the correct materials where they are needed, on time, and without carrying unnecessary inventory.

_____ 27. System of policies, practices, and procedures implemented throughout the company to create and produce quality goods and services.

_____ 28. Producing customized goods and services through mass production techniques.

_____ 29. Information systems that transmit documents such as invoices and purchase orders between computers, thereby lowering ordering costs and paperwork.

_____ 30. System for determining the right quantity of various items to have on hand and keeping track of their location, use, and condition.

_____ 31. Minimizing cost by maximizing the level of output from each resource.

_____ 32. Continuous system that pulls materials through the production process, making sure that all materials arrive just when they are needed with minimal inventory and waste.

_____ 33. Production system using computer-controlled machines that can adapt to various versions of the same operation.

_____ 34. Method of arranging a facility so that production proceeds along a line of workstations.

_____ 35. Planning, routing, scheduling, dispatching, and following up on production so as to achieve efficiency and high quality.

_____ 36. Specifying the sequence of operations and the path the work will take through the production facility.

_____ 37. Use of machines to do work previously done by people.

_____ 38. Global standards set by the International Organization for Standardization establishing a minimum level of acceptable quality.

_____ 39. Bar chart used to control schedules by showing how long each part of a production process should take and when it should take place.

_____ 40. Method of arranging a facility so that production tasks are carried out in separate departments containing specialized equipment and personnel.

_____ 41. Manufacture of uniform products in great quantities.

_____ 42. In a PERT network diagram, the sequence of operations that requires the longest time to complete.

_____ 43. Uniformity in goods or parts, making them interchangeable.

_____ 44. The use of computer-generated three-dimensional images and computerized calculations that allow engineers to test products.

_____ 45. Process of determining how long each production operation takes and then setting a starting and ending time for each.

_____ 46. Planning tool that managers of complex projects use to determine the optimal order of activities, the expected time for project completion, and the best use of resources.

_____ 47. Process of performing a mechanical operation with the absolute minimum of human intervention.

WORD SCRAMBLE

1. *Production*
donroptuci

2. *operations*
atpersonio

3. *quality*
layquit

LEARNING OBJECTIVES--POTENTIAL SHORT ANSWER OR ESSAY QUESTIONS

Learning Objective #1: "Explain the strategic importance of production and operations management." (226-227)

Learning Objective #2: "Describe the evolution of production efficiency." (227-228)

Learning Objective #3: "Discuss the role of computers and automation technology in production." (228-233)

Learning Objective #4: "Identify the key issues managers must consider when designing operations." (233-236)

Learning Objective #5: "**Explain the strategic importance of managing inventory, and review the management systems used to control it.**" (236-241)

Learning Objective #6: "**Describe the advantages and disadvantages of just-in-time (JIT) systems in production planning.**" (240-241)

Learning Objective #7: "**Discuss the differences between quality control and quality assurance.**" (141-244)

Learning Objective #8: "**Define the five basic steps in production control.**" (244-248)

CRITICAL THINKING QUESTIONS

1. Which type of facility layout characterizes your college or university in its production of educational services?

2. If your company produces a specialized equipment where modifications are common and small orders are typical, then what type of production design would be most appropriate? Why?

BRAIN TEASER

1. What would a point outside the upper or lower control limits on a statistical process control chart imply about the production process being observed? What should management do to enhance the quality of their product over time?

ANSWERS

True-False--*Answers*

1. False: A *synthetic* production system combines two or more materials to form a single product; an *analytic* production system breaks raw materials into one or more distinct products, which may or may not resemble the original material in form and function.
2. True
3. True
4. False: Production efficiency is *minimizing* cost by *maximizing* the level of output from each resource.
5. True
6. False: *Mass production* is the manufacture of uniform products in great quantities.
7. True
8. True
9. True

10. True
11. True
12. False: A *cellular* layout is a method of arranging a facility so that parts with similar shapes or processing requirements are processed together in work centers.
13. True
14. False: *Manufacturing resource planning (MRP II)* is a computer-based system that integrates data from all departments to manage inventory and production planning and control.
15. True
16. True
17. True
18. False: Quality *control* focuses on measuring finished products against a preset standard and weeding out any defects; quality *assurance* is a system of company-wide policies, practices, and procedures that build quality into a product and assure that each product meets quality standards.
19. True

Multiple Choice--*Answers*

1. d	5. a	9. c	13. a
2. d	6. b	10. a	14. b
3. c	7. a	11. b	15. d
4. d	8. d	12. c	

Jeopardy---*Answers*

	Production	**Operations**	**Quality Control and Assurance**
$100	production efficiency	capacity planning	quality control
$200	mass customization	facility location planning	quality assurance
$300	a flexible manufacturing system (FMS)	facility layout planning	statistical quality control (SQC)
$400	computer-integrated manufacturing (CIM)	purchasing management, inventory management, quality assurance, and production control	the five steps in production control
$500	if the basic process creates the wrong products or involves needless steps, and from using technology without properly training workers to operate it	material requirements planning (MRP)	program evaluation and review technique (PERT)

Match the Terms and Concepts to Their Definitions--*Answers*

1. e	7. j	13. n	19. jj	25. ee	31. gg	37. z	43. rr
2. b	8. uu	14. a	20. vv	26. y	32. t	38. s	44. h
3. hh	9. aa	15. ll	21. qq	27. kk	33. o	39. p	45. pp
4. dd	10. g	16. tt	22. i	28. w	34. cc	40. bb	46. ii
5. f	11. ss	17. nn	23. v	29. m	35. ff	41. x	47. c
6. l	12. q	18. d	24. u	30. r	36. oo	42. k	

Word Scramble---*Answers*

1. production   2. operations   3. quality

Learning Objectives--Potential Short Answer or Essay Questions--*Answers*

Learning Objective #1:

Production and operations management (POM) is the coordination of an organization's resources for manufacturing goods or producing services, using the basic functions of planning, organizing, leading, and controlling. Companies are using POM to improve quality and competitiveness by focusing on high efficiency, few defects, fast production, low costs, excellent customer service, broad market reach, innovative products and processes, less waste, and high flexibility.

Learning Objective #2:

Since the Industrial Revolution 200 years ago, a series of technological advances have made production more efficient. The first was mechanization--the use of machines to perform tasks. This led to standardization--the production of uniform, interchangeable parts. Henry Ford introduced the assembly line, where an item is put together as it progresses past a number of workstations. Eventually, many areas achieved automation--the process of performing a mechanical operation with the absolute minimum of human intervention. As technology advanced, so did mass production.

Learning Objective #3:

Computers and automation technology improve the production process in several ways: (1) Robots perform repetitive or mundane tasks quickly and with great precision; (2) AGVs move materials easily around factory floors; (3) CAD and CAE systems allow engineers to design and test virtual models of products; (4) CAM systems easily translate CAD data into production instructions; (5) CIM systems link the people, machines, databases, and decisions involved in each step of producing a good; (6) flexible manufacturing systems (FMS) reduce setup costs and time by linking programmable, multifunctional machine tools through a computer network and an automated material handling system; and (7) EDI systems make ordering supplies faster and easier.

Learning Objective #4:

Managers must first consider capacity, which is the volume of manufacturing or service delivery that an organization possesses. Second, they must find a facility location that minimizes regional costs (the cost of land, construction, labor, local taxes, leasing, and energy), transportation costs, and raw materials costs. Finally, managers need to consider facility layout, the arrangement of production work centers, and other facilities (such as material, equipment, and support departments) needed for the processing of goods and services. The four possible layouts include the process layout, the product layout, the cellular layout, and the fixed position layout.

Learning Objective #5:

The goods and materials kept in stock for production or sale make up inventory, which must be managed to minimize costs and ensure that the right supplies are in the right place at the right time. Many companies use material requirements planning (MRP) and perpetual inventory systems to determine when materials are needed, when they should be ordered, and when they should be delivered. A more advanced system is manufacturing resource planning (MRP II), which brings together data from all parts of a company (including financial, design, and engineering departments) to better manage inventory and production planning and control.

Learning Objective #6:

Just-in-time (JIT) systems reduce waste and improve quality in the following ways: (1) The manufacturer produces only enough to fill orders when they are due, thus eliminating finished-goods inventory; (2) workers on the production line take from the previous station only those parts or materials that they can process immediately, thus pulling the work through the system rather than pushing it through; and (3) the manufacturer orders supplies only when they are needed, thus eliminating raw materials inventories. This system encourages efficiency and teamwork. However, JIT systems are more susceptible to disruptions in the flow of raw materials, and they can place a heavy burden on suppliers.

Learning Objective #7:

Quality control focuses on measuring finished products against a preset standard and weeding out any defects. On the other hand, quality assurance is a system of company-wide policies, practices, and procedures that build quality into a product and assure that each product meets quality standards.

Learning Objective #8:

(1) Planning is the analysis of what to produce and how much to produce, as well as where and how to produce it. (2) Routing is figuring out how production will proceed. (3) Scheduling establishes the time frame for the production process. (4) Dispatching is sending production orders. (5) Following up is making sure that everything proceeds according to plan and figuring out how to cope with problems as they arise.

Critical Thinking Questions---*Answers*

1. Colleges and universities utilize a process layout where different tasks are carried out in separate departments---classrooms, labs, recreation facilities, living quarters, etc., are separate areas each containing specialized equipment and personnel.

2. A flexible manufacturing system (FMS) would be appropriate because it facilitates the changing from one design to another, and it saves time and setup costs compared to other production designs.

Brain Teaser--*Answer*

1. Any point outside the upper or lower control limits would imply that the process is out of control. Although variation in any process is to be expected, variation outside the control limits is unacceptable. Whenever management observes this, it must try to determine what caused the unacceptable variation and correct for it, thus enhancing quality over time.

Chapter 9

Human Relations, Motivation, and Performance

LEARNING OBJECTIVES

After studying this chapter, you should be able to:

1. List the three main components of good human relations within an organization. (258-259)
2. Explain how the five levels in Maslow's hierarchy of needs relate to employee motivation. (260-261)
3. Identify the two factors affecting employee motivation in Herzberg's two-factor theory. (261-263)
4. Describe how Theory X, Theory Y, and Theory Z link employee motivation and management style. (263-264)
5. Explain how changes in work-force demographics have complicated the challenge of motivating employees. (265-268)
6. Explain how changes in the economy create barriers to employee motivation. (268-272)
7. Describe how corporate cultures must change in order to keep employees motivated. (272-274)
8. Discuss the use of goal setting, behavior modification, investing in employees, and an improved quality of work life as motivational techniques. (274-280)

TRUE-FALSE

Indicate whether the statement is generally true or false by placing a "T" or "F" in the space provided. If it is a false statement, correct it so that it becomes a true statement.

_____ 1. Leadership, motivation, and communication are the major elements that contribute to good human relations.

_____ 2. The key to effective motivation is to demonstrate to employees that their individual needs are different than the needs of the organization.

_____ 3. In Frederick Taylor's view, people were motivated almost exclusively by money, and he advocated a piecework system.

_____ 4. The most basic of needs according to Maslow's hierarchy are the self-actualization needs.

_____ 5. In Maslow's hierarchy of needs, the need for esteem can be met through job security and pension plans.

_____ 6. Hygiene factors such as working conditions, company policies, and job security have a bad effect on motivation only if they are deficient.

_____ 7. Motivators such as achievement, recognition, and responsibility are related negatively to increases in productivity.

_____ 8. In attempting to motivate employees, Theory Y emphasizes management authority, and Theory X emphasizes employee growth and self-direction.

_____ 9. Theory Z assumes that the best management involves employees at all levels of the organization and treats employees like family.

_____ 10. The challenges that make motivating workers difficult stem from changes in the economy, the work force, and organizational cultures.

_____ 11. An increasing cultural diversity brings a wider range of work skills traditions, and attitudes to the workplace, which affect behavior on the job.

_____ 12. Because of changes in the work-force demographics, managers need to find new ways of keeping employees happy and productive on the job.

_____ 13. Because of global competition, work-saving technologies, and the pursuit of short-term profit, business require many highly skilled employees to work longer hours, which can lead to low morale and burnout.

_____ 14. Two significant effects of economic and technological change that are apparent in the United States today are: (1) downsizing and restructuring and (2) a growing income gap between highly-skilled and low-skilled workers.

_____ 15. To reduce turnover, corporate cultures need to begin emphasizing job advancement as the primary source of job satisfaction.

_____ 16. Goal setting is most effective as a means of increasing employee motivation when those goals are imposed from above.

_____ 17. Employee empowerment can be an effective motivational tool.

_____ 18. Job sharing is a scheduling system in which employees are allowed certain options regarding time of arrival and departure.

_____ 19. Job enrichment reduces specialization and makes work more meaningful by expanding each job's responsibilities.

MULTIPLE CHOICE

Circle the one best answer for each of the following questions.

1. Managers need to
    a. realize the importance of maintaining good relations with their employees.
    b. create a climate of openness and trust with their employees.
    c. realize that leadership, motivation and communication are the major elements that contribute to good human relations.
    d. do all of the above.

2. Which of the following statements is true?
    a. Morale is the force that moves individuals to take action.
    b. Motivation is an attitude an individual has toward his or her job and employer.
    c. Effective leadership and motivation depend heavily on communication.
    d. All of the above are true.

3. Frederick Taylor
    a. developed scientific management, a management approach that seeks to improve employee efficiency through the scientific study of work.
    b. believed workers are primarily motivated by a need to be loved and to feel a sense of belonging.
    c. abolished the piecework system of payment.
    d. did all of the above.

4. According to Maslow's hierarchy of needs,
    a. the higher levels of the hierarchy need to be satisfied before the lower-level needs can be addressed.
    b. the lowest level is self-actualization--the need to become everything one is capable of.
    c. the need for esteem relates to the feelings of self-worth and respect from others.
    d. the social needs are the most basic requirements for human life, and are seldom strong motivators for modern wage earners.

5. Employers providing job security and pension plans would best fulfill which of the following needs of workers?
    a. Physiological
    b. Safety (or security) needs
    c. Social needs
    d. Esteem needs

6. Employers giving employees the opportunity to expand their skills and take on additional responsibility would help satisfy which need of workers?
    a. Safety (or security) needs
    b. Social needs
    c. Self-actualization needs
    d. Esteem needs

7. Frederick Herzberg's Two-Factor Theory emphasized which two factors?
    a. Hygiene factors and motivators
    b. Social needs and physiological needs
    c. Money and job security
    d. Job enrichment and job sharing

8. According to the Two-Factor Theory,
   a. management may lessen dissatisfaction by improving hygiene factors that concern employees, but such improvements won't influence satisfaction.
   b. management can help employees feel more motivated by paying attention to motivators such as achievement, recognition, responsibility, and other personally rewarding factors.
   c. a skilled, well-paid employee may be motivated to perform better if motivators are supplied, but a young, unskilled or insecure employee who earns low wages will probably still need the support of strong hygiene factors to reduce dissatisfaction before the motivators can be effective.
   d. all of the above are true.

9. Theory X assumes
   a. employees are irresponsible.
   b. employees are unambitious and dislike work.
   c. managers must use force, control, or threats to motivate workers.
   d. all of the above.

10. Which of the following is *not* associated with Theory Y?
    a. Employees like work.
    b. Employees are naturally committed to certain goals and are capable of creativity.
    c. Managers must use force, control, or threats to motivate workers.
    d. Employees seek out responsibility under the right circumstances.

11. Which of the following statements is true?
    a. The assumptions behind Theory X emphasize authority.
    b. The assumptions behind Theory Y emphasize growth and self-direction.
    c. Managers who adopt Theory Z believe that employees with a sense of identity and belonging are more likely to perform their jobs more enthusiastically to achieve company goals.
    d. All of the above are true.

12. Which of the following statements is true?
    a. Because of changes in work-force demographics, managers need to find new ways of keeping employees happy and productive on the job.
    b. Older employees are holding on to the high-paying jobs longer.
    c. Baby boomers and younger employees find it harder to advance, and they want more participation in work decisions and a balance between work and home life.
    d. All of the above are true.

13. Which of the following is *not* one of the factors contributing to the rapid economic change affecting the United States work force?
    a. The economy has been shifting from a manufacturing to a service economy.
    b. Many of the new higher-paying jobs require skills beyond those possessed by workers losing their jobs in the manufacturing sector.
    c. The growing influence of labor unions has resulted in fewer job opportunities.
    d. More sophisticated production techniques have resulted in some jobs becoming obsolete.

14. In order to reduce turnover, corporate culture needs to
    a. downplay job advancement as the primary source of job satisfaction.
    b. become more open in order to control rumors, improve morale, allow employees to concentrate on performance, and encourage employees to take risks.
    c. show more empathy for employees by finding ways to make work more enjoyable.
    d. do all of the above.

15. Companies are trying to motivate their workers more by
    a. allowing employees to set clear and challenging personal goals that support organizational goals.
    b. using behavioral modification.
    c. sponsoring training to sharpen employees' skills.
    d. doing all of the above.

16. Job enrichment is
    a. increasing work specialization and making work more meaningful by adding to the responsibility of each job.
    b. a scheduling system in which employees are allowed certain options regarding time arrival and departure.
    c. slicing a few hours off everybody's workweek and cutting pay to minimize layoffs.
    d. splitting a single full-time job between two employees for their convenience.

JEOPARDY

You have 5 seconds to complete the question to each of the following answers.

	Motivation Theory	Demographic Changes Affecting the Work Force	Motivational Techniques
$100	The two-factor theory emphasizes these two elements of motivation. (261-262) What is_____ _____?	What older, higher-paying workers are doing. (265-266) What is_____ _____?	The systematic use of rewards and punishments to change human behavior. (275) What is_____ _____?
$200	This theory assumes employees dislike work and that managers must use threats to motivate them. (263) What is_____ _____?	The changing nature of families. (266) What is_____ _____?	Scheduling system in which employees are allowed certain options regarding time of arrival and departure. (277) What is_____ _____?
$300	This theory emphasizes involving employees at all levels and treating them like family. (263) What is_____ _____?	The effect of cultural diversity. (266-267) What is_____ _____?	Reducing work specialization and making work more meaningful by adding to the responsibilities of each job. (276) What is_____ _____?
$400	This theory assumes employees like work and seek out responsibility. (263) What is_____ _____?	Two economic changes affecting the work force. (268-269) What is_____ _____?	Working from home and communicating with the company's main office via computer and communication devices. (278) What is_____ _____?
$500	Maslow's hierarchy of needs from the lowest to highest. (261) What is_____ _____?	This has caused many employees to have to carry a heavier workload than in the past. (271) What is_____ _____?	Splitting a single full-time job between two employees for their convenience. (279) What is_____ _____?

MATCH THE TERMS AND CONCEPTS TO THEIR DEFINITIONS

a. behavior modification (275)
b. flextime (277)
c. human relations (258)
d. hygiene factors (262)
e. job enrichment (276)
f. job sharing (279)

g. morale (259)
h. motivation (258)
i. motivators (262)
j. piecework system (260)
k. quality of work life (276)
l. scientific management (260)

m. telecommuting (279)
n. Theory X (263)
o. Theory Y (263)
p. Theory Z (263)
q. work sharing (279)

_____ 1. Management approach designed to improve employees' efficiency by scientifically studying their work.

_____ 2. Slicing a few hours off everybody's workweek and cutting pay to minimize layoffs.

_____ 3. Managerial assumption that employees are irresponsible, unambitious, and distasteful of work and that managers must use force, control, or threats to motivate them.

_____ 4. Working from home and communicating with the company's main office via computer and communication devices.

_____ 5. Force that moves someone to take action.

_____ 6. Compensation system that pays employees a certain amount for each unit produced.

_____ 7. Aspects of the work environment that are associated with dissatisfaction.

_____ 8. Splitting a single full-time job between two employees for their convenience.

_____ 9. Scheduling system in which employees are allowed certain options regarding time of arrival and departure.

_____ 10. Interaction among people within an organization for the purpose of achieving organizational and personal goals.

_____ 11. Managerial assumption that employees like work, are naturally committed to certain goals, are capable of creativity, and seek out responsibility under the right conditions.

_____ 12. Factors of human relations in business that may increase motivation.

_____ 13. Overall environment that results from job and work conditions.

_____ 14. Attitude an individual has toward his or her job and employer.

_____ 15. Reducing work specialization and making work more meaningful by adding to the responsibilities of each job.

_____ 16. Human relations approach that emphasizes involving employees at all levels and treating them like family.

_____ 17. Systematic use of rewards and punishments to change human behavior.

WORD SCRAMBLE

1. _____ _____   2. _____   3. _____
   krow   grashin   metfixel   roamel

LEARNING OBJECTIVES--POTENTIAL SHORT ANSWER OR ESSAY QUESTIONS

Learning Objective #1: "List the three main components of good human relations within an organization." (258-259)

Learning Objective #2: "Explain how the five levels in Maslow's hierarchy of needs relate to employee motivation." (260-261)

Learning Objective #3: "Identify the two factors affecting employee motivation in Herzberg's two-factor theory." (261-263)

Learning Objective #4: "Describe how Theory X, Theory Y, and Theory Z link employee motivation and management style." (263-264)

Learning Objective #5: "**Explain how changes in work-force demographics have complicated the challenge of motivating employees.**" (265-268)

Learning Objective #6: "**Explain how changes in the economy create barriers to employee motivation.**" (268-272)

Learning Objective #7: "**Describe how corporate cultures must change in order to keep employees motivated.**" (272-274)

Learning Objective #8: "**Discuss the use of goal setting, behavior modification, investing in employees, and an improved quality of work life as motivational techniques.**" (274-280)

CRITICAL THINKING QUESTIONS

1. For each of the following, determine which of Maslow's hierarchy of needs might management be trying to meet.
    a. The company offers workers a wage sufficient to pay "the rent."

    b. The company offers workers health care benefits, sick leave pay, and a company-paid vacation as well as a company-paid life insurance package.

    c. Management encourages employees to play on the company softball or bowling team, to bring their families to the annual picnic, and to come to the annual Christmas party, etc.

    d. The company initiates an annual awards banquet which is also a "roast and toast" opportunity.

    e. The company will compensate employees for coursework obtained at an accredited college or university or offer a sabbatical for the same or similar reasons.

2. Within the context of this chapter, can you provide a historical explanation for one reason why unions were developed?

BRAIN TEASER

1. Some managers of production facilities in a few less developed foreign countries with less aggressive work ethics have found it challenging to motivate their workers. From what you have read in this chapter, what would you propose?

ANSWERS

True-False--*Answers*
1. True
2. False: The key to effective motivation is to demonstrate to employees that their individual needs *dovetail with* the needs of the organization.
3. True
4. False: The most basic of needs according to Maslow's hierarchy are the *physiological needs.*
5. False: In Maslow's hierarchy of needs, the need for esteem can be met *by motivational techniques of recognition.*
6. True
7. False: Motivators such as achievement, recognition, and responsibility are related *positively* to increases in productivity.
8. False: In attempting to motivate employees, Theory *X* emphasizes management authority, and Theory *Y* emphasizes employee growth and self-direction.
9. True
10. True
11. True
12. True
13. True
14. True
15. False: To reduce turnover, corporate cultures need to *downplay* job advancement as the primary source of job satisfaction.
16. False: Goal setting is most effective as a means of increasing employee motivation when *employees have input into the creation of clear and challenging--but achievable--goals.*
17. True
18. False: *Flextime* is a scheduling system in which employees are allowed certain options regarding time of arrival and departure.
19. True

Multiple Choice--*Answers*

1. d	5. b	9. d	13. c
2. c	6. c	10. c	14. d
3. a	7. a	11. d	15. d
4. c	8. d	12. d	16. a

Jeopardy--*Answers*

	Motivation Theory	**Demographic Changes Affecting the Work Force**	**Motivational Techniques**
$100	hygiene factors and motivators	they are working longer	behavior modification
$200	Theory X	a growing number of two-career households	flextime
$300	Theory Z	a wider range of work skills, traditions, and attitudes	job enrichment
$400	Theory Y	a shifting toward a service economy and rapid technological change	telecommuting
$500	physiological, safety, social, esteem, and self-actualization needs	downsizing and restructuring	job sharing

Match the Terms and Concepts to Their Definitions--*Answers*

1. l	4. m	7. d	10. c	13. k	16. p
2. q	5. h	8. f	11. o	14. g	17. a
3. n	6. j	9. b	12. i	15. e	

Word Scramble--*Answers*

1. work sharing   2. flextime   3. morale

Learning Objectives--Potential Short Answer or Essay Questions--*Answers*

Learning Objective #1:

Leadership, motivation, and communication are the major elements that contribute to good human relations.

Learning Objective #2:

Physiological needs, the most basic requirements for human life, are seldom strong motivators for modern wage earners. Safety (or security) needs can be met through job security and pension plans. Social needs, which drive people to seek membership in informal groups, may be more important than financial considerations. Esteem needs, which relate to feelings of self-worth and respect from others, are met by motivational techniques of recognition. Self-actualization needs may be met by giving employees the opportunity to expand their skills and take on additional responsibility.

Learning Objective #3:

Hygiene factors--such as working conditions, company policies, and job security have a bad effect on motivation only if they are deficient. Motivators--achievement, recognition, and responsibility-- are related positively to increases in productivity.

Learning Objective #4:

Theory X and Theory Y describe two opposite sets of assumptions about employees' motives for working; Theory X emphasizes management authority, and Theory Y emphasizes employee growth and self-direction. Theory Z, which describes human relations within U.S. companies that have adopted certain Japanese management techniques, assumes that employees are part of a family and that their needs therefore deserve consideration.

Learning Objective #5:

Because of changes in work-force demographics, managers need to find new ways of keeping employees happy and productive on the job. Older employees are holding on to high-paying positions longer. Baby boomers and younger employees find it harder to advance, and they want more participation in work decisions and a balance between work and home life. Also, increasing cultural diversity brings a wider range of work skills, traditions, and attitudes to the workplace, which can affect behavior on the job.

Learning Objective #6:

Because of global competition, work-saving technologies, and the pursuit of short-term profit, businesses require many highly skilled employees to work longer hours, which can lead to low morale and burnout. At the other end of the spectrum, low-skilled employees are increasingly taking jobs in the service sector that offer little security and opportunity for advancement. Both situations make it difficult for managers to motivate employees.

Learning Objective #7:

To reduce turnover, corporate cultures have to downplay job advancement as the primary source of job satisfaction. At the same time, corporate cultures must become more open in order to control rumors, improve morale, allow employees to concentrate on performance, and encourage employees to take risks. Management can also improve morale by showing more empathy for employees and by finding ways to make work more enjoyable.

Learning Objective #8:

Some companies motivate their employees by allowing them to set clear and challenging personal goals that support organizational goals. With behavioral modification, managers seek to change employee behavior by systematically encouraging actions that are desirable and discouraging those that are not. To motivate employees who are worried about job security, employers can sponsor training that will sharpen employee skills. Improving the quality of work life leads to better work conditions, which give employees the chance to use their special abilities and build their skills.

Critical Thinking Questions--*Answers*

1. a. Physiological
    b. Safety (security)
    c. Social
    d. Esteem (and social)
    e. Self-actualization

2. Generally, and historically speaking, unions were developed because management did a poor job of fulfilling workers' needs. Moreover, too many managers were operating under the assumptions of Theory X which emphasizes management authority. Most workers have resented that kind of treatment.

Brain Teaser--*Answer*

1. There is no "correct" answer for this question. However, according to Maslow's theory, a satisfied need is not a motivator. Therefore, it may be helpful to try to get the employees to find new "needs" and to inform them of the things they can afford to buy (washing machines, better cloth, etc.) if they simply work harder and receive the higher compensation as a consequence of their hard work. Evidence indicates that this has been somewhat successful in increasing some foreign workers' productivity. Nevertheless, assuming hygiene factors are met, then other motivators (working conditions, company policies, job security, etc.) need to be focused on. Those motivators need to be adapted to the foreign culture.

Chapter *10*

Human Resources Management

LEARNING OBJECTIVES
After studying this chapter, you should be able to:

1. List the six main functions of human resources departments. (290-318)
2. Identify the six stages in the hiring process. (297)
3. Explain why companies use training and development programs. (300-303)
4. State two general methods for compensating employees. (306)
5. Describe the main components of employee pay. (306-309)
6. Explain five employee benefits. (309-313)
7. Describe five ways an employee's status may change. (313-317)
8. Identify the two reasons that employers may terminate employment. (315-316)

TRUE-FALSE
Indicate whether the statement is generally true or false by placing a "T" or "F" in the space provided. If it is a false statement, correct it so that it becomes a true statement.

_____ 1. Human resource management is the specialized function of planning how to obtain employees, oversee their training, evaluate them, and compensate them.

_____ 2. Human resource management has become a major challenge in global business.

_____ 3. The first step in staffing business organizations is to train and develop employees.

_____ 4. The gap is widening between what employers will require of new employees in the years ahead and the actual skills of these employees.

_____ 5. After job analysis has been completed, the human resources manager develops a job description, then a job specification.

_____ 6. The first stage in the hiring process is to interview each candidate for the job.

_____ 7. Tests used in the hiring process are much debated and typically take the form of job-skills tests, psychological tests, and drug tests--job-skills tests being the most common.

_____ 8. Interviewing is the session or procedure for acclimating a new employee to the organization.

_____ 9. Job-skills training teaches mathematics and language to help employees master skills for working with each other, with customers, and with suppliers, whereas basic-skills training teaches employees how to perform specific work tasks.

_____ 10. Many companies have developed performance appraisal systems to objectively evaluate employees according to set criteria.

_____ 11. Two general methods for compensating employees are through wages and salaries.

_____ 12. Wages (for hourly employees) and salaries (for nonhourly employees) are the most typical components of employee pay.

_____ 13. Profit sharing is a cash payment in addition to the regular wage or salary, which serves as a reward for achievement.

_____ 14. A commission is a system for distributing a portion of the company's profits to employees.

_____ 15. Broadbanding is a payment system that uses wide pay grades, enabling the company to give pay raises without promotion.

_____ 16. Pay for performance is pay tied to an employee's acquisition of skills; also called skill-based pay.

_____ 17. The most popular types of benefits are health and retirement benefits.

_____ 18. A pension plan is a program enabling employees to become partial owners of a company.

_____ 19. A layoff is the termination of employees for economic or business reasons.

MULTIPLE CHOICE
Circle the one best answer for each of the following questions.

1. Which of the following is *not* one of the functions of human resource management?
   a. Planning, recruiting, and selecting new employees
   b. Training and developing employees
   c. Managing employees
   d. Appraising and compensating employees

2. Which of the following statements is true?
    a. Keeping track of the labor market is quite easy.
    b. Many of the growing occupations are service-oriented and require specialized skills or training, whereas the shrinking occupations involve activities that require fewer skills or that are increasingly being automated.
    c. More jobs are available today for low-skilled factory employees in traditional "smokestack" industries.
    d. The part-time labor force has shrunk in recent years.

3. A reason why companies are hiring more part-time workers is because
    a. a large percentage of the work force is made up of temporary employees.
    b. of outsourcing.
    c. they do not have to offer benefits like health care.
    d. of all of the above.

4. After job analysis has been completed, then human resource managers must
    a. develop a job description followed by a job specification.
    b. develop a job specification followed by a job description.
    c. continue to the next step which is to recruit potential workers.
    d. continue to the next step which is to interview candidates for a position.

5. Which of the following correctly describes the steps involved in the hiring process?
    a. Narrow down candidates; interview them; administer employment test (optional); evaluate candidates; conduct reference checks; and select the right candidate.
    b. Narrow down candidates; interview them; evaluate candidates; conduct reference checks; administer employment test (optional); and select the right candidate.
    c. Narrow down candidates; conduct reference checks; interview them; administer employment test (optional); evaluate candidates; and select the right candidate.
    d. Narrow down candidates; evaluate candidates; interview them; administer employment test (optional); conduct reference checks; and select the right candidate.

6. Which of the following would *not* be an appropriate question to ask of a candidate during an interview?
    a. Why do you wish to change employment?
    b. What are your expectations of this position?
    c. What is your religious affiliation?
    d. What are your long-term goals?

7. Training to teach employees how to perform specific work tasks is called
    a. orientation training.
    b. job-skills training.
    c. basic-skills training.
    d. management-development training.

8. Which of the following is true?
    a. A growing number of companies are helping their employees while they help themselves by offering college degree programs.
    b. The biggest problem with appraisal systems is finding a way to measure performance.
    c. Two general ways employees are compensated is through wages and salaries, and through benefits.
    d. All of the above are true.

9. Which of the following is *false* concerning compensation?
   a. Wages are earned by hourly employees while salaries are earned by nonhourly employees.
   b. Comparable worth is a concept of equal pay for jobs that are equal in value to the organization and require similar levels of education, training, and skills.
   c. A bonus is a cash payment in addition to the regular wage or salary, which serves as a reward for achievement.
   d. Profit sharing is a payment to employees equal to a certain percentage of sales made.

10. Accepting a lower base pay in exchange for bonuses based on meeting production or other goals is
    a. knowledge-based pay.
    b. pay for performance.
    c. broadbanding.
    d. a comparable worth pay scheme.

11. A company-sponsored program for providing retirees with income is
    a. a pension plan
    b. a stock option plan
    c. an employee stock-ownership plan.
    d. broadbanding.

12. Which of the following statements is true?
    a. Flexible benefit plans allow employees to choose the unique combination of benefits that suit their needs.
    b. Family benefit programs include maternity and paternal leave, child-care assistance, and elder-care assistance.
    c. Health and safety programs (including fitness and wellness programs) help keep employees at peak productivity.
    d. All of the above are true.

13. Which of the following is one of the ways an employee's status may change?
    a. Promotion or reassignment
    b. Termination or voluntary resignation
    c. Retirement
    d. All of the above are.

14. Which of the following statements is true?
    a. Ergonomics is the study of how tasks, equipment, and the environment relate to human performance and is of interest to human resource managers.
    b. An employee assistance program (EAP) is a company-sponsored counseling or referral plan for employees with personal problems.
    c. Benefits such as company cars and paid country club memberships are often referred to as perks, or perquisites.
    d. All of the above are true.

15. Which of the following is true?
    a. Fewer and fewer employees are willing to accept promotional transfers.
    b. Layoffs occur because of a downturn in business or because company strategy requires a leaner work force; they are not performance-related job losses.
    c. Firings are permanent removals of employees because of poor performance.
    d. All of the above are true.

JEOPARDY

You have 5 seconds to complete the question to each of the following answers.

	Hiring and Training	**Compensation**	**Employee Status Changes**
$100	This lists the tasks the job involves and the conditions under which those tasks are performed. (294-295) What is_____ _____?	The two general methods for compensating employees. (306) What is_____ _____?	The problem with this is that it may result in someone getting a job beyond his or her capabilities. (314) What is_____ _____?
$200	At these two stages of the hiring process human resource managers must be particularly careful not to break the law. (297-298) What is_____ _____?	The most popular type of benefit. (309) What is_____ _____?	Act of getting rid of an employee though layoffs or firing. (315) What is_____ _____?
$300	Programs used to help new and experienced managers sharpen their skills. (302) What is_____ _____?	Payments to employees equal to a certain percentage of sales made. (307) What is_____ _____?	Termination of employees for economic or business reasons. (315)) What is_____ _____?
$400	Training to teach employees how to perform a specific task. (301) What is_____ _____?	Company-sponsored programs for providing retirees with income. (310) What is_____ _____?	Required dismissal of an employee who reaches a certain age. (316) What is_____ _____?
$500	The overriding goal of this is to attract and keep good employees. (300-303) What is_____ _____?	This law entitles employees up to 2 weeks of unpaid leave for childbirth or the care of a family member. (311) What is_____ _____?	Distribution of financial incentives to employees who voluntarily depart, usually undertaken in order to shrink the payroll. (317) What is_____ _____?

MATCH THE TERMS AND CONCEPTS TO THEIR DEFINITIONS

a. bonus (307)
b. broadbanding (308)
c. commissions (307)
d. comparable worth (306)
e. compensation (306)
f. employee assistance program (EAP) (314)
g. employee benefits (309)
h. employee stock-ownership program (ESOP) (310)
i. employment at will (316)
j. ergonomics (313)

k. gain sharing (308)
l. human resources management (HRM) (290)
m. incentives (307)
n. job analysis (294)
o. job description (294)
p. job specification (294)
q. knowledge-based pay (308)
r. layoffs (315)
s. mandatory retirement (316)
t. orientation (300)
u. pay for performance (308)

v. pension plans (310)
w. performance appraisal (303)
x. profit sharing (308)
y. recruiting (294)
z. resume (297)
aa. salaries (306)
bb. stock option plan (310)
cc. termination (315)
dd. wages (306)
ee. worker buyout (317)
ff. wrongful discharge (316)

_____ 1. Payments to employees equal to a certain percentage of sales made.

_____ 2. Payment system that uses wide pay grades, enabling the company to give pay raises without promotions.

_____ 3. Process of attracting appropriate applicants for an organization's jobs.

_____ 4. Program enabling employees to become partial owners of a company.

_____ 5. Cash payment in addition to the regular wage or salary, which serves as a reward for achievement.

_____ 6. Evaluation of an employee's work according to specific criteria.

_____ 7. Study of how tasks, equipment, and the environment relate to human performance.

_____ 8. Specialized function of planning how to obtain employees, oversee their training, evaluate them, and compensate them.

_____ 9. Required dismissal of an employee who reaches a certain age.

_____ 10. Compensation other than wages, salaries, and incentive programs.

_____ 11. Act of getting rid of an employee through layoffs or firing.

_____ 12. Cash payments to employees who produce at a desired level or whose unit (often the company as a whole) produces at a desired level.

_____ 13. Termination of employees for economic or business reasons.

_____ 14. Session or procedure for acclimating a new employee to the organization.

_____ 15. Firing an employee with inadequate advance notice or explanation.

_____ 16. Cash payment based on the number of hours the employee has worked or the number of units the employee has produced.

_____ 17. Fixed weekly, monthly, or yearly cash compensation for work.

_____ 18. Program enabling employees to purchase a certain amount of stock at a discount after they have worked for the company a specified length of time or after the company's stock reaches a specific market price.

_____ 19. Money, benefits, and services paid to employees for their work.

_____ 20. Statement describing the kind of person who would be best for a given job--including the skills, education, and previous experience that the job requires.

_____ 21. Employer's right to keep or terminate employees as it wishes.

_____ 22. Statement of the tasks involved in a given job and the conditions under which the holder of the job will work.

_____ 23. Plan for rewarding employees not on the basis of overall profits but in relation to achievement of goals such as cost savings from higher productivity.

_____ 24. System for distributing a portion of the company's profits to employees.

_____ 25. Process by which jobs are studied to determine the tasks and dynamics involved in performing them.

_____ 26. Pay tied to an employee's acquisition of skills; also called skill-based pay.

_____ 27. Company-sponsored programs for providing retirees with income.

_____ 28. Accepting a lower base pay in exchange for bonuses based on meeting production or other goals.

_____ 29. Company-sponsored counseling or referral plan for employees with personal problems.

_____ 30. Brief description of education, experience, and personal data compiled by a job applicant.

_____ 31. Distribution of financial incentives to employees who voluntarily depart, usually undertaken in order to shrink the payroll.

_____ 32. Concept of equal pay for jobs that are equal in value to the organization and require similar levels of education, training, and skills.

WORD SCRAMBLE

1. _____   2. _____   3. _____ _____
   busno   simmocison   rongwulf   ischadrge

LEARNING OBJECTIVES--POTENTIAL SHORT ANSWER OR ESSAY QUESTIONS

Learning Objective #1: "List the six main functions of human resources departments." (290-318)

Learning Objective #2: "Identify the six stages in the hiring process." (297)

Learning Objective #3: "Explain why companies use training and development programs." (300-303)

Learning Objective #4: " State two general methods for compensating employees." (306)

Learning Objective #5: "Describe the main components of employee pay." (306-309)

Learning Objective #6: "Explain five employee benefits." (309-313)

Learning Objective #7: **"Describe five ways an employee's status may change."** (313-317)

Learning Objective #8: **"Identify the two reasons that employers may terminate employment."** (315-316)

CRITICAL THINKING QUESTIONS

1. How might management by objectives (discussed in Chapter 6) help in the performance appraisal process?

2. What do you think are the benefits and cost of hiring someone to fill a new position from within the company? What about filling the job by hiring someone outside the company?

BRAIN TEASER

1. Why are many people opposed to comparable worth pay systems?

ANSWERS

True-False--*Answers*

1. True
2. True
3. False: The first step in staffing business organizations is to *plan, or to forecast future staffing needs.*
4. True
5. True
6. False: The first stage in the hiring process is to *select a small number of qualified candidates from all of the applications received.*
7. True
8. False: *Orientation* is the session or procedure for acclimating a new employee to the organization.
9. False: *Basic-skills* training teaches mathematics and language to help employees master skills for working with each other, with customers, and with suppliers whereas *job-skills* training teaches employees how to perform specific work tasks.
10. True
11. False: Two general methods for compensating employees are through wages and salaries, *and through benefits and services.*
12. True
13. False: *A bonus* is a cash payment in addition to the regular wage or salary, which serves as a reward for achievement.
14. False: *Profit sharing* is a system for distributing a portion of the company's profits to employees.
15. True
16. False: *Knowledge-based pay* is pay tied to an employee's acquisition of skills; also called skill-based pay.
17. True
18. False: *An employee stock-ownership plan (ESOP)* is a program enabling employees to become partial owners of a company.
19. True

Multiple Choice--*Answers*

1. c	5. a	9. d	13. d
2. b	6. c	10. b	14. d
3. d	7. b	11. a	15. d
4. a	8. d	12. d	

Jeopardy—*Answers*

	Hiring and Training	Compensation	Employee Status Changes
$100	job description	wages and salaries, and benefits	promotion
$200	interviewing and testing	health benefits	termination
$300	management-development programs	a commission	layoffs
$400	job-skills training	pension plans	mandatory retirement
$500	training and development programs	The Family Medical and Leave Act (FMLA)	worker buyout

Match the Terms and Concepts to Their Definitions--*Answers*

1. c	5. a	9. s	13. r	17. aa	21. i	25. n	29 f
2. b	6. w	10. g	14. t	18. bb	22. o	26. q	30. z
3. y	7. j	11. cc	15. ff	19. e	23. k	27. v	31. ee
4. h	8. l	12. m	16. dd	20. p	24. x	28. u	32. d

Word Scramble--*Answers*

1. bonus   2. commission   3. wrongful discharge

Learning Objectives--Potential Short Answer or Essay Questions--*Answers*

Learning Objective #1:

Human resources departments engage in planning, recruiting and selecting new employees, training and developing employees, appraising employee performance, compensating employees, and accommodating changes in employment status.

Learning Objective #2:

The stages in the hiring process are (1) narrowing down the number of qualified candidates, (2) interviewing, (3) administering employment tests (optional), (4) evaluating candidates, (5) conducting reference checks, and (6) selecting the right candidate.

Learning Objective #3:

Companies use orientation training to help new employees learn procedures, policies, and goals. They use job-skills training to teach employees how to perform specific work tasks, and they use basic-skills training in mathematics and language to help employees master skills for working with each other and with customers and suppliers. Management-development programs are used to help new and experienced managers sharpen their skills.

Learning Objective #4:

Employees are compensated through payments, such as wages and salaries, and through benefits and services.

Learning Objective #5:

Wages (for hourly employees) and salaries (for nonhourly employees) are the most typical components of employee pay. Some employees also receive incentive payments (bonuses, commissions, profit sharing, and gain sharing), which are cash payments tied to employee, group, or company performance in order to encourage higher performance.

Learning Objective #6:

The most popular type of benefits are health benefits, which help protect employees and their families when they become ill. Retirement benefits are also popular as a means of helping people save for later years. Employee stock-ownership plans (ESOPs) and stock options are ways for employees to receive or purchase shares of the company's stock, and they give employees a stake in the company. Family-benefit programs include maternity and paternity leave, child-care assistance, and elder-care assistance. Flexible benefit plans allow employees to choose the unique combination of benefits that suit their needs. Health and safety programs (including fitness and wellness programs) help keep employees at peak productivity.

Learning Objective #7:

An employee's status may change through promotion to a higher-level position, through reassignment to a similar or lower-level position, through termination (removal from the company's payroll), through voluntary resignation, or through retirement.

Learning Objective #8:

Layoffs occur because of a downturn in business or because company strategy requires a leaner work force. Such terminations are not performance related. Firings are permanent removals of employees because of poor performance.

Critical Thinking Questions--*Answers*

1. Management by objectives essentially means that managers and their employees work together in defining the specific objectives or criteria the employee will be judged by at performance appraisal time. A management by objective approach should make the measurement of performance at appraisal time easier because the criteria by which performance will be measured would have been largely worked out in advance.

2. A benefit of hiring from within the firm is that the employee is already familiar with the organization and its culture. Another benefit is that it rewards hard work by reminding people that promotions are a realistic possibility. Some of the costs of hiring from within include the loss of an opportunity to "bring in new blood," and it may create some undesired animosity by those employees passed over.

    The benefits and costs of hiring from outside the company are the converse of those described above. That is, hiring from outside provides an opportunity to bring in new ideas, and it precludes the necessity of having to chose from many current qualified employees. The costs include having to train and assimilate the new employee into the company.

Brain Teaser--*Answer*

1. Comparable worth pay systems are essentially comparable pay for comparable work. Comparable worth pay systems are opposed by some because of the difficulty in determining what is comparable. Who is going to determine what is comparable? Moreover, comparable worth reduces the ability of market forces (demand and supply forces) to operate and to determine wages. The fear is that this could give rise to some shortages or surpluses of certain types of workers. Nevertheless, everyone is in agreement that in some cases the "market forces" at play in real-world labor markets have given rise to inequities.

Chapter 11
Employee-Management Relations

LEARNING OBJECTIVES

After studying this chapter, you should be able to:

1. Identify two main types of labor unions. (326-327)
2. Outline the organizational structure of unions. (330-331)
3. Explain the two steps unions take to become the bargaining agent for a group of employees.
4. Describe the four stages in collective bargaining. (332-341)
5. List five general issues that may be addressed in a labor contract. (336-340)
6. Discuss four options that unions have when negotiations with management break down. (341-343)
7. Discuss four options that management has when negotiations with the union break down. (343-344)
8. Explain how employee-management relations are changing to meet the challenges of today's business environment. (344-349)

TRUE-FALSE

Indicate whether the statement is generally true or false by placing a "T" or "F" in the space provided. If it is a false statement, correct it so that it becomes a true statement.

_____ 1. Industrial unions, which developed first, are composed of people who perform a particular type of skilled work, such as carpentry.

_____ 2. Most labor legislation was enacted in the 1930s and 1940s.

_____ 3. There has been an increase in the percentage of the labor force who are members of labor unions in the last couple of decades.

_____ 4. National unions are composed of local unions; labor federations are composed of national unions and unaffiliated local unions.

_____ 5. A national union is responsible for such activities as organizing new areas or industries, negotiating industrywide contracts, assisting locals with negotiations, administering benefits, lobbying Congress, and lending assistance in the event of a strike.

_____ 6. A business agent is a union member and employee who is elected to represent other union members and who attempts to resolve employee grievances with management.

_____ 7. The first step in unionizing is to request a certification election.

_____ 8. Authorization cards are sign-up cards designating a union as the signer's preferred bargaining agent.

_____ 9. Collective bargaining is the process used by unions and management to negotiate work contracts.

_____ 10. The union cannot legally call for a strike vote before or during negotiations.

_____ 11. Givebacks are concessions made by union members to give up promised increases in wages or benefits in order to enhance the company's competitive position.

_____ 12. The four stages in collective bargaining are: (1) preparing to meet, (2) negotiating, (3) forming a tentative agreement, and (4) ratifying the proposed contract.

_____ 13. Once a union is established, the contracts it negotiates begin with a provision guaranteeing the security of the union.

_____ 14. Very few unions negotiate for better pay and working conditions.

_____ 15. A two-tier wage plan is a clause in a union contract ensuring that wages will rise in proportion to inflation.

_____ 16. If negotiations break down with management, labor has the option of a strike, decreasing employee productivity to pressure management.

_____ 17. If workers walk off their jobs, management can legally replace them with strikebreakers.

_____ 18. An injunction is a court order prohibiting union workers from taking certain actions.

_____ 19. To survive tough foreign and domestic competition, employees and management alike are having to change the way they relate to each other.

_____ 20. One strategy for building better labor-management relations is the establishment of employee grievance systems.

_____ 21. One strategy for building better labor-management relations is involving employees more in decision making and daily business operations.

MULTIPLE CHOICE

Circle the one best answer for each of the following questions.

1. Which of the following is true concerning unions?
   a. An industrial union is made up of skilled artisans belonging to a single profession or practicing a single craft.
   b. A craft union represents both skilled and unskilled employees from all phases of a particular industry.
   c. Not all employees support labor unions.
   d. All of the above are true.

2. Which of the following is true about unions?
   a. Union membership peaked in 1946 at 36% of the labor force, but now accounts for only approximately 14% of the labor force.
   b. Today's unions fight for many of the same rights unions have always sought--good wages, safe working conditions, and benefits.
   c. As more manufacturing jobs move to developing countries, U.S. unions are also expanding their efforts to organize employees globally.
   d. All of the above.

3. Which of the following is a reason for the decline in union influence in recent years?
   a. Increased global competition has shifted to other countries many jobs that were traditionally unionized.
   b. A strong anti-sentiment among managers in many companies.
   c. Workers fear losing their jobs due to downsizing and restructuring.
   d. All of the above are.

4. Which of the following is a reason why workers join unions?
   a. Workers are dissatisfied with their current job and employment conditions.
   b. Workers believe that unionization can be helpful in improving job conditions.
   c. Workers are willing to overlook negative stereotypes that have surrounded unions in recent years.
   d. All of the above are.

5. Which of the following is *false* about the organizational structure of unions?
   a. Labor federations are relatively small union groups, usually part of a national union, that represent members who work in a single facility or in a certain geographic area.
   b. Each local union has a hierarchy consisting of rank-and-file members, an elected president, elected shop stewards, and perhaps a business agent.
   c. National unions consist of delegates elected by the local unions, who in turn elect officers; staff experts and organizers are hired to carry out the union's programs
   d. A shop steward is a union member and employee who is elected to represent other union members and who attempts to resolve employee grievances with management.

6. The first step in forming a union is to have
   a. at least 75% of the workers sign authorization cards; and then the management must recognize the union.
   b. at least 30% of the workers sign authorization cards; and then, if management objects to recognizing the union, the union asks the National Labor Relations Board to sponsor a certification election.
   c. at least 50% of the workers sign authorization cards; then management must recognize the union.

d. workers request an election from the National Labor Relations Board; if at least 30% of the workers vote for authorization, then the union is certified and issues authorization cards to its members.

7. Which of the following is true about the four stages in collective bargaining?
   a. The first stage is to prepare to meet, which may involve a strike vote.
   b. The second stage is actually negotiating; the third stage is forming a tentative agreement.
   c. The fourth stage is ratifying a contract.
   d. All of the above are true.

8. Which of the following is true of negotiations between a union and management?
   a. Permissive subjects are topics that must be discussed in collective bargaining.
   b. Mediation is the process for resolving a labor contract dispute in which an impartial third party studies the issues and makes a binding decision.
   c. Ratification is a process by which union members vote on a contract negotiated by union leaders.
   d. All of the above are true.

9. A workplace in which the employer may hire new employees at will, but where the employees are required to join the union after a probationary period, is called
   a. a closed shop.
   b. a union shop.
   c. an open shop.
   d. an agency shop.

10. Issues that may be subject to negotiation in the collective bargaining process include
    a. union security and management rights.
    b. compensation and job security.
    c. work rules and employee safety and health.
    d. All of the above may be.

11. Featherbedding refers to
    a. the practice of requiring employees to be kept on the payroll for work they do not do or for work that is not necessary.
    b. laws giving employees the explicit right to keep a job without joining a union.
    c. employee complaints about management's violating some aspect of a labor contract.
    d. a system of procedures and mechanisms for ensuring fair treatment on the job.

12. Which of the following is an option for labor in the event that negotiations with management break down?
    a. Employ strikebreakers.
    b. Institute a lockout.
    c. Impose a boycott.
    d. Seek an injunction.

13. Which of the following is an option for management in the event that negotiations with labor break down?
    a. Go on strike.
    b. Seek a pact with other companies in the industry.
    c. Exercise financial and political influence.
    d. All of the above are.

14. Which of the following is true concerning labor-management relations?
    a. Employees and managers are becoming more cooperative and less adversarial.
    b. To enhance labor-management relations, management could offer better pay and working conditions, establish grievance procedures, comply with legislation that protects employee rights, and involve workers in the operation of the business.
    c. To enhance labor-management relations, labor could help management find ways to cut costs, accept more flexible compensation packages, and reduce cumbersome work rules.
    d. All of the above.

JEOPARDY

You have 5 seconds to complete the question to each of the following answers.

	Types and Organizational Structure of Unions	Collective Bargaining	Options When Negotiations Break Down
$100	Unions representing both skilled and unskilled employees from all phases of a particular industry. (327) What is_____ _____?	The four steps in collective bargaining. (332-341) What is_____ _____?	Strike activity in which union members march before company entrances to persuade customers to cease business with the company. (341) What is_____ _____?
$200	The recent trend in union membership. (329) What is_____ _____?	Topics that may be omitted from collective bargaining. (335) What is_____ _____?	Nonunion workers hired to replace striking workers. (343) What is_____ _____?
$300	Nationwide organizations made up of locals that represent employees in locations around the country. (330) What is_____ _____?	Process for resolving a labor contract dispute in which a neutral third party meets with sides and attempts to steer them toward a resolution. (335) What is_____ _____?	Union activity in which members and sympathizers refuse to buy or handle the product of a target company. (342) What is_____ _____?
$400	Umbrella organization of national unions and unaffiliated local unions that undertakes large-scale activities on behalf of their members and that resolves conflicts between unions. (331) What is_____ _____?	Some of the issues subject to negotiations. (5) What is_____ _____?	Management tactic in which union members are prevented from entering a business during a strike in order to force union acceptance of management's last contract proposal. (344) What is_____ _____?
$500	The two steps in creating a union. (331) What is_____ _____?	System of procedures and mechanisms for ensuring fair treatment on the job. (340) What is_____ _____?	Court order prohibiting certain actions by striking workers. (344) What is_____ _____?

MATCH THE TERMS AND CONCEPTS TO THEIR DEFINITIONS

a. agency shop (336)
b. arbitration (336)
c. authorization cards (331)
d. boycott (342)
e. business agent (331)
f. certification (331)
g. closed shop (336)
h. collective bargaining (332)
i. cost-of-living adjustment (COLA) (338)
j. craft unions (326)
k. decertification (331)
l. due process (340)

m. featherbedding (340)
n. givebacks (334)
o. grievances (340)
p. industrial unions (327)
q. injunction (344)
r. labor federation (331)
s. labor unions (326)
t. locals (330)
u. lockouts (344)
v. mandatory subjects (335)
w. mediation (335)
x. national union (330)
y. open shop (336)

z. pattern bargaining (336)
aa. permissive subjects (335)
bb. picketing (341)
cc. ratification (336)
dd. right-to-work laws (336)
ee. shop steward (331)
ff. slowdown (341)
gg. strike (341)
hh. strikebreakers (343)
ii. two-tier wage plan (337)
jj. union shop (336)
kk. work rules (339)

_____ 1. Nonunion workers hired to replace striking workers.

_____ 2. Strike activity in which union members march before company entrances to persuade nonstriking employees to walk off the job and to persuade customers and others to cease doing business with the company.

_____ 3. Full-time union staffer who negotiates with management and enforces the union's agreements with companies.

_____ 4. Management tactic in which union members are prevented from entering a business during a strike in order to force union acceptance of management's last contract proposal.

_____ 5. Laws giving employees the explicit right to keep a job without joining a union.

_____ 6. Topics that may be omitted from collective bargaining.

_____ 7. Organizations of employees formed to protect and advance their members' interests.

_____ 8. Court order prohibiting certain actions by striking workers.

_____ 9. Process for resolving a labor-contract dispute in which an impartial third party studies the issues and makes a binding decision.

_____ 10. Topics that must be discussed in collective bargaining.

_____ 11. Workplace in which union membership is voluntary and employees need not join or pay dues.

_____ 12. Union activity in which members and sympathizers refuse to buy or handle the product of a target company.

_____ 13. Union member and employee who is elected to represent other union members and who attempts to resolve employee grievances with management.

_____ 14. System of procedures and mechanisms for ensuring fair treatment on the job.

_____ 15. Concessions made by union members to give up promised increases in wages or benefits in order to enhance the company's competitive position.

_____ 16. Negotiating similar wages and benefits for all companies within a particular industry.

_____ 17. Sign-up cards designating a union as the signer's preferred bargaining agent.

_____ 18. Process for resolving a labor-contract dispute in which a neutral third party meets with both sides and attempts to steer them toward a solution.

_____ 19. Process by which union members vote on a contract negotiated by union leaders.

_____ 20. Umbrella organization of national unions and unaffiliated local unions that undertakes large-scale activities on behalf of their members and that resolves conflicts between unions.

_____ 21. Workplace requiring nonunion employees who are covered by agreements negotiated by the union to pay service fees to that union.

_____ 22. Employee complaints about management's violating some aspect of a labor contract.

_____ 23. Compensation agreement in which new employees are put on a wage scale lower than that of veteran employees.

_____ 24. Unions representing both skilled and unskilled employees from all phases of a particular industry.

_____ 25. Relatively small union groups, usually part of a national union or a labor federation, that represent members who work in a single facility or in a certain geographic area.

_____ 26. Clause in a union contract ensuring that wages will rise in proportion to inflation.

_____ 27. Temporary work stoppage by employees who want management to accept their union's demands.

_____ 28. Process employees use to take away a union's official right to represent them.

_____ 29. Workplace in which the employer may hire new employees at will, but where the employees are required to join the union after a probationary period.

_____ 30. Unions made up of skilled artisans belonging to a single profession or practicing a single craft.

_____ 31. Nationwide organization made up of locals that represent employees in locations around the country.

_____ 32. Practice of requiring employees to be kept on the payroll for work they do not do or for work that is not necessary.

_____ 33. Process used by unions and management to negotiate work contracts.

_____ 34. Decreasing employee productivity to pressure management.

_____ 35. Process by which a union is officially recognized by the National Labor Relations Board as the bargaining agent for a group of employees.

_____ 36. Workplace in which union membership is a condition of employment.

_____ 37. Policies set during collective bargaining that govern what type of work union members will do and the conditions under which they will work.

WORD SCRAMBLE

1. _____   2. _____   3. _____   _____
   kirste   injtionncu   onuni   pohs

LEARNING OBJECTIVES--POTENTIAL SHORT ANSWER OR ESSAY QUESTIONS

Learning Objective #1: "Identify two main types of labor unions." (326-327)

Learning Objective #2: "Outline the organizational structure of unions." (330-331)

Learning Objective #3: "Explain the two steps unions take to become the bargaining agent for a group of employees." (331)

<u>Learning Objective #4:</u> "Describe the four stages in collective bargaining." (332-341)

<u>Learning Objective #5:</u> "List five general issues that may be addressed in a labor contract." (336-340)

<u>Learning Objective #6:</u> "Discuss four options that unions have when negotiations with management break down." (341-343)

<u>Learning Objective #7:</u> "Discuss four options that management has when negotiations with the union break down." (343-344)

Learning Objective #8: "**Explain how employee-management relations are changing to meet the challenges of today's business environment.**" (344-349)

CRITICAL THINKING QUESTIONS

1. What are three real-world examples of industrial unions? What are three real-world examples of craft unions?

2. What do you think could give rise to a resurgence in union membership in the United States? How likely do you think this is?

BRAIN TEASER

1. Can you think of some specific tactics used by craft unions that are not used by industrial unions in attempting to increase their members' wages?

ANSWERS

True-False--*Answers*

1. False: *Craft* unions, which developed first, are composed of people who perform a particular type of skilled work, such as carpentry.
2. True
3. False: There has been *a decrease* in the percentage of the labor force who are members of labor unions in the last couple decades.
4. True
5. True
6. False: A *shop steward* is a union member and employee who is elected to represent other union members and who attempts to resolve employee grievances with management.
7. False: The first step in unionizing is to *issue authorization cards*.
8. True
9. True
10. False: The union *can* legally call for a strike vote before or during negotiations.
11. True
12. True
13. True
14. False: *Most* unions negotiate for better pay and working conditions.
15. False: A *cost-of-living adjustment (COLA)* is a clause in a union contract ensuring that wages will rise in proportion to inflation.
16. False: If negotiations break down with management, labor has the option of a *slowdown,* decreasing employee productivity to pressure management.
17. True
18. True
19. True
20. True
21. True

Multiple Choice--*Answers*

1. c	5. a	9. b	13. b
2. d	6. b	10. d	14. d
3. d	7. d	11. a	
4. d	8. c	12. c	

Jeopardy—*Answers*

	Types and Organizational Structure of Unions	Collective Bargaining	Options When Negotiations Break Down
$100	industrial unions	preparing to meet, negotiating, forming an agreement, and ratifying the contract	picketing
$200	decreasing in membership	permissive subjects	strikebreakers (scabs)
$300	national unions	mediation	a boycott
$400	a labor federation	union security and management rights, compensation, job security, work rules, and employee safety and health	lockouts

$500	getting authorization cards signed and then getting certified	due process	an injunction

Match the Terms and Concepts to Their Definitions--*Answers*

1. hh	6. aa	11. y	16. z	21. a	26. i	31. x	36. g
2. bb	7. s	12. d	17. c	22. o	27. gg	32. m	37. kk
3. e	8. q	13. ee	18. w	23. ii	28. k	33. h	
4. u	9. b	14. l	19. cc	24. p	29. jj	34. ff	
5. dd	10. v	15. n	20. r	25. t	30. j	35. f	

Word Scramble--*Answers*

1. strike   2. injunction   3. union shop

Learning Objectives--Potential Short Answer or Essay Questions--*Answers*

Learning Objective #1:

Craft unions, which developed first, are composed of people who perform a particular type of skilled work, such as carpentry. Industrial unions organize people who perform different types of work within a single industry, such as the automobile and steel industries.

Learning Objective #2:

National unions are composed of local unions; labor federations are composed of national unions and unaffiliated local unions. Each local has a hierarchy consisting of rank-and-file members, an elected president, elected shop stewards, and perhaps a business agent. National unions and federations consist of delegates elected by the local unions, who in turn elect officers; staff experts and organizers are hired to carry out the unions' programs.

Learning Objective #3:

First, unions distribute authorization cards to employees, which designate the union as bargaining agent, and if at least 30% (but usually a majority) of the target group sign the cards, the union asks management to recognize it. Second, if management is unwilling to do so, the union asks the National Labor Relations Board to sponsor a certification election. If a majority of the employees vote in favor of being represented by the union, the union becomes the official bargaining agent for the employees.

Learning Objective #4:

The first stage is preparing to meet, which may involve a strike vote. The second stage is actually negotiating. The third stage is forming a tentative agreement. The fourth stage is ratifying the proposed contract.

Learning Objective #5:

Among the issues that may be subject to negotiation are union security and management rights, compensation, job security, work rules, and employee safety and health.

<u>Learning Objective #6:</u>

Unions can conduct strikes, organize boycotts, exercise financial and political influence, and use publicity to pressure management into complying with union proposals.

<u>Learning Objective #7:</u>

To pressure a union into accepting its proposals, management may continue running the business with strikebreakers and managers, institute a lockout of union members, seek an injunction against a strike or other union activity, or seek a pact with other companies in the industry.

<u>Learning Objective #8:</u>

Employees and managers are becoming more cooperative and less adversarial. Specific actions by management include making more efforts to meet the life needs of employees, establishing employee grievance systems, complying with legislation that protects employee rights, and involving employees more in decision making and daily business operations. Actions by employees include helping management find ways to cut costs and improve efficiency, accepting more flexible compensation systems to help the company weather hard times, and reducing cumbersome work rules.

Critical Thinking Questions--*Answers*

1. Three real-world examples of industrial unions are the United Auto Workers (UAW), the United Mine Workers (UMW), and the Teamsters. Three real-world examples of craft unions are the local electricians union, the local bricklayers union, and the local painters union typically found on commercial construction sites.

2. A resurgence in union membership in the United States could be caused by the same general conditions which gave rise to their creation in the first place: low wages, poor working conditions, and a lack of benefits. How likely this is to happen in large part depends on how management treats workers in the future.

Brain Teaser---*Answer*

1. Industrial unions generally use the threat of a strike to try to restrict the supply of their labor to zero below the wage the union is striking for. Although, craft unions also try to restrict their supply in order to receive higher wages, they are often unable to effectively use the threat of a strike. Instead, they restrict the number of people able to practice their trade through long apprenticeship programs (e.g., the printers, plumbers, and electricians unions), licensing requirements--and only so many licenses will be granted (e.g., cosmetologists, barbers, and beauticians), stringent educational requirements (e.g. doctors and lawyers--the American Medical Association and the local Bar Association is essentially a union), or by issuing only so many membership cards--and those cards proving membership are required to practice the trade or craft (e.g., bricklayers, carpenters, and other commercial construction trades). Anything which restricts the supply of workers who are able to practice the trade or craft, short of a strike, is generally the type of tactics used by craft unions which are not practiced by industrial unions.

Chapter 12
Marketing and Customer Satisfaction

LEARNING OBJECTIVES
After studying this chapter, you should be able to:

1. Explain what marketing is. (358-359)
2. Describe the four utilities created by marketing. (359)
3. Clarify how technology is shaping the marketing function. (359-363)
4. List the benefits of delivering quality products and superior customer service. (363-367)
5. Define market segmentation, and review the five factors used to identify segments. (367-371)
6. List five factors that influence the buyer's purchase decision. (371)
7. Discuss how marketing research helps the marketing effort, and highlight its limitations. (372-373)
8. Distinguish between relationship marketing, database marketing, and one-to-one marketing. (373-376)

TRUE-FALSE
Indicate whether the statement is generally true or false by placing a "T" or "F" in the space provided. If it is a false statement, correct it so that it becomes a true statement.

_____ 1. Marketing involves all decisions related to determining a product's characteristics, prices, production specifications, market-entry date, sales, and customer service.

_____ 2. Place marketing is the identification and marketing of a social issue, cause, or idea to selected target markets

_____ 3. Utility is the power of a good or service to satisfy a human need and can take the form of form utility, time utility, place utility, and possession utility.

_____ 4. Form utility is created by making the product available when the consumer wants to buy it.

_____ 5. Place utility is created when a product is make available at a location that is convenient for the consumer.

_____ 6. A seller's market is a marketplace characterized by an abundance of products.

_____ 7. Most companies have adopted the marketing concept, an approach to business management that stresses customer needs and wants, seeks long-term profitability, and integrates marketing with other functional units within the organization.

_____   8. Technology is making it possible to mass-customize products.

_____   9. One way companies can learn about customer preferences is through relationship marketing, a focus on developing and maintaining long-term relationships with customers, suppliers, and distributors for mutual benefit.

_____ 10. Delivering quality products backed with good customer service improves customer satisfaction, enhances customer loyalty, decreases marketing costs, and increases profits.

_____ 11. Market segmentation is designed to shut some customers out of the market.

_____ 12. Geographic segmentation is the classification of customers on the basis of their psychological makeup.

_____ 13. Behavioral segmentation is the categorization of customers according to their relationship with products or response to product characteristics.

_____ 14. Niche marketing simply takes segmentation one step further by dividing a market segment into microsegments.

_____ 15. As one way to pave the way for repeat customers, companies address cognitive dissonance with guarantees, phone calls to check on customer's satisfaction, user hot lines, follow-up letters, and so on.

_____ 16. Factors that influence buying behavior include culture, social class, reference groups, self-image, and situational factors.

_____ 17. Customer markets are customers who buy goods or services for resale or for use in conducting their own operations.

_____ 18. Marketing research is simply one of the tools used by managers to understand the market; it is not a substitute for judgement.

_____ 19. Marketing research is a good indicator of what will excite customers in the future.

_____ 20. Database marketing is the process of building, maintaining, and using customer databases for the purpose of contacting customers and transacting business.

MULTIPLE CHOICE

Circle the one best answer for each of the following questions.

1. Marketing can be thought of as a series of strategic steps that involves
   a. defining market segments and niches.
   b. analyzing consumer buying behavior.
   c. choosing value disciplines.
   d. all of the above.

2. Marketing involves
   a. selling a product ("a bundle of value") for a profit.
   b. selling services.
   c. selling ideas and causes.
   d. all of the above.

3. Consumer value created by converting raw materials and other inputs into finished goods and services refers to
   a. form utility.
   b. time utility
   c. place utility.
   d. possession utility.

4. Consumer value created when someone takes ownership of a product refers to
   a. form utility.
   b. time utility
   c. place utility.
   d. possession utility.

5. Consumer value added by making a product available in a convenient location refers to
   a. form utility.
   b. time utility
   c. place utility.
   d. possession utility.

6. The marketing concept
   a. is an approach to business management that stresses customer needs and wants.
   b. seeks long-term profitability.
   c. integrates marketing with other functional units within the organization.
   d. is/does all of the above.

7. Which of the following statements is *false* about technology?
   a. It is making it easier to conduct a dialogue with customers and build long-term relationships.
   b. It is making relationship marketing more difficult.
   c. It is providing marketers with new ways to learn consumer preferences and buying behavior.
   d. It is opening up new shopping alternatives while creating new marketing opportunities and challenges.

8. Delivering quality products backed with good customer service will do all of the following *except*
    a. will improve customer satisfaction.
    b. will increase profits.
    c. will increase marketing costs.
    d. will increase customer loyalty.

9. Which of the following is *not* one of the common factors used to identify market segments?
    a. Micrographics
    b. Demographics
    c. Psychographics
    d. Behavior

10. Categorization of customers according to their relationship with products or response to product characteristics is which of the following market segmentation approaches?
    a. Demographic segmentation
    b. Behavioral segmentation
    c. Geodemographic segmentation
    d. Geographics segemetation

11. Which of the following are factors that influence buying behavior?
    a. Culture and social class
    b. Reference groups
    c. Self-image and situational factors
    d. All of the above are.

12. Marketing research can help companies
    a. set goals, develop new products, and measure customer satisfaction.
    b. segment markets and plan future marketing programs.
    c. evaluate the effectiveness of a marketing program and to keep an eye on competition.
    d. do all of the above.

13. The practice of building long-term satisfying relationship with customers by focusing on two-way communication is called
    a. customer marketing.
    b. database marketing.
    c. relationship marketing.
    d. one-to-one marketing.

14. When marketers record customer interactions and customer data, this is called
    a. customer marketing.
    b. database marketing.
    c. relationship marketing.
    d. one-to-one marketing.

15. When marketers treat each customer individually, this is called
    a. customer marketing.
    b. database marketing.
    c. relationship marketing.
    d. one-to-one marketing.

JEOPARDY
You have 5 seconds to complete the questions to each of the following answers.

	Utilities Created by Marketing; Effects of Technology	Benefits of Delivering Quality Products; Market Segmentation	Factors Affecting the Buyer's Decision; Marketing Approaches
$100	Consumer value added by making a product available at a convenient time. (359) What is_____ _____?	A few benefits of delivering quality products. (363-367) What is_____ _____?	Behavior exhibited by consumers as they consider and purchase various products. (370) What is_____ _____?
$200	Consumer value added by making a product available in a convenient location. (359) What is_____ _____?	Method of combining geographic data with demographic data to develop profiles of neighborhood segments. (369) What is_____ _____?	Anxiety following a purchase that prompts buyers to seek reassurance about the purchase; commonly known as *buyer's remorse*. (370) What is_____ _____?
$300	Consumer value created when someone takes ownership of a product. (359) What is_____ _____?	Categories of customers according to their relationship with products or response to product characteristics. (369) What is_____ _____?	A few factors that influence buying behavior. (371) What is_____ _____?
$400	Consumer value created by converting raw materials and other inputs into finished goods and services. (359) What is_____ _____?	This simply takes segmentation one step further by dividing a market segment into microsegments. (369) What is_____ _____?	A marketing approach that treats each customer individually. (370) What is_____ _____?
$500	A few ways technology is shaping the marketing function. (359-363) What is_____ _____?	Study of statistical characteristics of a population. (368) What is_____ _____?	A marketing approach designed to build a long-term satisfying relationship with customers. (361) What is_____ _____?

MATCH THE TERMS AND CONCEPTS TO THEIR DEFINITIONS

a. behavioral segmentation (369)
b. buyer's market (360)
c. cause-related marketing (359)
d. cognitive dissonance (370)
e. consumer buying behavior (370)
f. consumer markets (372)
g. database marketing (375)
h. demographics (368)
i. exchange process (359)
j. form utility (359)

k. geodemographics (369)
l. geographic segmentation (368)
m. market (367)
n. market segmentation (368)
o. marketing (358)
p. marketing concept (360)
q. marketing research (372)
r. need (359)
s. organizational market (371)
t. place marketing (359)

u. place utility (360)
v. possession utility (360)
w. psychographics (368)
x. relationship marketing (361)
y. sellers' markets (360)
z. time utility (360)
aa. transaction (359)
bb. utility (359)
cc. wants (359)

_____   1. Individuals or households that buy goods or services for personal use.

_____   2. Marketplace characterized by a shortage of products.

_____   3. People or businesses who need or want a product and have the money to buy it.

_____   4. Exchange between parties.

_____   5. Division of total market into smaller, relatively homogeneous groups.

_____   6. Collection and use of information for marketing decision making.

_____   7. Consumer value added by making a product available in a convenient location.

_____   8. Process of building, maintaining, and using customer databases for the purpose of contacting customers and transacting business.

_____   9. Act of obtaining a desired object from another party by offering something of value in return.

_____   10. Marketplace characterized by an abundance of products.

_____   11. Power of a good or service to satisfy a human need.

_____   12. Consumer value created when someone takes ownership of a product.

_____   13. Difference between a person's actual state and his or her ideal state; provides the basic motivation to make a purchase.

_____   14. Customers who buy goods or services for resale or for use in conducting their own operations.

_____   15. Anxiety following a purchase that prompts buyers to seek reassurance about the purchase; commonly known as buyer's remorse.

_____   16. Study of statistical characteristics of a population.

_____   17. Things that are desirable in light of a person's experiences, culture, and personality.

_____   18. Approach to business management that stresses customer needs and wants, seeks long-term profitability, and integrates marketing with other functional units within the organization.

_____   19. Process of planning and executing the conception, pricing, promotion, and distribution of ideas, goods, and services to create and maintain relationships that satisfy individual and organizational objectives.

_____   20. Behavior exhibited by consumers as they consider and purchase various products.

_____   21. Categorization of customers according to their geographic location.

_____   22. Identification and marketing of a social issue, cause, or idea to selected target markets.

_____ 23. Categorization of customers according to their relationship with products or response to product characteristics.

_____ 24. Method of combining geographic data with demographic data to develop profiles of neighborhood segments.

_____ 25. Consumer value created by converting raw materials and other inputs into finished goods and services.

_____ 26. Classification of customers on the basis of their psychological makeup.

_____ 27. Focus on developing and maintaining long-term relationships with customers, suppliers, and distributors for mutual benefit.

_____ 28. Marketing efforts to attract people and organizations to a particular geographic area.

_____ 29. Consumer value added by making a product available at a convenient time.

WORD SCRAMBLE

1. _____   2. _____   3. _____
    sementgation   moderpicgahs   yutilit

LEARNING OBJECTIVES--POTENTIAL SHORT ANSWER OR ESSAY QUESTIONS

Learning Objective #1: "Explain what marketing is." (358-359)

Learning Objective #2: "Describe the four utilities created by marketing." (359)

Learning Objective #3: "Clarify how technology is shaping the marketing function." (359-363)

Learning Objective #4: "List the benefits of delivering quality products and superior customer service." (363-367)

Learning Objective #5: "Define market segmentation, and review the five factors used to identify segments." (367-371)

Learning Objective #6: "List five factors that influence the buyer's purchase decision." (371)

Learning Objective #7: **"Discuss how marketing research helps the marketing effort, and highlight its limitations."** (372-373)

Learning Objective #8: **"Distinguish between relationship marketing, database marketing, and one-to-one marketing."** (373-376)

CRITICAL THINKING QUESTIONS

1. How might a toy store use relationship and database marketing to improve customer loyalty?

2. Marketers often refer to the "4 Ps" of marketing? What are they?

BRAIN TEASER

1. Price discrimination occurs when a company sells a good or service at different prices to different people, where those price differences are not a reflection of cost differences. The purpose of price discrimination is to charge some customers a higher price than others, and to therefore increase company profits. What two conditions must exist in order for price discrimination to occur? What are some examples of price discrimination?

ANSWERS

True-False--*Answers*

1. True
2. False: *Cause-related* marketing is the identification and marketing of a social issue, cause, or idea to selected target markets
3. True
4. False: *Time* utility is created by making the product available when the consumer wants to buy it.
5. True
6. False: A *buyer's* market is a marketplace characterized by an abundance of products.
7. True
8. True
9. True
10. True
11. False: Market segmentation is designed to *divide the total market into smaller, realtively homogenous groups.*
12. False: *Psychographic* segmentation is the classification of customers on the basis of their psychological makeup.
13. True
14. True
15. True
16. True
17. False: *Organizational* markets are customers who buy goods or services for resale or for use in conducting their own operations.
18. True
19. False: Marketing research is a *poor* indicator of what will excite customers in the future.
20. True

Multiple Choice--*Answers*

1. d	5. c	9. a	13. c
2. d	6. d	10. b	14. b
3. a	7. b	11. d	15. d
4. d	8. c	12. d	

Jeopardy—*Answers*

	Utilities Created by Marketing; Effects of Technology	Benefits of Delivering Quality Products; Market Segmentation	Factors Affecting the Buyer's Decision; Marketing Approaches
$100	time utility	it increases customer satisfaction, loyalty, and profits while it decreases marketing costs	consumer buying behavior
$200	place utility	geodemographics	cognitive dissonance
$300	possession utility	behavioral segmentation	culture, social class, reference groups, self-image, and situational factors
$400	form utility	niche marketing	one-to-one marketing
$500	it is making new shopping, mass-customization, and increased communication with customers possible	demographics	relationship marketing

Match the Terms and Concepts to Their Definitions--*Answers*

1. f	5. n	9. i	13. r	17. cc	21. l	25. j	29. z
2. y	6. q	10. b	14. s	18. p	22. c	26. w	
3. m	7. u	11. bb	15. d	19. o	23. a	27. x	
4. aa	8. g	12. v	16. h	20. e	24. k	28. t	

Word Scramble---*Answers*

1. segmentation　　　　2. demographics　　　　3. utility

Learning Objectives--Potential Short Answer or Essay Questions--*Answers*

Learning Objective #1:
　　Marketing is the process of planning and executing the conception, pricing, promotion, and distribution of ideas, goods, and services to create exchanges that satisfy individual and organizational objectives.

Learning Objective #2:
　　Form utility is created when companies turn raw materials into finished goods desired by consumers. Time utility is created by making the product available when the consumer wants to buy it. Place utility is created when a product is made available at a location that is convenient for the consumer. Possession utility is created by facilitating the transfer of ownership from seller to buyer.

Learning Objective #3:
　　Technology is making it possible to mass-customize products. It is making it easier to conduct a dialogue with customers and build long-term relationships. It is providing marketers with new ways to learn about consumer preferences and buying behavior. Finally, it is opening up new shopping alternatives while creating new marketing opportunities and challenges.

Learning Objective #4:

Delivering quality products backed with good customer service improves customer satisfaction, enhances customer loyalty, decreases marketing costs, and increases profits. These benefits can give companies a competitive advantage in the marketplace.

Learning Objective #5:

Market segmentation is the process of subdividing a market into homogeneous groups in order to identify potential customers and to devise marketing approaches geared to their needs and interests. The five most common factors used to identify segments are demographics, geographics, psychographics, geodemographics, and behavior.

Learning Objective #6:

The purchase decision is influenced by the buyer's culture, social class, reference groups, self-image, and situational factors.

Learning Objective #7:

Marketing research can help companies set goals, develop new products, segment markets, plan future marketing programs, evaluate the effectiveness of a marketing program, keep an eye on competition, and measure customer satisfaction. On the other hand, marketing research is a poor predictor of what will excite consumers in the future, and it can be ineffective--especially when conducted in an artificial setting.

Learning Objective #8:

Relationship marketing is the practice of building long-term satisfying relationships with customers. It focuses on two-way communication. Database marketing is the tool for recording customer interactions and customer data. One-to-one marketing treats customers individually. It requires a thorough understanding of a customer's preferences, which are entered into a detailed customer information file or database.

Critical Thinking Questions--*Answers*

1. A database can be collected on who buys what. The store could then send promotional materials inviting the customer to a special "invitation-only" sale of the items relevant for that aged child before the sale is advertised to the general public.

2. The "4 Ps" of marketing are Product, Price, Place, and Promotion.

Brain Teaser--*Answer*

1. The company must be able to segment its markets--to determine who is willing to pay a higher price. The second condition that must be present in order for price discrimination to take place is that it must be difficult for the good or service to be resold (for obvious reasons). Examples are doctors (if you have health insurance coverage, you may be charged more than someone who does not) and lawyers (how nervous are you?), the electric company (it charges higher prices to residential customers than commercial customers), movie theaters (the matinee showing is cheaper than the evening showing), car dealerships (how bad do you want that new car, etc. Can you think of any more?

Chapter 13
Product and Pricing Decisions

LEARNING OBJECTIVES
After studying this chapter, you should be able to:

1. Outline the ten steps in the strategic marketing planning process. (385-389)
2. Identify the four basic components of the marketing mix. (387)
3. Specify the four stages in the life cycle of a product. (392-393)
4. Describe the six stages of product development. (394-395)
5. Identify four ways of expanding a product line. (395-398)
6. Cite three levels of brand loyalty. (398-399)
7. Discuss the functions of packaging. (401-402)
8. List seven factors that influence pricing decisions. (402-405)

TRUE-FALSE
Indicate whether the statement is generally true or false by placing a "T" or "F" in the space provided. If it is a false statement, correct it so that it becomes a true statement.

_____ 1. The strategic marketing planning process involves three steps: evaluating your current marketing situation, analyzing your opportunities, and then developing your marketing strategy.

_____ 2. Stage One of the strategic marketing planning process involves assessing your opportunities and setting your objectives.

_____ 3. A marketing strategy is the overall plan for marketing a product.

_____ 4. A firm's marketing mix consists of the four Ps of the marketing strategy: product, price, place (distribution), and promotion.

_____ 5. Positioning is the firm's portion of the total sales in a market.

_____ 6. Target markets are specific groups of customers to whom a company wants to sell a particular product.

_____ 7. Products move from the introductory phase through a maturity phase; then they pass into a growth phase and eventually decline.

_____ 8. A business must introduce new products periodically to balance sales losses as older products decline.

_____ 9. The first two stages of product development involve generating and screening ideas to isolate those with the most potential.

_____ 10. A product mix is a series of related products offered by a firm.

_____ 11. A product line could be expanded by filling gaps in the market.

_____ 12. Brand names are a portion of a brand that cannot be expressed verbally.

_____ 13. A trademark is a brand that has been given legal protection so that its owner has exclusinve rights to its use.

_____ 14. The first level of brand loyalty is brand insistence, in which the buyer will accept no substitute.

_____ 15. Brand awareness is the level of brand loyalty at which people habitually buy a product if it is available.

_____ 16. Private brands are brands owned by a manufacturer and distributed nationally.

_____ 17. Packaging provides protection, makes products easier to display, and attracts attention.

_____ 18. Factors affecting price include marketing objectives, government regulations, and price-quality relationships.

_____ 19. Penetration pricing is introducing a new product at a low price in hopes of building sales volume quickly.

_____ 20. Skimming is the method of calculating the minimum volume of sales needed at a given price to cover all costs.

_____ 21. One of the biggest marketing decisions in international business is deciding whether to standardize your marketing mix or customize it to accommodate the local lifestyles and habits of your target market.

MULTIPLE CHOICE

Circle the one best answer for each of the following questions.

1. Which of the following is part of the strategic planning process?
   a. Evaluate your current marketing strategies.
   b. Examine your opportunities and objectives.
   c. Develop your marketing mix.
   d. All of the above are.

2. Which of the following is *not* part of the first stage in the strategic marketing planning process?
   a. Develop your marketing mix.
   b. Review past/current performance.
   c. Evaluate the competition, and examine your internal strengths and weaknesses.
   d. Analyze the external environment.

3. Which of the following is *not* part of the firm's marketing mix?
   a. Product
   b. Price
   c. Perception
   d. Promotion

4. A promotional strategy intended to differentiate a good or service from those of competitors in the mind of the prospective buyer is called
   a. positioning your product.
   b. skimming.
   c. co-branding.
   d. penetration pricing.

5. Which of the following statements is true?
   a. When positioning your products in your target markets, you need to take into consideration the four marketing mix elements plus the external environment.
   b. Organizational products are products sold to firms.
   c. Target markets are specific groups of customers to whom a company wants to sell a particular product.
   d. All of the above are true.

6. The four stages of the product life cycle begin with
   a. the introduction of the product, then its maturity, growth and finally its decline.
   b. the introduction of the product, then its growth, its maturity, and finally its decline.
   c. the introduction of the product, then its growth, its decline, and finally its maturity.
   d. its growth, its maturity, its decline, and then its reintroduction.

7. Which of the following correctly describes the stages of product development?
   a. Screening of ideas, business analysis, prototype development, product testing, and then commercialization.
   b. Prototype development, product testing, screening of ideas, business analysis, and then commercialization.
   c. Business analysis, screening of ideas, prototype development, product testing, and then commercialization.
   d. Product testing, business analysis, prototype development, screening of idea, and then commercialization.

8. Which of the following statements is true?
    a. Commercialization is the product development stage in which a product is sold on a limited a limited basis for trial introduction.
    b. A product line is a large-scale production and distribution of a product.
    c. A product mix is a complete list of all products that a company offers for sale.
    d. All of the above are true.

9. A product line can be expanded by
    a. line filling.
    b. line or brand extensions.
    c. line stretching.
    d. all of the above.

10. The highest level of brand loyalty is
    a. brand awareness.
    b. brand preference.
    c. brand insistence.
    d. brand substitution.

11. A brand that has been given legal protection so that its owner has exclusive rights to its use is
    a. brand name.
    b. a trademark.
    c. brand mark.
    d. brand new.

12. Which of the following statements is true?
    a. Private brands are brands that carry the label of a retailer or wholesaler rather than a manufacturer.
    b. National brands are characterized by a plain label, with no advertising or trademark.
    c. Co-branding is using a brand name on a variety of products.
    d. All of the above are true.

13. Packaging is designed to:
    a. protect the product.
    b. make products easier to display.
    c. attract attention.
    d. do all of the above.

14. Which of the following is *false*?
    a. Many companies today simplify the pricing task by using cost-based pricing (also know as cost plus pricing).
    b. Skimming is charging a high price for a new product during the introductory stage and lowering the price later.
    c. Penetration pricing is introducing a new product at a low price in hopes of building sales volume quickly.
    d. Break-even analysis attempts to find that volume of production for which variable costs equal fixed costs.

JEOPARDY

You have 5 seconds to complete the question to each of the following answers.

	Strategic Marketing Planning Process	**Product Management**	**Pricing Strategies and Decisions**
$100	Specific groups of customers to whom a company wants to sell a particular product. (387) What is_____ _____?	The four stages of the product life cycle. (392) What is_____ _____?	Factors affecting pricing decisions. (403) What is_____ _____?
$200	Promotional strategy intended to differentiate a good or service from those of competitors in the mind of the prospective buyer. (388) What is_____ _____?	The first stage of new product development. (394) What is_____ _____?	Pricing a product by adding a certain profit margin on top of the cost of production. (403-404) What is_____ _____?
$300	The stage of the strategic marketing planning process that examines the current marketing situation. (385) What is_____ _____?	The four ways to expand a product line. (398) What is_____ _____?	Charging a high price for a new product during the introductory stage and lowering the price later. (404) What is_____ _____?
$400	The stage of the strategic marketing planning process that analyzes opportunities and objectives. (385) What is_____ _____?	The highest level of brand loyalty. (399) What is_____ _____?	Introducing a new product at a low price in hopes of building sales volume quickly. (404) What is_____ _____?
$500	The stage of the strategic marketing planning process that develops the marketing strategy. (385) What is_____ _____?	The purposes of packaging. (401-402) What is_____ _____?	Method of calculating the minimum volume of sales needed at a given price to cover all costs. (404) What is_____ _____?

MATCH THE TERMS AND CONCEPTS TO THEIR DEFINITIONS

a. brand (398)
b. brand awareness (399)
c. brand insistence(399)
d. brand loyalty (399)
e. brand marks (398)
f. brand names (398)
g. brand preference (399)
h. break-even analysis (404)
i. break-even point (404)
j. co-branding (400)
k. commercialization (395)

l. discount pricing (405)
m. family branding (400)
n. fixed costs (404)
o. generic products (399)
p. market share (387)
q. marketing mix (387)
r. marketing strategy (387)
s. national brands (399)
t. penetration pricing (404)
u. positioning (388)
v. private brands (399)

w. product (390)
x. product life cycle (392)
y. product line (395)
z. product mix (395)
aa. skimming (404)
bb. target markets (387)
cc. test marketing (395)
dd. trademark (398)
ee. Universal Product Codes (UPCs) (402)
ff. variable costs (404)

_____ 1. A bar code on a product's package that provides information read by optical scanners.

_____ 2. Specific groups of customers to whom a company wants to sell a particular product.

_____ 3. Offering a reduction in price.

_____ 4. Large-scale production and distribution of a product.

_____ 5. Products characterized by a plain label, with no advertising and no brand name.

_____ 6. Partnership between two or more companies to closely link their brand names together for a single product.

_____ 7. Charging a high price for a new product during the introductory stage and lowering the price later.

_____ 8. Good or service used as the basis of commerce.

_____ 9. Complete list of all products that a company offers for sale.

_____ 10. Commitment to a particular brand.

_____ 11. A series of related products offered by a firm.

_____ 12. Measure of a firm's portion of the total sales in a market.

_____ 13. Brands owned by the manufacturer and distributed nationally.

_____ 14. Level of brand loyalty at which people are familiar with a product as they recognize it.

_____ 15. Brands that carry the label of a retailer or wholesaler rather than a manufacturer.

_____ 16. Level of brand loyalty at which people habitually buy a product if it is available.

_____ 17. Method of calculating the minimum volume of sales needed at a given price to cover all costs.

_____ 18. Overall plan for marketing a product.

_____ 19. Level of brand loyalty at which people will accept no substitute for a particular product.

_____ 20. Promotional strategy intended to differentiate a good or service from those of competitors in the mind of the prospective buyer.

_____ 21. Introducing a new product at a low price in hopes of building sales volume quickly.

_____ 22. Sales volume at a given price that will cover all of a company's costs.

_____ 23. A name, term, sign, symbol, design, or combination used to identify the products of a firm and differentiate them from competing products.

_____ 24. The four key elements of marketing strategy: product, price, distribution, and promotion.

_____ 25. Using a brand name on a variety of related products.

_____ 26. Business costs that increase with the number of units produced.

_____ 27. Product-development stage in which a product is sold on a limited basis as a trial introduction.

_____ 28. Business costs that remain constant regardless of the number of units produced.

_____ 29. Portion of a brand that can be expressed orally, including letters, words, or numbers.

_____ 30. Portion of a brand that cannot be expressed verbally.

_____ 31. Four basic stages through which a product progresses: introduction, growth, maturity, and decline.

_____ 32. Brand that has been given legal protection so that its owner has exclusive rights to its use.

WORD SCRAMBLE

1. _____   2. _____   3. _____
   tucdrop   gimksmin   dranb

LEARNING OBJECTIVES--POTENTIAL SHORT ANSWER OR ESSAY QUESTIONS

Learning Objective #1: "Outline the ten steps in the strategic marketing planning process." (385-389)

Learning Objective #2: "Identify the four basic components of the marketing mix." (387)

Learning Objective #3: **"Specify the four stages in the life cycle of a product."** (392-393)

Learning Objective #4: **"Describe the six stages of product development."** (394-395)

Learning Objective #5: **"Identify four ways of expanding a product line."** (395-398)

Learning Objective #6: **"Cite three levels of brand loyalty."** (398-399)

Learning Objective #7: "Discuss the functions of packaging." (401-402)

Learning Objective #8: "List seven factors that influence pricing decisions." (402-405)

CRITICAL THINKING QUESTIONS

1. What can be done to extend the life of a mature product?

2. What is the break-even volume of sales needed for a firm that sells its product at $4 per unit and has fixed costs of $20,000 and variable costs per unit of $3?

BRAIN TEASER

1. Sometimes we hear about "predatory" pricing. What is that?

ANSWERS

True-False--*Answers*

1. True
2. False: Stage *Two* of the strategic marketing planning process involves assessing your opportunities and setting your objectives.
3. True
4. True
5. False: *Market share* is the firm's portion of the total sales in a market.
6. True
7. False: Products move from the introductory phase through a *growth* phase; then they pass into a *maturity* phase and eventually decline.
8. True
9. True
10. False: A product *line* is a series of related products offered by a firm.
11. True
12. False: Brand *marks* are a portion of a brand that cannot be expressed verbally.
13. True
14. False: The *final* level of brand loyalty is brand insistence, in which the buyer will accept no substitute.
15. False: Brand *preference* is the level of brand loyalty at which people habitually buy a product if it is available.
16. False: *National* brands are brands owned by a manufacturer and distributed nationally.
17. True
18. True
19. True
20. False: *Break-even analysis* is the method of calculating the minimum volume of sales needed at a given price to cover all costs.
21. True

Multiple Choice--*Answers*

1. d	5. d	9. d	13. d
2. a	6. b	10. c	14. d
3. c	7. a	11. b	
4. a	8. c	12. a	

Jeopardy—*Answers*

	Strategic Marketing Planning Process	**Product Management**	**Pricing Strategies and Decisions**
$100	target market	introduction, growth, maturity, and decline	marketing objectives, government regulations, and price-quality relationships.
$200	positioning	the screening of ideas	cost-based pricing
$300	stage one	line filling, line extensions, brand extensions, line stretching	skimming
$400	stage two	brand insistence	penetration pricing
$500	stage three (the last stage)	to provide protection, to make products easier to display, and to attract attention	break-even analysis

Match the Terms and Concepts to Their Definitions--*Answers*

1. ee	5. o	9. z	13. s	17. h	21. t	25. m	29. f
2. bb	6. j	10. d	14. b	18. r	22. i	26. ff	30. e
3. l	7. aa	11. y	15. v	19. c	23. a	27. cc	31. x
4. k	8. w	12. p	16. g	20. u	24. q	28. n	32. dd

Word Scramble--*Answers*

1. product   2. skimming   3. brand

Learning Objectives--Potential Short Answer or Essay Questions--*Answers*

Learning Objective #1:

The ten steps in the strategic marketing planning process are reviewing your past performance, evaluating your competition, examining your internal strengths and weaknesses, analyzing the external environment, assessing your opportunities, setting your objectives, segmenting your market, choosing your target markets, positioning your product, and developing a marketing mix to satisfy that market.

Learning Objective #2:

The marketing mix consists of the four Ps: product, price, place (distribution), and promotion.

Learning Objective #3:

Products move from the introductory phase through a growth phase; then they pass into maturity and eventually decline.

Learning Objective #4:

The first two stages of product development involve generating and screening ideas to isolate those with the most potential. Promising ideas are analyzed to determine their likely profitability. Those that appear worthwhile enter the prototype development stage, in which a limited number of the products are created. In the next stage, the product is test-marketed to determine buyer response. Products that survive the testing process are then commercialized.

Learning Objective #5:

A product line can be expanded by filling gaps in the market, extending the line to include new varieties of existing products, extending the brand to new product categories, and stretching the line to include lower- or higher-priced items.

Learning Objective #6:

The first level of brand loyalty is brand awareness, in which the buyer is familiar with the product. The next level is brand preference, in which the buyer will select the product if it is available. The final level is brand insistence, in which the buyer will accept no substitute.

Learning Objective #7:

Packaging provides protection, makes products easier to display, and attracts attention. In addition, packaging enhances the convenience of the product and communicates its attributes to the buyer.

Learning Objective #8:

Pricing decisions are influenced by a firm's marketing objectives, government regulations, consumer perceptions, manufacturing and selling costs, competition, consumer demand, and the needs of wholesalers and retailers who distribute the product to the final customer.

Critical Thinking Questions--*Answers*

1. Generally, a company can extend the life of a mature product by broadening its appeal or making minor improvements. In addition, some companies have extended the life of their mature products by aggressively introducing their products in less developed nations.

2. Break-even point = $20,000/($4 - $3) = 20,000 units.

Brain Teaser--*Answer*

1. Predatory pricing is often used to refer to a company which prices its product below its own costs (or below "fair" market value) in order to drive their competitors out of business (on the assumption they can sustain losses longer than their competitors can).

Chapter 14
Distribution

LEARNING OBJECTIVES
After studying this chapter, you should be able to:

1. List the eight functions performed by marketing intermediaries. (415-416)
2. Explain what a distribution channel is, and discuss the major factors that influence channel design and selection. (417-421)
3. Differentiate between intensive, selective, and exclusive market-coverage strategies. (418)
4. Highlight the main advantage of a vertical marketing system, and explain how it differs from a conventional marketing channel. (422-423)
5. Discuss how the internet is influencing marketing channels. (423)
6. Explain what is meant by the wheel of retailing. (425)
7. Identify at least six types of store retailers and four types of nonstore retailers. (424-431)
8. Specify the activities included in physical distribution, and list the five most common ways of transporting goods. (431-436)

TRUE-FALSE
Indicate whether the statement is generally true or false by placing a "T" or "F" in the space provided. If it is a false statement, correct it so that it becomes a true statement.

_____ 1. Distribution channels are an organized network of firms that work together to get goods and services from producer to consumer.

_____ 2. Most producers lack the financial resources to carry out direct marketing so they use marketing intermediaries.

_____ 3. Marketing intermediaries have a sole purpose, and that is to stock and deliver the product.

_____ 4. Despite the common assumption that buying directly from the producer saves money, intermediaries actually reduce the price we pay for many goods and services.

_____ 5. Intermediaries do not create any utility.

_____ 6. Although most businesses purchase their goods directly from producers, channels for consumer goods generally have more than one level and are more complex.

_____ 7. Channel design and selection has little to do with the type of product; target market; company strengths, weaknesses, and objectives; desired market coverage; distribution costs; and desire for control.

_____ 8. With a selective distribution strategy, a company attempts to saturate the market with its products by offering them in every available outlet.

_____ 9. Channels (like products) have life cycles too--they emerge, grow, mature and eventually wane.

_____ 10. The main advantage of a vertical marketing system is channel control.

_____ 11. In a conventional marketing channel, the producer, wholesaler, and retailer act as a unified system to conduct distribution activities.

_____ 12. The internet is a sales, delivery, and repair marketing channel that moves forward and backward.

_____ 13. "Wheel of training" is a term used to describe the evolution of stores from low-priced, limited-service establishments to higher-priced outlets that provide more services.

_____ 14. Retailers are firms that sell products to other firms for resale or for organizational use.

_____ 15. A full-service merchant wholesaler provides a wide variety of services to its customers, such as storage, delivery, and marketing support.

_____ 16. Discount stores are a discount chain that sells only one category of products.

_____ 17. A mail-order firm is an example of a retail outlet.

_____ 18. The steps in the distribution system can be divided into in-house operations and transportation.

_____ 19. In-house operations include activities such as forecasting, order processing, inventory control, warehousing, and materials handling.

_____ 20. The five most common ways of transporting goods are via trucks, railroads, ships, airplanes, and pipelines.

MULTIPLE CHOICE

Circle the one best answer for each of the following questions.

1. Marketing intermediaries
   a. provide a sales force, market information, and promotional support.
   b. sort, standardize, and divide merchandise as well as carry stock and deliver products.
   c. assume risks, provide financing, and perform a preliminary buying function for users.
   d. do all of the above.

2. Which of the following describes a type of distribution channel?
   a. Producer to consumer
   b. Producer to retailer to consumer
   c. Producer to wholesaler to retailer to consumer
   d. All of the above do.

3. Which of the following statements is true?
   a. Most services are distributed directly by the producer to the consumer.
   b. Reverse channels are designed to move the product from the producer to the consumer.
   c. A distribution mix is businesspeople and organizations that channel goods and services from producers to consumers.
   d. All of the above are true.

4. Choosing one distribution channel over another depends on
   a. the number of outlets where the product is available.
   b. the cost of distribution.
   c. the need for control over the product as it moves through the channel to the final consumer.
   d. all of the above.

5. A market coverage strategy that tries to place a product in as many outlets as possible is
   a. a reverse channel strategy.
   b. an intensive distribution.
   c. a selective distribution.
   d. an exclusive distribution.

6. An exclusive distribution is market coverage that
   a. is designed to move products from the consumer to the producer.
   b. tries to place a product in as many outlets as possible.
   c. gives intermediaries exclusive rights to sell a product in a specific geographical area.
   d. selects a limited number of outlets to distribute products.

7. The distribution channel selected depends on
   a. the product.
   b. the customer.
   c. the company's capabilities.
   d. all of the above.

8. Vertical marketing systems
   a. may be corporate, administered, or contractual.
   b. are characterized by the producer, wholesaler, and retailer acting together as a unified system in the distribution channel.

   c.   are much different than conventional marketing channels because in conventional channels wholesalers and retailers are independent.

   d.   are all of the above.

9. Which of the following is true about channel conflict?

   a.   It may occur when companies sell products in multiple channels.

   b.   It may occur when markets are oversaturated with channel intermediaries.

   c.   Not all channel conflict is bad; the challenge is not to eliminate it but to control it.

   d.   All of the above are true.

10. Many companies are modifying their channel structures to include the internet which

   a.   is causing some channel conflict.

   b.   is the driving force behind the increased use of electronic catalogs and electronic storefronts for retail sales.

   c.   offers tremendous potential for direct marketing and interactive shopping.

   d.   does all of the above.

11. Which of the following is true?

   a.   Basically, intermediaries are of two main types: wholesalers and retailers.

   b.   Wholesalers are firms that sell goods and services to individuals for their own use rather than for resale.

   c.   Retailers are firms that sell products to other firms for resale or for organizational use.

   d.   All of the above are true.

12. Independent wholesalers that do not take title to the goods they distribute, but may or may not take possession of those goods, are called:

   a.   rack jobbers.

   b.   agents and brokers.

   c.   full-service merchant wholesalers.

   d.   limited-service merchant wholesalers.

13. Which of the following is a common type of store retailer?

   a.   Vending machines

   b.   Mail-order firms

   c.   Convenience stores

   d.   Telemarketers

14. Which of the following is a common type of nonstore retailer?

   a.   Virtual storefronts

   b.   Discount stores

   c.   Specialty stores

   d.   Supermarkets

15. Which of the following is true?

   a.   The average life cycle of a retail store is considerably longer than it used to be.

   b.   Physical distribution encompasses transportation and in-house activities.

   c.   Transportation activities include forecasting, order processing, inventory control, warehousing, and materials handling.

   d.   In-house activities include dealing with trucks, railroads, ships, airplanes, and pipelines.

JEOPARDY

You have 5 seconds to complete the questions to each of the following answers.

	Developing a Distribution Strategy	Choosing Intermediaries	Managing Physical Distribution
$100	The three general roles of marketing intermediaries. (415-416) What is_____ _____?	The two basic types of intermediaries. (423) What is_____ _____?	All of the activities required to move finished products from the producer to the consumer. (431) What is_____ _____?
$200	A system for moving goods and services from producers to customers. (415) What is_____ _____?	The most common type of wholesaler--they take legal title of goods they distribute. (424) What is_____ _____?	The two major types of physical distribution. (431-436) What is_____ _____?
$300	With this type of distribution channel, a company attempts to saturate the market with its products by offering them in every available outlet. (418) What is_____ _____?	Examples of these types of outlets include department stores, discount stores, specialty stores, supermarkets, convenience stores, and category killers. (424-427) What is_____ _____?	Examples include forecasting, order processing, inventory control, warehousing, and material handling. (433-434 What is_____ _____?
$400	With this type of distribution strategy, a company selects a limited number of outlets to distribute products. (418) What is_____ _____?	These types of outlets include mail-order firms, vending machines, telemarketers, and virtual storefronts. (428-430) What is_____ _____?	This includes the use of trucks, railroads, ships, airplanes, and pipelines. (434-436) What is_____ _____?
$500	A marketing system in which the producer, wholesaler, and retailer act as a unified system to conduct distribution activities in order to gain more channel control. (422) What is_____ _____?	A term describing the evolution of stores from low-priced, limited-service establishments to higher-priced outlets that provide more services. (425) What is_____ _____?	The overall objective of the physical distribution process. (432) What is_____ _____?

MATCH THE TERMS AND CONCEPTS TO THEIR DEFINITIONS

a. agents and brokers (424)
b. branch office (424)
c. category killers (426)
d. channel captain (421)
e. common carriers (435)
f. contract carriers (435)
g. customer-service standards (432)

o. full-service merchant wholesalers (424)
p. industrial distributors (423)
q. intensive distribution (418)
r. limited-service merchant wholesalers (424)
s. logistics (431)
t. mail-order firms (429)

bb. retailers (423)
cc. reverse channels (418)
dd. sales office (424)
ee. scrambled merchandising (425)
ff. selective distribution (418)
gg. specialty shops (425)

h. discount stores (426)
i. distribution centers (434)
j. distribution channels (415)
k. distribution mix (415)
l. distribution strategy (415)
m. drop shippers (424)
n. exclusive distribution (418)

u. marketing intermediaries (415)
v. materials handling (434)
w. merchant wholesalers (424)
x. order processing (433)
y. physical distribution (431)
z. private carriers (435)
aa. rack jobbers (424)

hh. vertical marketing systems (VMS) (421)
ii. warehouse (434)
jj. wheel of retailing (425)
kk. wholesalers (423)

_____ 1. Merchant wholesalers that provide a wide variety of services to their customers, such as storage, delivery, and marketing support.

_____ 2. The planning, movement, and flow of goods and related information throughout the supply chain.

_____ 3. Evolutionary process by which stores that feature low prices are gradually upgraded until they forfeit their appeal to price-sensitive shoppers and are replaced by new competitors.

_____ 4. Specialized freight haulers that serve selected companies under written contract.

_____ 5. Distribution channels designed to move products from the customer back to the producer.

_____ 6. Movement of goods within a firm's warehouse terminal, factory, or store.

_____ 7. Firms that sell goods and services to individuals for their own use rather than for resale.

_____ 8. Planned distribution channels in which members coordinate their efforts to optimize distribution activities.

_____ 9. Specifications for the quality of service that a firm will provide for its customers.

_____ 10. Merchant wholesalers that are responsible for setting up and maintaining displays in a particular section of a retail store.

_____ 11. Systems for moving goods and services from producers to customers; also known as marketing channels.

_____ 12. Producer-owned office that markets products but doesn't carry any stock.

_____ 13. Independent wholesalers that take legal title to goods they distribute.

_____ 14. Merchant wholesalers that offer fewer services than full-service wholesalers; they often specialize in particular markets, such as agriculture.

_____ 15. Channel member that is able to influence the activities of the other members of the distribution channel.

_____ 16. Policy of carrying merchandise that is ordinarily sold in a different type of outlet.

_____ 17. Combination of intermediaries and channels that a producer uses to get a product to end users.

_____ 18. Transportation operations owned by a company to move its own products and not those of the general public.

_____ 19. Market coverage strategy that tries to place a product in as many outlets as possible.

_____ 20. Warehouse facilities that specialize in collecting and shipping merchandise.

_____ 21. Producer-owned marketing intermediary that carries stock and sells it; also called a sales branch.

_____ 22. All the activities required to move finished products from the producer to the consumer.

_____ 23. Market coverage strategy that gives intermediaries exclusive rights to sell a product in a specific geographical area.

_____ 24. Stores that carry only particular types of goods.

_____ 25. Wholesalers that sell to industrial customers, rather than to retailers.

_____ 26. Retailers that sell a variety of goods below the market price by keeping their overhead low.

_____ 27. Functions involved in preparing and receiving an order.

_____ 28. Firm's overall plan for moving products to intermediaries and final customers.

_____ 29. Independent wholesalers that do not take title to the goods they distribute, but may or may not take possession of those goods.

_____ 30. Transportation companies that offer their services to the general public.

_____ 31. Companies that sell products through catalogs and ship them directly to customers.

_____ 32. Facility for storing inventory.

_____ 33. Businesspeople and organizations that channel goods and services from producers to consumers.

_____ 34. Firms that sell products to other firms for resale or for organizational use.

_____ 35. A discount chain that sells only one category of products.

_____ 36. Market coverage strategy that selects a limited number of outlets to distribute products.

_____ 37. Merchant wholesalers that assume ownership of goods but do not take physical possession; commonly used to market agricultural and mineral products.

WORD SCRAMBLE

1. _____   _____   2. _____   _____   3. _____
      sluvexcie   buttridision   plahysic   tribdistuion   selaitrer

LEARNING OBJECTIVES--POTENTIAL SHORT ANSWER OR ESSAY QUESTIONS

Learning Objective #1: "**List the eight functions performed by marketing intermediaries.**" (415-416)

Learning Objective #2: "**Explain what a distribution channel is, and discuss the major factors that influence channel design and selection.**" (417-421)

Learning Objective #3: "**Differentiate between intensive, selective, and exclusive market-coverage strategies.**" (418)

Learning Objective #4: **"Highlight the main advantage of a vertical marketing system and explain how it differs from a conventional marketing channel."** (422-423)

Learning Objective #5: **"Discuss how the internet is influencing marketing channels."** (423)

Learning Objective #6: **"Explain what is meant by the wheel of retailing."** (425)

Learning Objective #7: **"Identify at least six types of store retailers and four types of nonstore retailers."** (424-431)

Learning Objective #8: **"Specify the activities included in physical distribution, and list the five most common ways of transporting goods."** (431-436)

CRITICAL THINKING QUESTION

1. The factors involved in selecting the appropriate distribution channel basically depends on the product, the customer, and the company's capabilities. For each of the following factors, explain the distribution channel which should be selected.

   a. There are a large number of transactions necessary in getting the product to the consumer.

   b. The value of each transaction in the distribution channel is high.

   c. The market is growing very rapidly.

   d. Customers are clustered in a limited geographic area.

   e. The product is complex, innovative, and specialized.

BRAIN TEASER

1. Why do companies need to modify their marketing channel distribution strategies periodically?

ANSWERS

True-False--*Answers*

1. True
2. True
3. False: Marketing intermediaries have *at least eight functions, one of which* is to stock and deliver the product.
4. True
5. False: Intermediaries *do* create utility: *they create time, place, and possession utility.*
6. True
7. False: Channel design and selection *are influenced by* the type of product; target market; company strengths, weaknesses, and objectives; desired market coverage; distribution costs; and desire for control.
8. False: With *an intensive* distribution strategy, a company attempts to saturate the market with its products by offering them in every available outlet.
9. True
10. True
11. False: In a *vertical* marketing channel, the producer, wholesaler, and retailer act as a unified system to conduct distribution activities.
12. True
13. True
14. False: *Wholesalers* are firms that sell products to other firms for resale or for organizational use.
15. True
16. False: *Category killers* are a discount chain that sells only one category of products.
17. False: A mail-order firm is an example of a *nonstore retailer.*
18. True
19. True
20. True

Multiple Choice--*Answers*

1. d	5. b	9. d	13. c
2. d	6. c	10. d	14. a
3. a	7. d	11. a	15. b
4. d	8. d	12. b	

Jeopardy—*Answers*

	Developing a Distribution Strategy	Choosing Intermediaries	Managing Physical Distribution
$100	they provide a sales force, market information, and promotional support	wholesalers and retailers	physical distribution
$200	a distribution channel	merchant wholesalers	transportation and in-house activities
$300	an intensive distribution strategy	store retailers	in-house activities
$400	an exclusive distribution strategy	nonstore retailers	transportation
$500	a vertical marketing system	wheel of retailing	to provide a target level of customer service at the lowest overall cost.

Match the Terms and Concepts to Their Definitions--*Answers*

1. o	6. v	11. j	16. ee	21. b	26. h	31. t	36. ff
2. s	7. bb	12. dd	17. k	22. y	27. x	32. ii	37. m
3. jj	8. hh	13. w	18. z	23. n	28. l	33. u	
4. f	9. g	14. r	19. q	24. gg	29. a	34. kk	
5. cc	10. aa	15. d	20. i	25. p	30. e	35. c	

Word Scramble--*Answers*

1. exclusive distribution   2. physical distribution   3. retailers

Learning Objectives--Potential Short Answer or Essay Questions--*Answers*

Learning Objective #1:

Marketing intermediaries provide a sales force, market-information, and promotional support. They sort, standardize, and divide merchandise; and they also carry stock and deliver products. In addition, they assume risks, provide financing, and perform a preliminary buying function for users.

Learning Objective #2:

A distribution channel is an organized network of firms that work together to get a product from a producer to consumers. Channel design and selection are influenced by the type of product; target market; company strengths, weaknesses, and objectives; desired market coverage; distribution costs; and desire for control.

Learning Objective #3:

With an intensive distribution strategy, a company attempts to saturate the market with its products by offering them in every available outlet. Companies that use a more selective approach to distribution choose a limited number of retailers that can adequately support the product. Firms that use exclusive distribution grant a single wholesaler or retailer the exclusive right to sell the product within a given geographic area.

Learning Objective #4:

The main advantage of a vertical marketing system is channel control. In a vertical marketing system, the producer, wholesaler, and retailer act as a unified system to conduct distribution activities. By contrast, in a conventional marketing channel, wholesalers and retailers are independent.

Learning Objective #5:

The internet is a sales, delivery, and repair marketing channel that moves forward and backward. Many companies are modifying their channel structures to include the internet in their distribution mix, and such change is causing channel conflict. The internet is the driving force behind the increased use of electronic catalogs and electronic storefronts for retail sales. It offers tremendous potential for direct marketing and interactive shopping.

Learning Objective #6:

Wheel of retailing is a term used to describe the evolution of stores from low-priced, limited-service establishments to higher-priced outlets that provide more services. As stores are upgraded, lower-priced competitors move in to fill the gap.

Learning Objective #7:

Some of the most common types of store retailers are department stores, discount stores, specialty stores, supermarkets, convenience stores, and category killers. Common nonstore retailers are mail-order firms, vending machines, telemarketers, and virtual storefronts.

Learning Objective #8:

Physical distribution encompasses transportation and in-house activities such as forecasting, order processing, inventory control, warehousing, and materials handling. The five most common ways of transporting goods are trucks, railroads, ships, airplanes, and pipelines.

Critical Thinking Question--*Answer*

1. See Exhibit 14.3 on page 420 of the textbook for detailed explanations.

Brain Teaser--*Answer*

1. In short, companies need to modify their marketing channel distribution strategies periodically to remain competitive. We live in a rapidly changing, dynamic, and increasingly competitive market environment. Battles over how products will be distributed are inevitable. Firms must remain flexible and willing to change distribution channels (and the companies they are doing business with) if they wish to survive the competition. Unfortunately, some businesses will be hurt by this change. See also the "Thinking About Ethics" boxed section on page 420 of the textbook.

Chapter 15
Promotion

LEARNING OBJECTIVES
After studying this chapter, you should be able to:

1. Identify the five basic categories of promotion. (447-449)
2. Distinguish between push and pull strategies of promotion. (450-451)
3. List the seven steps in the personal-selling process. (453-455)
4. Differentiate between institutional, product, and competitive advertising. (456-457)
5. Define interactive advertising, and discuss the challenge it presents to marketers. (457)
6. Discuss the difference between logical and emotional advertising appeals. (457-459)
7. Distinguish between the two main types of sales promotion, and give at least two examples of each. (463-466)
8. Explain the role of public relations in marketing. (466-467)

TRUE-FALSE
Indicate whether the statement is generally true or false by placing a "T" or "F" in the space provided. If it is a false statement, correct it so that it becomes a true statement.

_____ 1. The five basic categories of promotion are personal selling, advertising, direct marketing, sales promotion, and public relations.

_____ 2. Reminder advertising is intended to encourage product sampling and brand switching.

_____ 3. Public concern about potential misuse of promotion has led to the passage of government regulations that limit promotional abuses.

_____ 4. Personal selling involves direct communication, other than personal sales contacts designed to effect a measurable response.

_____ 5. Advertising is the nonsales communication that businesses have with their various audiences.

_____ 6. Direct marketing is both a nonretail sales vehicle and a form of promotion.

_____ 7. Coupons, rebates, in-store demonstrations, free samples, trade shows, and point of purchase displays all fall into the category of direct marketing.

_____ 8. Advertising tries to encourage favorable reviews of products in newspapers and magazines and on radio and television.

_____ 9. The basics of integrated marketing communications (IMC) are quite simple: communicating in one voice and one message to the marketplace.

_____ 10. In the push strategy, the approach depends on stimulating enough consumer demand to "push" a product through the distribution channel.

_____ 11. Consumer products are more likely to rely on pull strategies; organizational products are more often pushed.

_____ 12. The seven steps in the personal selling process are prospecting, preparing, approaching the prospects, making the sales presentation, handling objections, closing, and following up after the sale has been made.

_____ 13. Product advertising is advertising that specifically highlights how a product is better than its competitors.

_____ 14. Institutional advertising promotes a company's overall image, not any particular product.

_____ 15. Local advertising is sponsored by a local merchant.

_____ 16. Interactive advertising is a two-way exchange between a merchant and a potential customer.

_____ 17. Logical advertising appeals to the head; emotional advertising appeals to the heart.

_____ 18. Two main types of sales promotions are consumer promotion and trade promotion.

_____ 19. When media planners use the term "frequency," they are referring to the total number of audience members who will be exposed to a message at least once in a given period.

_____ 20. Trade promotions are sales-promotion efforts aimed at inducing distributors or retailers to push a product's products.

_____ 21. Smart companies use public relations to build and protect their reputations.

MULTIPLE CHOICE

Circle the one best answer for each of the following questions.

1. Which of the following is *not* part of the promotional mix?
   a. Personal selling
   b. Pricing
   c. Advertising
   d. Public relations

2. Personal selling
   a. involves direct, person-to-person communication, either face-to-face or by phone.
   b. has the disadvantage of being relatively expensive.
   c. has the advantages of allowing for immediate interaction between buyers and sellers, and enables sellers to adjust their message to the specific needs and interests of their individual customers.
   d. does all of the above.

3. Which of the following is a disadvantage of advertising?
   a. It is expensive to create an advertising campaign.
   b. It cannot always motivate customers.
   c. Traditional forms of advertising cannot provide direct feedback, as personal selling can, and they are also difficult to personalize.
   d. All of the above are.

4. Direct marketing as defined by the Direct Marketing Association is any direct communication to a consumer or business recipient designed to generate
   a. a response in the form of an order.
   b. a request for further information.
   c. a visit to a store or other place of business for purchase of a specific product or service.
   d. all of the above.

5. The principle vehicle for direct marketing is
   a. telemarketing.
   b. television infomercials.
   c. direct mail.
   d. electronic media.

6. Which of the following is statements is true?
   a. Sales promotions are the most difficult promotional element to define because they involve a wide variety of events and activities designed to stimulate interest in the product.
   b. Examples of advertising include coupons, rebates, contests, in-store demonstrations, free samples, trade shows, and point of purchase displays.
   c. Sales promotions are designed to encourage favorable reviews of products in newspapers and magazines and on radio and television programs.
   d. All of the above are true.

7. The strategy of coordinating and integrating communications and promotional efforts with customers to ensure greater efficiency and effectiveness is
   a. advertising.
   b. integrated marketing communications.
   c. public relations.
   d. sales promotion.

8. Which of the following statements is true?
   a. The promotional mix is influenced by the size and concentration of the market.
   b. In markets with relatively few customers, particularly when they are clustered in a limited area, personal selling is a practical promotional alternative.
   c. Many marketers use a combination of methods, often relying on advertising and public relations to build awareness and interest, following up with personal selling to complete the sale.
   d. All of the above.

9. Which of the following is true?
   a. The global approach to international advertising, as opposed to the local approach, tries to allow its divisions or representatives in each country to design an implement their own advertising.
   b. Reminder advertising is intended to remind existing customers of a product's availability and benefits.
   c. Firms rarely use a combination of push and pull strategies to increase the impact of their promotional efforts.
   d. All of the above are true.

10. Which of the following is true?
    a. In the push strategy, the producer "pushes" an item to distributors, who in turn promote the product to end users.
    b. The "pull" approach depends on stimulating enough consumer demand to "pull" a product through the distribution channel.
    c. Consumer products are more likely to rely on pull strategies; organizational products are more often pushed.
    d. All of the above are true.

11. Which of the following is not one of three most common types of sales support personnel?
    a. Order takers
    b. Technical salespeople
    c. Trade salespeople
    d. Missionary salespeople

12. Which of the following is not one of the seven steps in the personal-selling process?
    a. Approaching the prospect
    b. Making the Presentation
    c. Delivering the product
    d. Handling objections

13. Which of the following statements is *false*?
    a. Product advertising emphasizes the products themselves; competitive advertising emphasizes the differences between a product and its competitors.
    b. The advantages with interactive advertising is that no one can control when the message is received and that consumers must actively choose to participate.
    c. Logical advertising appeals try to convince the audience with facts, reason, and rational conclusions; emotional appeals persuade through emotion--which can range from heart-warming tenderness to stark fear.
    d. Nearly all ads contain a mixture of both logic and emotion; most just lean heavily in one direction or the other.

14. Which of the following statements is true?
    a. Consumer promotions are intended to motivate the final consumer to try new products or to experiment with the company's brands; examples include coupons, cross-promotion, specialty advertising, premiums, point-of-purchase displays, and special events.
    b. Trade promotions are designed to induce wholesalers and retailers to stimulate sales of a producer's products; examples include trade allowances, trade shows, display premiums, dealer contests, and travel bonus programs.
    c. Because consumers and investors support companies with good reputations, smart companies use public relations to build and protect their reputations.
    d. All of the above are true.

JEOPARDY

You have 5 seconds to complete the questions to each of the following answers.

	The Promotional Mix and Personal Selling	**Adverting and Direct Marketing**	**Sales Promotion and Public Relations**
$100	The five elements of the promotional mix. (447) What is_____ _____?	Advertising that tries to sell specific goods and services, generally by describing features, benefits, and, occasionally, price. (456) What is_____ _____?	The two basic categories of sales promotions. (463) What is_____ _____?
$200	This element of the promotional mix involves in-person communication between a seller and one or more potential buyers. (448) What is_____ _____?	Advertising that seeks to create goodwill and to build a desired image for a company rather than to sell specific products. (456) What is_____ _____?	This is designed to induce wholesalers and retailers to stimulate sales of a producer's product. (466) What is_____ _____?
$300	Seller process used by order getters, which involves determining customer needs, devising strategies to explain product benefits, and persuading customers to buy. (452) What is_____ _____?	Advertising sent directly to potential customers, usually through the U.S. Postal Service; the most common type of direct marketing. (460) What is_____ _____?	Examples include coupons, cross-promotion, specialty advertising, premiums, point-of-purchase display, and special events. (463-466) What is_____ _____?
$400	The three most common types of sales support personnel. (453) What is_____ _____?	The three most popular direct-marketing categories. (460) What is_____ _____?	Discount offered by producers to wholesalers and retailers. (466) What is_____ _____?
$500	The seven steps in the personal-selling process. (453-454) What is_____ _____?	The disadvantages of interactive advertising. (457) What is_____ _____?	The overriding objective of public relations by a firm. (466-467) What is_____ _____?

MATCH THE TERMS AND CONCEPTS TO THEIR DEFINITIONS

a. advertising (448)
b. advocacy advertising (456)
c. artwork (459)
d. canned approach (454)
e. closing (454)
f. comparative advertising (456)
g. competitive advertising (456)
h. consumer promotions (463)
i. continuity (461)
j. cooperative advertising (457)
k. copy (459)
l. cost per thousand (CPM) (461)
m. couponing (463)
n. creative selling (452)
o. cross-promotion (465)
p. direct mail (460)
q. direct marketing (448)
r. forward buying (466)
s. frequency (461)
t. institutional advertising (456)

u. integrated marketing communications (IMC) (449)
v. interactive advertising (457)
w. local advertising (457)
x. media (460)
y. media mix (460)
z. media plan (460)
aa. missionary salespeople (453)
bb. national advertising (457)
cc. need-satisfaction approach (454)
dd. order getters (452)
ee. order takers (453)
ff. personal selling (448)
gg. persuasive advertising (446)
hh. point-of-purchase display (464)
ii. premiums (465)
jj. press conference (467)
kk. press relations (467)
ll. press release (467)

nn. product advertising (456)
oo. promotion (446)
pp. promotional mix (447)
qq. promotional strategy (446)
rr. prospecting (453)
ss. public relations (449)
tt. pull strategy (450)
uu. push strategy (450)
vv. qualified prospects (453)
xx. reach (461)
yy. reminder advertising (446)
zz. sales promotion (449)
a1. sales support personnel (453)
a2. specialty advertising (465)
a3. technical salespeople (453)
a4. telemarketing (460)
a5. trade allowance (466)
a6. trade promotions (466)
a7. trade salespeople (453)
a8. trade show (466)

_____ 1. Advertising sponsored by companies that sell products on a nationwide basis; refers to the geographic reach of the advertiser, not the geographic coverage of the ad.

_____ 2. Brief statement or video program released to the press announcing new products, management changes, sales performance, and other potential news items; also called a news release.

_____ 3. Total number of audience members who will be exposed to a message at least once in a given period.

_____ 4. Potential buyers who have both the money needed to make the purchase and the authority to make the purchase decision.

_____ 5. Strategy of coordinating and integrating communications and promotions efforts with customers to ensure greater efficiency and effectiveness.

_____ 6. Advertising sponsored by a local merchant.

_____ 7. Selling method based on a fixed, memorized presentation.

_____ 8. Verbal (spoken or written) part of an ad.

_____ 9. Wide variety of persuasive techniques used by companies to communicate with their target markets and the general public.

_____ 10. Process of finding and qualifying potential customers.

_____ 11. Customer-seller communication in which the customer controls the amount and type of information received.

_____ 12. Advertising that appears on various items such as coffee mugs, pens, and calendars, designed to help keep a company's name in front of customers.

_____ 13. Nonsales communication that businesses have with their various audiences (includes both communication with the general public and press relations).

_____ 14. Promotional approach designed to motivate wholesalers and retailers to push a product's purchase.

_____ 15. Selling method that starts with identifying the customer's needs and then creating a presentation that addresses those needs; this is the approach used by most professional salespeople.

_____ 16. Statement or document that defines the direction and scope of the promotional activities that a company will use to meet its marketing objectives.

_____ 17. Process of communicating with reporters and editors from newspapers, magazines, and radio and television networks and stations.

_____ 18. Joint efforts between local and national advertisers, in which producers of nationally sold products share the costs of local advertising with local merchants and wholesalers.

_____ 19. Wide range of events and activities (including coupons, rebates, contests, in-store demonstrations, free samples, trade shows, and point-of-purchase displays) designed to stimulate interest in a product.

_____ 20. Visual, graphic part of an ad.

_____ 21. Gathering of media representatives at which companies announce new information; also called a press briefing.

_____ 22. Salespeople who sell to and support marketing intermediaries by giving in-store demonstrations, offering samples, and so on.

_____ 23. Advertising designed to encourage product sampling and brand switching.

_____ 24. Jointly advertising two or more noncompeting brands.

_____ 25. Selling process used by order getters, which involves determining customer needs, devising strategies to explain product benefits, and persuading customers to buy.

_____ 26. Point at which a sale is completed.

_____ 27. Direct communication other than personal sales contacts designed to effect a measurable response.

_____ 28. Promotional strategy that stimulates consumer demand, which then exerts pressure on wholesalers and retailers to carry a product.

_____   29. Advertising sent directly to potential customers, usually through the U.S. Postal Service.

_____   30. Salespeople who generally process incoming orders without engaging in creative selling.

_____   31. Combination of various media options that a company uses in an advertising campaign.

_____   32. Paid, nonpersonal communication to a target market from an identified sponsor using mass communications channels.

_____   33. Advertising that tries to sell specific goods or services, generally by describing features, benefits, and, occasionally, price.

_____   34. Retailers' taking advantage of trade allowances by buying more products at discounted prices than they hope to sell.

_____   35. Cost of reaching 1,000 people with an ad.

_____   36. Advertising intended to remind existing customers of a product's availability and benefits.

_____   37. Salespeople who facilitate the selling effort by providing such services as prospecting, customer education, and customer service.

_____   38. Advertising or other display materials set up at retail locations to promote products to potential customers as they are making their purchase decisions.

_____   39. Pattern according to which an ad appears in the media; it can be spread evenly over time or concentrated during selected periods.

_____   40. Ads that specifically highlight how a product is better than its competitors.

_____   41. Written plan that outlines how a company will spend its media budget, including how the money will be divided among the various media and when the advertisements will appear.

_____   42. Salespeople who support existing customers, usually wholesalers and retailers.

_____   43. Advertising that seeks to create goodwill and to build a desired image for a company rather than to sell specific products.

_____   44. Communications channels, such as newspapers, radio, and television.

_____   45. Discount offered by producers to wholesalers and retailers.

_____   46. In-person communication between a seller and one or more potential buyers.

_____   47. Sales promotions aimed at final consumers.

_____   48. Specialists who contribute technical expertise and other sales assistance.

_____   49. Ads that present a company's opinions on public issues such as education and health.

_____ 50. Particular blend of personal selling, advertising, direct marketing, sales promotion, and public relations that a company uses to reach potential customers.

_____ 51. Distribution of certificates that offer discounts on particular items.

_____ 52. Selling or supporting the sales process over the telephone.

_____ 53. Advertising technique in which two or more products are explicitly compared.

_____ 54. Free or bargain-priced items offered to encourage consumers to buy a product.

_____ 55. Gathering where producers display their wages to potential buyers; nearly every industry has one or more focused on particular types of products.

_____ 56. Average number of times that each audience member is exposed to the message (equal to the total number of exposures divided by the total audience population).

_____ 57. Salespeople who are responsible for generating new sales and for increasing sales to existing customers.

_____ 58. Sales-promotion efforts aimed at inducing distributors or retailers to push a producer's products.

WORD SCRAMBLE

1. _____   2. _____   _____   3. _____   _____
    stingidaver   lasse   romontopi   clipub   snaletior

LEARNING OBJECTIVES--POTENTIAL SHORT ANSWER OR ESSAY QUESTIONS

Learning Objective #1: "Identify the five basic categories of promotion." (447-449)

Learning Objective #2: "Distinguish between push and pull strategies of promotion." (450-451)

Learning Objective #3: **"List the seven steps in the personal-selling process."** (453-455)

Learning Objective #4: **"Differentiate between institutional, product, and competitive advertising."** (456-457)

Learning Objective #5: **"Define interactive advertising, and discuss the challenge it presents to marketers."** (457)

Learning Objective #6: **"Discuss the difference between logical and emotional advertising appeals."** (457-459)

Learning Objective #7: **"Distinguish between the two main types of sales promotion, and give at least two examples."** (463-466)

Learning Objective #8: **"Explain the role of public relations in marketing."** (466-467)

CRITICAL THINKING QUESTIONS

1. What are the advantages and disadvantages of using each of the following advertising medium?

    a. Newspapers

    b. Television

    c. Direct mail

    d. Radio

    e. Magazines

2. Suppose a firm has developed a new product. The company is so excited about its new product that it states, "this good will sell itself!" Does this mean that a promotional strategy is not important? Generally, what kind of marketing strategy would you recommend for this good?

BRAIN TEASER

1. Advertising agencies often argue that "advertising doesn't cost; it pays!" What do they mean? Is that possible? Generally, what is the recommended amount of advertising dollars which should be spent by a company in promoting its good or service?

ANSWERS

True-False--*Answers*

1. True
2. False: *Persuasive* advertising is intended to encourage product sampling and brand switching.
3. True
4. False: *Direct marketing* involves direct communication, other than personal sales contacts designed to effect a measurable response.
5. False: *Public relations* is the nonsales communication that businesses have with their various audiences.
6. True
7. False: Coupons, rebates, in-store demonstrations, free samples, trade shows, and point of purchase displays all fall into the category of *sales promotion.*
8. False: *Public relations* tries to encourage favorable reviews of products in newspapers and magazines and on radio and television.
9. True
10. False: In the *pull* strategy, the approach depends on stimulating enough consumer demand to *"pull"* a product through the distribution channel.
11. True
12. True
13. False: *Competitive* advertising is advertising that specifically highlights how a product is better than its competitors.
14. True
15. True
16. True
17. True
18. True
19. False: When media planners use the term *"reach,"* they are referring to the total number of audience members who will be exposed to a message at least once in a given period.
20. True
21. True

Multiple Choice--*Answers*

1. b	5. c	9. b	13. b
2. d	6. a	10. d	14. d
3. d	7. b	11. a	
4. d	8. d	12. c	

Jeopardy—*Answers*

	The Promotional Mix and Personal Selling	Adverting and Direct Marketing	Sales Promotion and Public Relations
$100	personal selling, advertising, direct marketing, sales promotion, and public relations	product advertising	consumer promotion and trade promotion
$200	personal selling	institutional advertising	trade promotions
$300	creative selling	direct mail	consumer promotions
$400	missionary, technical, and trade salespeople	direct mail, telemarketing, and infomercials	trade allowance
$500	prospecting, preparing, approaching the prospect, making the presentation, handling objections, closing, and following up	it cannot control when the message is received, and consumers must actively participate	to enhance a company's reputation with consumers and investors

Match the Terms and Concepts to Their Definitions--*Answers*

1. bb	9. oo	17. kk	25. n	33. nn	41. z	49. b	57. dd
2. ll	10. rr	18. j	26. e	34. r	42. aa	50. pp	58. a6
3. xx	11. v	19. zz	27. q	35. l	43. t	51. m	
4. vv	12. a2	20. c	28. tt	36. yy	44. x	52. a4	
5. u	13. ss	21. jj	29. p	37. al	45. a5	53. f	
6. w	14. uu	22. a7	30. ee	38. hh	46. ff	54. ii	
7. d	15. cc	23. gg	31. y	39. i	47. h	55. a8	
8. k	16. qq	24. o	32. a	40. g	48. a3	56. s	

Word Scramble--*Answers*

1. advertising   2. sales promotion   3. public relations

Learning Objectives--Potential Short Answer or Essay Questions--*Answers*

Learning Objective #1:

The five basic categories of promotion are personal selling, advertising, direct marketing, sales promotion, and public relations.

Learning Objective #2:

In the push strategy, the producer "pushes" an item to distributors, who in turn promote the product to end users. The pull approach depends on stimulating enough consumer demand to "pull" a product through the distribution channel. Consumer products are more likely to rely on pull strategies; organizational products are more often pushed.

Learning Objective #3:

The seven steps are prospecting (finding prospects and qualifying them), preparing, approaching the prospects, making the sales presentation, handling objections, closing, and following up after the sale has been made.

Learning Objective #4:

Institutional advertising promotes a company's overall image, not any particular products. Product advertising, however, emphasizes the products themselves. Competitive advertising emphasizes the differences between a product and its competitors.

Learning Objective #5:

Interactive advertising is a two-way exchange between a merchant and a potential customer. The biggest challenge it presents is that marketers cannot control when the message is received and that consumers must actively choose to participate.

Learning Objective #6:

You can view the difference between logical and emotional appeals as the difference between appealing to the head and appealing to the heart. Logical appeals try to convince the audience with facts, reasons, and rational conclusions. Emotional appeals, as the name implies, persuade through emotion--which can range from heart-warming tenderness to stark fear. It is important to remember, however, that nearly all ads contain a mixture of both logic and emotion; most just lean heavily in one direction or the other.

Learning Objective #7:

The two main types of sales promotion are consumer promotion and trade promotion. Consumer promotions are intended to motivate the final consumer to try new products or to experiment with the company's brands. Examples include coupons, cross-promotion, specialty advertising, premiums, point-of-purchase displays, and special events. Trade promotions are designed to induce wholesalers and retailers to stimulate sales of a producer's products. Examples include trade allowances, trade shows, display premiums, dealer contests, and travel bonus programs.

Learning Objective #8:

Because consumers and investors support companies with good reputations, smart companies use public relations to build and protect their reputations. They communicate with consumers, investors, industry analysts, and government officials through the media. They pursue and maintain press relations so that they can give effective press releases and hold effective press conferences.

Critical Thinking Questions--*Answers*

1. See Exhibit 15.3 on page 462 for a detailed list of the advantages and disadvantages for each.

2. If a good "sells itself," then this means it will likely be very popular with consumers. Therefore, sales are likely to pick up over a relatively short period of time as consumers become familiar with its existence. However, this does not mean that a promotional strategy is not important. Generally, the company would want to undertake a promotional strategy that would expose the product to as many customers as possible so that it can "sell itself."

Brain Teaser--*Answer*

1. Advertising, if properly undertaken, can increase sales revenues more than it increases a company's cost. Advertising can increase a firm's profits. A firm should continue to undertake advertising (through whatever medium) for as long as it generates more sales revenues than it costs the company.

Chapter 16
Computers and Information Technology

LEARNING OBJECTIVES
After studying this chapter, you should be able to:

1. Distinguish between data and information, and explain the characteristics of useful information. (477-478)
2. Identify the major ways companies use information systems. (478-482)
3. List seven common business computer applications. (482-485)
4. Describe the four classes of computers. (485-487)
5. Identify the major components of a computer system. (488-492)
6. Describe the primary components of computer networks. (493-498)
7. Explain the business uses of the internet. (498-499)
8. Discuss the drawbacks to business computing. (499-500)

TRUE-FALSE
Indicate whether the statement is generally true or false by placing a "T" or "F" in the space provided. If it is a false statement, correct it so that it becomes a true statement.

_____ 1. Data are recorded facts and statistics; information is created when data are arranged in such a manner as to be meaningful for a particular problem or situation.

_____ 2. In order to be useful, information needs to be accurate, timely, complete, relevant, and concise, and it must reach the right people at the right time.

_____ 3. The computer systems companies use to meet their needs generally fall into two major categories: operations information systems and management information systems.

_____ 4. A process control system is a computer system that manages the production of goods and services by controlling production lines, robots, and other machinery.

_____ 5. Management information systems include transaction processing systems, process and production control systems, and office automation systems.

_____ 6. The use of information systems by companies falls into five major categories: transaction processing; process and production control; office automation; design and engineering; and the managerial tasks of analysis, planning, and decision making as they relate to the company's various functional areas.

_____ 7. A management information system is a computerized system that provides managers with information and support for making effective decisions.

_____ 8. Seven common business computer applications are word processing, spreadsheets, desktop publishing, database management, business graphics, communications, and internet publishing.

_____ 9. Supercomputers are a class of computers with the basic size and shape of microcomputers but with the speed of traditional midsize computers; often used for design, engineering, and scientific applications.

_____ 10. Microcomputers, such as Apple Macintosh and the IBM PC, are the smallest and cheapest computers.

_____ 11. Hardware and software are the two major aspects of a computer.

_____ 12. Hardware is divided into operating systems, applications, and computer languages.

_____ 13. Multimedia refers to computer activity that involves sound, photographic images, animation, and video in addition to traditional computer data.

_____ 14. A network is a collection of computers, communication software, and transmission media (such as telephone lines) that allows computers to communicate.

_____ 15. Powerful software packages called groupware, such as Lotus Notes, enable users to collaborate on projects, schedule meetings, brainstorm, hold electronic conferences, and generally share information from dispersed locations as easily as if they were in the same room.

_____ 16. The internet is the world's largest computer network.

_____ 17. A modem would be considered to be software.

_____ 18. Bandwidth is the maximum capacity of a data transmission medium

_____ 19. For business, maintaining computer security (including guarding against hackers and viruses) poses an important problem.

MULTIPLE CHOICE
Circle the one best answer for each of the following questions.

1. Which of the following statements is true?
    a. A database is a collection of data that is usually stored in a computerized form.
    b. Data are just statistics that answer no particular question and solve no particular problem.
    c. Information is created when data are arranged in such a manner as to be meaningful for a particular problem or situation.
    d. All of the above are true.

2. Companies use information to
    a. increase organizational efficiency.
    b. stay ahead of competitors and to find new customers.
    c. plan, organize, lead, and control the organization.
    d. do all of the above.

3. Which of the following statements is *false*?
    a. Production control systems monitor conditions such as temperature or pressure change in physical processes.
    b. Operations information systems typically support daily operations and decision making for lower-level management and supervisors.
    c. Much of the daily flow of data into and out of a typical business organization is handled by a transaction processing system (TCP), which takes care of customer orders, billing, employee payroll, inventory changes, and other essential transactions.
    d. Effective information management is of such strategic importance in business today that many companies now have a top-level executive, sometimes called the chief information officer.

4. Computer systems that manage production by controlling production line, robots, and other machinery and equipment are a
    a. transactions processing system (TPS).
    b. process control system.
    c. production control system.
    d. office automation system.

5. Which of the following statements is true?
    a. Whereas a management information system (MIS) provides structured, routine information for managerial decision making, a decision support system (DSS) assists managers in solving highly unstructured and nonroutine problems with the use of decision models, specialized databases, and even artificial intelligence.
    b. Compared with an MIS, a DSS is more interactive (allowing the user to interact with the system instead of simply receiving information), and it usually relies on both internal and external information.
    c. An executive information system (EIS) is similar to a decision support system, but it is customized to the strategic needs of executives.
    d. All of the above are true.

6. The applications of business computing include
    a. word processing and spreadsheets.
    b. desktop publishing and database management.
    c. business graphics, communications, and internet publishing.
    d. all of the above.

7. Which of the following statements is *false*?
   a. Workstations are similar in size and shape to microcomputers but are a step up in price and performance.
   b. Mainframes are the fastest and most expensive computers available today.
   c. Supercomputers are often used for applications that rely on virtual reality.
   d. Microcomputers, often referred to as a personal computer or PC, are the smallest and cheapest computers.

8. Which of the following statements is *false*?
   a. Many mainframes are being replaced by client-server systems composed of groups of smaller computers.
   b. Minicomputers are scaled-down versions of mainframes.
   c. Like mainframes, microcomputers (or personal computers) are built using many microprocessors.
   d. Workstations are a class of computers with the basic size and shape of microcomputers but with the speed of traditional midsize computers; they are often used for design, engineering, and scientific applications.

9. Which of the following is *not* part of computer hardware?
   a. Operating systems
   b. Input and storage devices
   c. A central processing unit
   d. Output devices

10. Which of the following is one of the general categories of software?
    a. Operating systems
    b. Applications programs
    c. Computer languages
    d. All of the above.

11. Networks are composed of
    a. hardware such as modems, front-end processors, multiplexes, and routers.
    b. network transmission media such as telephone lines, coaxial cable, fiber optic cable, microwave stations, and satellites.
    c. network software such as groupware and Web browsers.
    d. all of the above.

12. Businesses use the internet to
    a. find new partners and to recruit employees.
    b. sell products and to order supplies.
    c. distribute information and to invest funds.
    d. do all of the above.

13. Which of the following statements is *false*?
    a. Computers enhance productivity in many ways, but they can also create new hassles and distractions for employees.
    b. For businesses, maintaining computer security (including guarding against hackers and viruses) poses an important problem.
    c. The internet is mistakenly viewed as a network.
    d. Until recently, the primary power of the internet has been in communicating and sharing information.

JEOPARDY

You have 5 seconds to complete the question to each of the following answers.

	Information and Computers in Today's Business Environment	Information Processing Technology	Networks; Drawbacks to Business Computing
$100	Collection of related data that can be cross-referenced in order to extract information. (477) What is_____ _____?	These computers represent the traditional notion of large and powerful computers. (486) What is_____ _____?	Collection of computers, communications software, and transmission media (such as telephone lines) that allows computers to communicate. (494) What is_____ _____?
$200	This is created when data is arranged in such a manner as to be meaningful. (477) What is_____ _____?	These computers are very often called personal computers or PCs. (486) What is_____ _____?	Computing arrangement in which teams can easily work together on projects. (497) What is_____ _____?
$300	Two major categories of information computer systems. (479) What is_____ _____?	Class of computers with the basic size and shape of microcomputers but with the speed of traditional midsize computers. (487) What is_____ _____?	Computer network that encompasses a small area, such as an office or a university campus. (494) What is_____ _____?
$400	Computer system that supplies information to assist in managerial decision making. (480) What is_____ _____?	This includes input devices, central processing units, and output devices. (488-489) What is_____ _____?	Software that enables users in different locations to share information, collaborate on projects, and perform other tasks together. (497) What is_____ _____?
$500	These types of information systems include transaction processing systems, process and production control systems that typically support daily operations. (479) What is_____ _____?	Advanced integrated circuit that combines most of the basic function of a computer onto a single chip. (488) What is_____ _____?	Two significant problems businesses face as a result of business computing. (499) What is_____ _____?

MATCH THE TERMS AND CONCEPTS TO THEIR DEFINITIONS

a. application software (491)
b. artificial intelligence (480)
c. bandwidth (496)
d. CD-ROMs (490)
e. central processing
    unit (CPU) (488)

t. expert system (481)
u. fiber optic cable (496)
v. fourth-generation
    languages (4GLs) (491)
w. graphical user
    interface (GUI) (491)

kk. office automation
    systems (OAS) (480)
ll. operating systems (490)
nn. parallel processing (489)
oo. primary storage device (489)
pp. process control system (479)

f. chief information officer (CIO) (478)
g. client/server system (496)
h. computer languages (491)
i. computer viruses (500)
j. data (476)
k. data communications (494)
l. data mining (480)
m. data warehousing (480)
n. database (476)
o. database management (483)
p. decision support system (DSS) (480)
q. desktop publishing (DTP) (483)
r. disk drive (489)
s. executive information system (EIS) (480)
x. groupware (497)
y. hardware (488)
z. hypertext markup language (HTML) (485)
aa. local area network (LAN) (494)
bb. mainframe computer (486)
cc. management information system (MIS) (480)
dd. microcomputer (486)
ee. microprocessor (488)
ff. minicomputers (486)
gg. modem (496)
hh. multimedia (490)
ii. multitasking (491)
jj. network (494)
qq. production control system (479)
rr. programming (491)
ss. random-access memory (RAM) (489)
tt. read-only memory (ROM)(489)
uu. secondary storage (489)
vv. software (488)
xx. speech-recognition system(481)
yy. spreadsheet (482)
zz. supercomputers (487)
a1. transaction processing system (TPS) (479)
a2. wide area network (WAN)(494)
a3. wireless transceivers (497)
a4. workgroup computing (497)
a5. workstation (487)

_____ 1. Ability of computers to reason, to learn, and to simulate human sensory perceptions.

_____ 2. An internet publishing format that incorporates sound, graphics, and video with document text; it can also hyperlink documents together, making it easy for users to jump from one document to another.

_____ 3. Storage devices that use the same technology as music CDs; popular because of their low cost and large storage capacity.

_____ 4. Program that organizes and manipulates data in a row-column matrix.

_____ 5. Recorded facts and statistics; they need to be converted to information before they can help people solve business problems.

_____ 6. Sets of programmable rules and conventions for communicating with computers.

_____ 7. Special circuits that store data and programs permanently but do not allow users to record their own data or programs; a common use of ROM is for the programs that activate start-up routines when the computer is turned on.

_____ 8. Computer programs that can work their way into a computer system and erase or corrupt data or programs.

_____ 9. Sifting through huge amounts of data to identify what is valuable to a specific question or problem.

_____ 10. A user-friendly program running in conjunction with the operating system that enables computer operators to enter commands by clicking on icons and menus with a mouse.

_____ 11. Small hardware attachments that enable a computer to transmit and receive data.

_____   12. Computer systems that assist with the tasks that people in a typical business office face regularly, such as drawing graphs or processing documents.

_____   13. Class of software that controls the computer's hardware components.

_____   14. Cable that transmits data as laser-generated pulses of light; capable of transmitting data at speeds of 2.5 billion bits per second without a modem.

_____   15. Collection of related data that can be cross-referenced in order to extract information.

_____   16. Programs that perform specific functions for users, such as word processing or spreadsheet analysis.

_____   17. Computer system that recognizes human speech, enabling users to enter data and give commands vocally.

_____   18. Computer activity that involves sound, photographic images, animation, and video in addition to traditional computer data.

_____   19. Collective name applied to a variety of software tools that ease the task of interacting with computers; some let users give instructions in natural languages such as English.

_____   20. Computer system that supplies information to assist in managerial decision making.

_____   21. Computers with the highest level of performance; often boasting speeds greater than a trillion calculations per second.

_____   22. Computer storage for data and programs that are not needed at the moment.

_____   23. Computerized information system that processes the daily flow of customer, supplier, and employee transactions, including inventory, sales, and payroll records.

_____   24. Computing arrangement in which teams can easily work together on projects.

_____   25. Storage for data and programs while they are being processed by the computer.

_____   26. Computer system that simulates the thought processes of a human expert who is adept at solving particular problems.

_____   27. Maximum capacity of a data transmission medium.

_____   28. Running several programs at once and switching back and forth between them.

_____   29. Computer system that uses special sensing devices to monitor conditions in a physical process and makes necessary adjustments to the process.

_____   30. Computer system design in which one computer (the server) contains software and data used by a number of attached computers (the clients); the clients also have their own processing capabilities, and they share certain tasks with the server, enabling the system to run at optimum efficiency.

_____ 31. Creating, storing, maintaining, rearranging, and retrieving the contents of databases.

_____ 32. Programmed instructions that drive the activity of computer hardware.

_____ 33. Physical components of a computer system, including integrated circuits, keyboards, and disk drives.

_____ 34. Most common mechanism for secondary storage which can be of four types: a hard disk drive, a floppy disk drive, a zip drive, or a CD-ROM drive.

_____ 35. Process of creating the sets of instructions that direct computers to perform desired tasks.

_____ 36. Computer systems that manage production by controlling production lines, robots, and other machinery and equipment.

_____ 37. Computer network that encompasses a large geographic area.

_____ 38. Software that enables users in different locations to share information, collaborate on projects, and perform other tasks together.

_____ 39. A large and powerful computer, capable of storing and processing vast amounts of data.

_____ 40. Class of computers with the basic size and shape of microcomputers but with the speed of traditional midsize computers; often used for design, engineering, and scientific applications.

_____ 41. Information system that uses decision models, specialized databases, and artificial intelligence to assist managers in solving highly unstructured and nonroutine problems.

_____ 42. Use of multiple processors in a single computer unit, with the intention of increasing the speed at which complex calculations can be completed.

_____ 43. Smaller, less powerful, and less expensive mainframes; often referred to as midsize computers.

_____ 44. Top corporate executive with responsibility for managing information and information systems.

_____ 45. Similar to a decision support system, but customized to the strategic needs of executives.

_____ 46. Ability to prepare documents using computerized typesetting and graphics-processing capabilities.

_____ 47. Smallest and least expensive class of computers; often generally referred to as a personal computer.

_____ 48. Computer network that encompasses a small area, such as an office or a university campus.

_____ 49. Building an organized central database out of files and databases gathered from different functional areas, such as marketing, operations, and accounting.

_____ 50. Hardware device that allows a computer to communicate over a regular telephone line.

_____ 51. Core of the computer, performing the three basic functions of arithmetic (addition, etc.), logic (comparing numbers), and control/communication (managing the computer).

_____ 52. Primary storage devices allowing a computer to access any piece of data in such memory at random.

_____ 53. Collection of computers, communications software, and transmission media (such as telephone lines) that allows computers to communicate.

_____ 54. Advanced integrated circuit that combines most of the basic functions of a computer onto a single chip.

_____ 55. Process of connecting computers and allowing them to send data back and forth.

WORD SCRAMBLE

1. _____   2. _____   3. _____
   wardhare   woupgrare   omteropcrmicu

LEARNING OBJECTIVES--POTENTIAL SHORT ANSWER OR ESSAY QUESTIONS

Learning Objective #1: **"Distinguish between data and information, and explain the characteristics of useful information."** (477-478)

Learning Objective #2: **"Identify the major ways companies use information systems."** (478-482)

Learning Objective #3: **"List seven common business computer applications."** (482-485)

Learning Objective #4: **"Describe the four classes of computers."** (485-487)

Learning Objective #5: **"Identify the major components of a computer system."** (488-492)

Learning Objective #6: **"Describe the primary components of computer networks."** (493-498)

Learning Objective #7: **"Explain the business uses of the internet."** (498-499)

Learning Objective #8: **"Discuss the drawbacks to business computing."** (499-500)

CRITICAL THINKING QUESTIONS

1. Which layer of management principally uses operations information systems? Management information systems?

2. What have been the four most commonly used applications of business computing?

BRAIN TEASER

1. Will there likely be a larger market for the sale of consumer or industrial products on the internet?

ANSWERS

True-False--*Answers*

1. True
2. True
3. True
4. False: A *production* control system is a computer system that manages the production of goods and services by controlling production lines, robots, and other machinery.
5. False: *Operations information* systems include transaction processing systems, process and production control systems, and office automation systems.
6. True
7. True
8. True

9. False: *Workstations are* a class of computers with the basic size and shape of microcomputers but with the speed of traditional midsize computers; often used for design, engineering, and scientific applications.

10. True

11. True

12. False: *Software* is divided into operating systems, applications, and computer languages.

13. True

14. True

15. True

16. True

17. False: A modem would be considered to be *hardware*.

18. True

19. True

Multiple Choice--*Answers*

1. d	5. d	9. a	13. c
2. d	6. d	10. d	
3. a	7. b	11. d	
4. c	8. c	12. d	

Jeopardy—*Answers*

	Information and Computers in Today's Business Environment	Information Processing Technology	Networks; Drawbacks to Business Computing
$100	a database	mainframes	a network
$200	information	microcomputer	workgroup computing
$300	operations information systems and management information systems	workstations	a local area network
$400	operations information systems	hardware	groupware
$500	management information systems	microprocessor	guarding against hackers and viruses

Match the Terms and Concepts to Their Definitions--*Answers*

1. b	8. i	15. n	22. uu	29. pp	36. qq	43. ff	50. gg
2. z	9. l	16. a	23. a1	30. g	37. a2	44. f	51. e
3. d	10. w	17. xx	24. a4	31. o	38. x	45. s	52. ss
4. yy	11. a3	18. hh	25. oo	32. vv	39. bb	46. q	53. jj
5. j	12. kk	19. v	26. t	33. y	40. a5	47. dd	54. ee
6. h	13. ll	20. cc	27. c	34. r	41. p	48. aa	55. k
7. tt	14. u	21. zz	28. ii	35. rr	42. nn	49. m	

Word Scramble---*Answers*

1. hardware   2. groupware   3. microcomputer

Learning Objectives--Potential Short Answer or Essay Questions--*Answers*

Learning Objective #1:

Data are recorded facts and statistics; information is created when data are arranged in such a manner as to be meaningful for a particular problem or situation. In order to be useful, information needs to be accurate, timely, complete, relevant, and concise, and it must reach the right people at the right time.

Learning Objective #2:

The chapter discusses five major categories: transaction processing; process and production control; office automation; design and engineering; and the managerial tasks of analysis, planning, and decision making as they relate to the company's various functional areas.

Learning Objective #3:

The seven common applications discussed in the chapter are word processing, spreadsheets, desktop publishing, database management, business graphics, communications, and internet publishing.

Learning Objective #4:

Mainframes represent the traditional notion of large and powerful computers. They are capable of processing and storing huge amounts of data. Smaller mainframes are called midsize computers, or minicomputers. Microcomputers, such as the Apple Macintosh and the IBM PC, are the smallest and cheapest computers. Workstations are a step up in price and performance; similar in size and shape to microcomputers, they approach or equal the performance of minicomputers. Supercomputers are the fastest and most expensive computers available today. They are often used for applications that rely on virtual reality.

Learning Objective #5:

Hardware and software are the two major aspects of a computer. Hardware includes input devices (such as keyboards), central processing units, output devices (such as printers), and primary and secondary storage. Software is divided into operating systems, application software, and computer languages.

Learning Objective #6:

Networks are composed of hardware (such as modems, front-end processors, multiplexers, and routers), network transmission media (such as telephone lines, coaxial cable, fiber optic cable, microwave stations, and satellites), and network software (such as groupware and Web browsers).

Learning Objective #7:

Businesses use the internet to find new partners, sell products, order supplies, invest funds, distribute information, and recruit employees. Until recently, the primary power of the internet has been in communicating and sharing information. However, internet commerce is expected to boom as new users go online and internet security improves.

Learning Objective #8:

Computers enhance productivity in many ways, but they can also create new hassles and distractions for employees. For businesses, maintaining computer security (including guarding against hackers and viruses) poses an important problem.

Critical Thinking Questions--*Answers*

1. Operations information systems, because they typically support daily operations and decision making are principally used by lower-level managers and supervisors. On the other hand, management information systems, because they assist in managerial decision making are typically used by upper-level management.

2. The four most commonly used applications of business computing are word processing, spreadsheets, database management, and communications.

Brain Teaser--*Answer*

1. There will likely be a larger market for the sale of consumer products on the internet because consumer products are typically less sophisticated. On the other hand, industrial products are typically more sophisticated, and, as such, personal selling is generally more effective.

Chapter 17

Accounting

LEARNING OBJECTIVES
After studying this chapter, you should be able to:

1. Describe the importance of accounting information to managers, investors, creditors, and government agencies. (510-512)
2. Identify two major reasons why the work of accountants is changing. (512)
3. State the basic accounting equation, and explain the purpose of double-entry bookkeeping. (516-517)
4. Differentiate between cash basis and accrual basis accounting. (517-518)
5. Explain the purpose of the balance sheet, and identify its three main sections. (518-523)
6. Explain the purpose of the income statement, and the statement of cash flows. (523-525)
7. Explain the purpose of ratio analysis and list the four main categories of financial ratios. (528-531)
8. Explain how companies use what-if analysis and budgeting to plan for the future. (532-534)

TRUE-FALSE
Indicate whether the statement is generally true or false by placing a "T" or "F" in the space provided. If it is a false statement, correct it so that it becomes a true statement.

_____ 1. Accounting is important to business for two reasons: it helps managers plan and control a company's operation; it helps outsiders evaluate a business.

_____ 2. Generally accepted accounting principles (GAAP) are professionally approved standards and practices used by the accountants in the preparation of financial statements.

_____ 3. Even though published financial statements must comply with GAAP, they do not always tell the whole story.

_____ 4. The two major reasons why the work of accountants is changing are the increasing demands by users for more information and the integration of technology into the accounting process.

_____ 5. Management accounting is the area of accounting concerned with preparing financial information for users outside the organization.

_____ 6. Private accountants are independent of the businesses, organizations, and individuals they serve.

_____ 7. Certified management accountants (CMAs) are professionally licensed accountants who meet certain requirements for education and experience and who pass a comprehensive examination.

_____ 8. Cost accounting is an area of accounting focusing on the calculation of manufacturing and storage costs of products for use or sale in a business.

_____ 9. Assets = Liabilities - Owner's Equity is the basic accounting equation.

_____ 10. Double-entry bookkeeping is a system of recording financial transactions to keep the accounting equation in balance.

_____ 11. Accrual basis accounting recognizes revenue at the time payment is received, whereas cash basis accounting recognizes revenue at the time of sale, even if payment is not received.

_____ 12. The income statement provides a snapshot of the business at a particular time, whereas the balance sheet reflects the results of operations over a period of time.

_____ 13. Retained earnings are that portion of shareholder's equity earned by the compnay but not distributed to its owners in the form of dividends.

_____ 14. The statement of cash flows indicates a firm's cash receipts and cash payments that presents information on its sources and uses of cash.

_____ 15. Trend analysis is a comparison of a firm's financial data from year to year to see how they have changed.

_____ 16. Financial ratios provide information for analyzing the health and future prospects of a business while allowing for comparisons between different size companies.

_____ 17. Most of the important financial ratios fall into one of four categories: profitability ratios, liquidity ratios, activity ratios, and debt ratios.

_____ 18. Companies use what-if analysis to analyze the cost and benefits of a particular decision.

_____ 19. Companies use budgets to control costs and to plan for future spending.

_____ 20. The internal auditor is the highest ranking accountant in a company.

MULTIPLE CHOICE
Circle the one best answer for each of the following questions.

1. Accounting information
    a. helps managers make business decisions and spot problems and opportunities.
    b. provides investors, suppliers, and creditors with the means to analyze a business
    c. supports the government's efforts to collect taxes and regulate business.
    d. does all of the above.

2. Which of the following statements is true?
    a. Bookkeeping is the record-keeping, clerical phase of accounting.
    b. The International Accounting Standards Committee (IASC), founded in 1973, has established itself as the recognized body for the development of International Accounting Standards (IAS) for use in the presentation of financial statements.
    c. In the United States, the Financial Accounting Standards Board (FASB) controls the rule making.
    d. All of the above are true.

3. The area of accounting concerned with preparing data for use by managers within the organization is
    a. financial accounting.
    b. managerial accounting.
    c. public accounting.
    d. tax accounting.

4. The process of evaluating a company's performance and analyzing the cost and benefits of a strategic action is
    a. cost accounting.
    b. an internal audit.
    c. financial analysis.
    d. cost analysis.

5. In the accounting equation,
    a. assets equal liabilities plus owner's equity.
    b. assets are a claim against a firm by a creditor.
    c. liabilities are anything of value owned or leased by a company.
    d. all of the above are true.

6. Which of the following is statements is true?
    a. Double-entry bookkeeping is a way of recording financial transactions that require two entries for every transaction so that the accounting equation is always kept in balance.
    b. Accrual basis accounting is a method in which revenue is recorded when a sale is made and expense is recorded when incurred.
    c. Cash basis accounting is a method in which revenue is recorded when payment is received and expense is recorded when cash is paid.
    d. All of the above are true.

7. Which of the following statements is *false*?
    a. Depreciation is an accounting procedure for systematically spreading the cost of a tangible asset over its estimated useful life.
    b. Owner's equity is anything of value owned or leased by a company.
    c. An audit is a formal evaluation of the fairness and reliability of a client's financial statements.

    d. Debtors are people or organizations who have to repay money they have borrowed.

8. A statement of a firm's financial position on a particular date, also known as a statement of financial position is
    a. a balance sheet.
    b. an income statement.
    c. a statement of cash flows.
    d. a cost of goods sold statement.

9. The balance sheet
    a. "balances" because it includes all elements in the accounting equation and shows the balance between assets on one side of the equation, and liabilities and owner's equity on the other side.
    b. shows how profitable the organization has been over a specific period of time, typically one year.
    c. unfortunately does not enable the reader to determine the size of the company nor what the major assets, liabilities or owner's equity is.
    d. does all of the above.

10. Which of the following statements is *false*?
    a. Dividends are distributions of corporate assets to shareholders in the form of cash or other assets.
    b. Net income is the profit or loss earned by a firm, determined by subtracting expenses from revenues; also known as the bottom line.
    c. Expenses are the amount of sales of goods or services and inflow from miscellaneous sources such as interest, rent, and royalties.
    d. Gross profit is the amount remaining when the cost of goods sold is deducted from net sales; also known as gross margin.

11. Ratios that measure the overall financial performance of a firm are called
    a. liquidity ratios.
    b. profitability ratios.
    c. activity ratios.
    d. debt ratios.

12. Ratios that measure a firm's ability to meet its short-term obligations when they are due are
    a. liquidity ratios.
    b. profitability ratios.
    c. activity ratios.
    d. debt ratios.

13. Ratios that measure a firm's reliance on debt financing of its operation are
    a. liquidity ratios.
    b. profitability ratios.
    c. activity ratios.
    d. debt ratios.

14. Which of the following statements is *false*?
    a. Companies use what-if analysis to analyze the costs and benefits of a particular decision.
    b. Companies use budgets to control costs and to plan for future spending.
    c. The three segments of an income statement are assets, liabilities, and owner's equity.
    d. The statement of cash flows shows how cash was received and spent in three areas: operations, investments, and financing.

JEOPARDY

You have 5 seconds to complete the question to each of the following answers.

	Types of Accountants; Accounting Concepts	Financial Statements	Financial Analysis
$100	In-house accountants employed by organizations and businesses other than a public accounting firm; also called corporate accountants. (515) What is _____ _____?	This provides a snapshot of the business at a particular point in time. (518) What is _____ _____?	Use of quantitative measures to evaluate a firm's financial performance. (528) What is _____ _____?
$200	Assets = Liabilities + Owner's Equity. (517) What is _____ _____?	Its three main sections are assets, liabilities, and owner's equity. (519) What is _____ _____?	Ratios that measure the overall financial performance of a firm. (529) What is _____ _____?
$300	This equals assets minus liabilities. (516-517) What is _____ _____?	This shows how profitable the organization has been over a specific period of time. (523) What is _____ _____?	Ratios that measure a firm's ability to meet its short-term obligations when they are due. (529) What is _____ _____?
$400	Area of accounting concerned with preparing data for use by managers within the organization. (513) What is _____ _____?	This shows how a company's cash was received and spent in three areas: operations, investments, and financing. (524-525) What is _____ _____?	Ratios that measure the effectiveness of the firm's use of its resources. (531) What is _____ _____?
$500	Accounting method in which revenue is recorded when a sale is made and expense is recorded when incurred.. (2) What is _____ _____?	Obligations that fall due more than one year from the date of the balance sheet. (522) What is _____ _____?	Ratios that measure a firm's reliance on debt financing of its operations (sometimes called coverage ratios). (531) What is _____ _____?

MATCH THE TERMS AND CONCEPTS TO THEIR DEFINITIONS

a. accounting (510)
b. accounting equation (517)
c. accounts receivable turnover ratio (531)
d. accrual basis (517)
e. activity ratios (531)
f. assets (516)
g. audit (513)
h   balance sheet (518)
i. bookkeeping (510)

v. current ratio (529)
w. debt ratios (531)
x. debt-to-equity ratio (531)
y. debt-to-total-assets ratio (531)
z. debtors (513)
aa. depreciation   (518)
bb. dividends (523)
cc. double-entry bookkeeping (517)

rr. liquidity ratios (529)
ss. long-term liabilities (522)
tt. management accounting (513)
uu. matching principle (517)
vv. net income (523)
xx. operating expenses (523)
yy. owners' equity (516)
zz. private accountants (515)
a1. profitability ratios (529)

j. budget (532)
k. calendar year (520)
l. cash basis (518)
m. certified management accountants (CMAs) (515)
n. certified public accountants (CPAs) (512)
o. closing the books (517)
p. controller (515)
q. cost accounting (515)
r. cost of goods sold (523)
s. creditors (513)
t. current assets (522)
u. current liabilities (522)

dd. earnings per share (529)
ee. expenses (523)
ff. financial accounting (513)
gg. financial analysis (515)
hh. fiscal year (521)
ii. fixed assets (522)
jj. general expenses (523)
kk. generally accepted accounting principles (GAAP) (511)
ll. gross profit (523)
nn. income statement (523)
oo. internal auditors (515)
pp. inventory turnover ratio (531)
qq. liabilities (516)

a2. public accountants (513)
a3. quick ratio (529)
a4. ratio analysis (528)
a5. retained earnings (523)
a6. return on investment (ROI) (529)
a7. return on sales (529)
a8. revenues (523)
a9. selling expenses (523)
b1. statement of cash flows (524)
b2. tax accounting (515)
b3. trend analysis (527)
b4. working capital (529)

_____ 1. Obligations that fall due more than a year from the date of the balance sheet.

_____ 2. Planning and control tool that reflects expected revenues, operating expenses, and cash receipts and outlays.

_____ 3. Distributions of corporate assets to shareholders in the form of cash or other assets.

_____ 4. Area of accounting focusing on the calculation of manufacturing and storage costs of products for use or sale in a business.

_____ 5. Twelve-month accounting period that begins on January 1 and ends on December 31.

_____ 6. All costs of operation that are not included under cost of goods sold.

_____ 7. Accounting method in which revenue is recorded when payment is received and expense is recorded when cash is paid.

_____ 8. Operating expenses, such as office and administrative expenses, not directly associated with creating or marketing a good or service.

_____ 9. Measure of a firm's short-term liquidity, calculated by adding cash, marketable securities, and receivables, and then dividing that sum by current liabilities; also known as the acid-test ratio.

_____ 10. People or organizations who have to repay money they have borrowed.

_____ 11. The portion of shareholders' equity earned by the company but not distributed to its owners in the form of dividends.

_____ 12. Accountants who have fulfilled the requirements for certification as specialists in management accounting.

_____ 13. Measure of a firm's profitability for each share of outstanding stock, calculated by dividing net income after taxes by shares of common stock outstanding.

_____   14. Area of accounting focusing on tax preparation and tax planning.

_____   15. Any 12 consecutive months used as an accounting period.

_____   16. Measuring, interpreting, and communicating financial information to support internal and external decision making.

_____   17. Accounting procedure for systematically spreading the cost of a tangible asset over its estimated useful life.

_____   18. Obligations that must be met within a year.

_____   19. Accounting method in which revenue is recorded when a sale is made and expense is recorded when incurred.

_____   20. Financial record of a company's revenues, expenses, and profits over a given period of time.

_____   21. Process of evaluating a company's performance and analyzing the costs and benefits of a strategic action.

_____   22. Statement of a firm's financial position on a particular date; also known as a statement of financial position.

_____   23. In-house accountants employed by organizations and businesses other than a public accounting firm; also called corporate accountants.

_____   24. Professionals who provide accounting services to other businesses and individuals for a fee.

_____   25. Record keeping, clerical phase of accounting.

_____   26. Cash and other items that can be turned back into cash within one year.

_____   27. Highest-ranking accountant in a company, responsible for overseeing all accounting functions.

_____   28. All the operating expenses associated with marketing goods or services.

_____   29. People or organizations that have loaned money or extended credit.

_____   30. Amount remaining when the cost of goods sold is deducted from net sales; also known as gross margin.

_____   31. Ratios that measure a firm's ability to meet its short-term obligations when they are due.

_____   32. Portion of a company's assets that belongs to the owners after obligations to all creditors have been met.

_____   33. Assets retained for long-term use, such as land, buildings, machinery, and equipment; also referred to as property, plant, and equipment.

_____   34. Current assets minus current liabilities.

_____ 35. Statement of a firm's cash receipts and cash payments that presents information on its sources and uses of cash.

_____ 36. Formal evaluation of the fairness and reliability of a client's financial statements.

_____ 37. Ratio between the net income earned by a company and total owner's equity; also known as return on equity.

_____ 38. Anything of value owned or leased by a business.

_____ 39. Measure of a firm's short-term liquidity, calculated by dividing current assets by current liabilities.

_____ 40. Comparison of a firm's financial data from year to year to see how they have changed.

_____ 41. Employees who analyze and evaluate the operation of company departments to determine their efficiency.

_____ 42. Cost of producing or acquiring a company's products for sale during a given period.

_____ 43. Ratios that measure the effectiveness of the firm's use of its resources.

_____ 44. Measure of the extent to which a business is financed by debt as opposed to invested capital, calculated by dividing the company's total liabilities by owner's equity.

_____ 45. Profit or loss earned by a firm, determined by subtracting expenses from revenues; also called the bottom line.

_____ 46. Fundamental principle requiring that expenses incurred in producing revenue be deducted from the revenues they generate during an accounting period.

_____ 47. Basic accounting equation that assets equals liabilities plus owner's equity.

_____ 48. Ratio between net income and net sales; also known as profit margin.

_____ 49. Area of accounting concerned with preparing data for use by managers within the organization.

_____ 50. Measure of a firm's ability to carry long-term debt. Calculated by dividing total liabilities by total assets.

_____ 51. Transferring the net revenue and expense account balances to retained earnings for the period.

_____ 52. Claim against a firm's assets by a creditor.

_____ 53. Measure of the time a company takes to turn its accounts receivables into cash, calculated by dividing sales by the average value of accounts receivable for a period.

_____ 54. Ratios that measure the overall financial performance of a firm.

_____ 55. Professionally licensed accountants who meet certain requirements for education and experience and who pass a comprehensive examination.

_____ 56. Costs created in the process of generating revenues.

_____ 57. Measure of the time a company takes to turn its inventory into sales, calculated by dividing cost of goods sold by the average value of inventory for a period.

_____ 58. Area of accounting concerned with preparing financial information for users outside the organization.

_____ 59. Ratios that measure a firm's reliance on debt financing of its operations (sometimes called coverage ratios).

_____ 60. Way of recording financial transactions that requires two entries for every transaction so that the accounting equation is always kept in balance.

_____ 61. Use of quantitative measures to evaluate a firm's financial performance.

_____ 62. Professionally approved standards and practices used by the accountants in the preparation of financial statements.

_____ 63. Amount of sales of goods or services and inflow from miscellaneous sources such as interest, rent, and royalties.

WORD SCRAMBLE

1. _____ _____   2. _____   3. _____
    tario   sasnaily   tessa   gincactoun

LEARNING OBJECTIVES--POTENTIAL SHORT ANSWER OR ESSAY QUESTIONS

Learning Objective #1: **"Describe the importance of accounting information to managers, investors, creditors, and government agencies."** (510-512)

Learning Objective #2: **"Identify two major reasons why the work of accountants is changing."** (512)

Learning Objective #3: "State the basic accounting equation, and explain the purpose of double-entry bookkeeping." (516-517)

Learning Objective #4: "Differentiate between cash basis and accrual basis accounting." (517-518)

Learning Objective #5: "Explain the purpose of the balance sheet, and identify its three main sections." (518-523)

Learning Objective #6: "Explain the purpose of the income statement and the statement of cash flows." (523-525)

Learning Objective #7: **"Explain the purpose of ratio analysis, and list the four main categories of financial ratios."** (528-531)

Learning Objective #8: **"Explain how companies use what-if analysis and budgeting to plan for the future."** (532-534)

CRITICAL THINKING QUESTIONS

1. Use the accounts below to answer the following questions.

Net sales	Accounts receivable	Advertising expense
Common stock	Equipment	Marketable securities
Salaries	Retained earnings	Long-term notes payable
Cash	Inventory	Rent

    a. Which of these would be considered a current asset? Why?

    b. Which of these would be considered a fixed asset? Why?

    c. Which of these would be considered a current liability? Why?

    d. Which of these would be considered a long-term liability ? Why?

    e. Which of these would be considered owner's equity?

f. Which of these would be considered a revenue?

g. Which of these would be considered an expense?

2. Indicate the ratio that would provide information on:

a. A firm's ability to meet short-term obligations.

b. A firm's ability to pay current debts.

c. A firm's ability to pay current debts on short notice.

d. A firm's overall financial performance.

e. The amount of profits earned for each share of common stock outstanding.

f. Net income compared to sales.

g. Owner's equity.

h. A firm's use of its resources.

i. The number of times merchandise moves through the business.

j. The extent to which the firm relies on financing.

k. The percentage of owner's investments to debt financing.

BRAIN TEASER

1. At the end of the year, Jan Nord, Inc. showed the following balances on accounts. Prepare a balance sheet for Jan Nord, Inc.

Land.............................	$70,000
Buildings.........................	320,000
Inventory.........................	110,000
Cash..............................	20,000
Accounts payable................	120,000
Marketable securities............	42,000
Retained earnings................	392,000
Common shares....................	80,000
(40,000 share @ $2)	
Notes payable....................	120,000
Equipment........................	60,000

ANSWERS

True-False--*Answers*

1. True
2. True
3. True
4. True
5. False: *Financial* accounting is the area of accounting concerned with preparing financial information for users outside the organization.
6. False: *Public* accountants are independent of the businesses, organizations, and individuals they serve.
7. False: Certified *public* accountants (*CPAs*) are professionally licensed accountants who meet certain requirements for education and experience and who pass a comprehensive examination.
8. True
9. False: Assets = Liabilities *plus* Owner's Equity is the basic accounting equation.
10. True
11. False: *Cash* basis accounting recognizes revenue at the time payment is received, whereas *accrual* basis accounting recognizes revenue at the time of sale, even if payment is not received.
12. False: The *balance sheet* provides a snapshot of the business at a particular time, whereas the *income statement* reflects the results of operations over a period of time.
13. True
14. True
15. True
16. True
17. True
18. True
19. True
20. False: The *controller* is the highest ranking accountant in a company.

Multiple Choice--*Answers*

1. d	5. a	9. a	13. d
2. d	6. d	10. c	14. c
3. b	7. b	11. b	
4. c	8. a	12. a	

Jeopardy---*Answers*

	Types of Accountants; Accounting Concepts	Financial Statements	Financial Analysis
$100	private accountants	a balance sheet	ratio analysis
$200	the accounting equation	a balance sheet	profitability ratios
$300	owner's equity	an income statement	liquidity ratios
$400	managerial accounting	a statement of cash flows	activity ratios
$500	accrual basis accounting	long-term liabilities	debt ratios

Match the Terms and Concepts to Their Definitions--*Answers*

1. ss	9. a3	17. aa	25 i	33. ii	41. oo	49. tt	57. pp
2. j	10. z	18. u	26. t	34. b4	42. r	50. y	58. ff
3. bb	11. a5	19. d	27. p	35. b1	43. e	51. o	59. w
4. q	12. m	20. nn	28. a9	36. g	44. x	52. qq	60. cc
5. k	13. dd	21. gg	29. s	37. a6	45. vv	53. c	61. a4
6. xx	14. b2	22. h	30. ll	38. f	46. uu	54. a1	62. kk
7. l	15. hh	23. zz	31. rr	39. v	47. b	55. n	63. a8
8. jj	16. a	24. a2	32. yy	40. b3	48. a7	56. ee	

Word Scramble--*Answers*

1. ratio analysis   2. asset   3. accounting

Learning Objectives--Potential Short Answer or Essay Questions--*Answers*

Learning Objective #1:
   Accounting information helps managers make business decisions and spot problems and opportunities; provides investors, suppliers, and creditors with the means to analyze a business; and supports the government's efforts to collect taxes and regulate business.

Learning Objective #2:
   The two principal reasons why the work of accountants is changing are the increasing demands by users for more information and the integration of technology into the accounting process.

Learning Objective #3:
   Assets = Liabilities + Owners' Equity is the basic accounting equation. Double-entry bookkeeping is a system of recording financial transactions to keep the accounting equation in balance.

Learning Objective #4:

Cash basis accounting recognizes revenue at the time payment is received, whereas accrual basis accounting recognizes revenue at the time of sale, even if payment is not made.

Learning Objective #5:

The balance sheet provides a snapshot of the business at a particular point in time. Its main sections are assets, liabilities, and owner's equity.

Learning Objective #6:

The income statement reflects the results of operations over a period of time. The statement of cash flows shows how a company's cash was received and spent in three areas; operations, investments, and financing.

Learning Objective #7:

Financial ratios provide information for analyzing the health and future prospects of a business while allowing for comparisons between different size companies. Most of the important ratios fall into one of four categories: profitability ratios, liquidity ratios, activity ratios, and debt ratios.

Learning Objective #8:

Companies use what-if analysis to analyze the costs and benefits of a particular decision. Companies use budgets to control costs and to plan for future spending.

Critical Thinking Questions--*Answers*

1. a. Cash, accounts receivable, inventory, and marketable securities would all be considered current assets. See page 522 of the textbook for a definition and a discussion.
    b. Equipment is the only fixed asset on this list. See page 522 of the textbook for a definition and a discussion.
    c. Salaries, advertising expenses and rent accrued are the current liabilities. See page 522 of the textbook for a definition and a discussion.
    d. Long-term notes payable are the only long-term liability on this list. See page 522 of the textbook for a definition and a discussion.
    e. Common stock and retained earnings are the owner's equity.
    f. Net sales and interest from marketable securities (and retained earnings if it is earning interest) constitutes the revenue.
    g. The expenses include: salaries, advertising expenses, interest on long-term notes payable, and rent (as well as depreciation on the equipment).

2. a. The liquidity ratios (the current and quick ratios).
    b. The current ratio (one of the liquidity ratios).
    c. The quick ratio (one of the liquidity ratios).
    d. The profitability ratios (earnings per share, return to sales, and return on equity).
    e. The earnings per share ratio (one of the profitability ratios).
    f. The return on sales ratio (one of the profitability ratios).
    g. The return on equity ratio (one of the profitability ratios).
    h. The activity ratio (for example, the inventory turnover ratio).
    i. The inventory ratio (one of the activity ratios).
    j. The debt ratios (for example, the debt-to-equity ratio).
    k. The debt-to-equity ratio (one of the debt ratios).

Brain Teaser--*Answer*

1.

Jan Nord, Inc.
<u>Balance Sheet</u>

<u>ASSETS</u>

Current Assets		
Cash	$110,000	
Marketable Securities	42,000	
Inventory	<u>110,000</u>	
Total Current Assets		*$262,000*
Fixed Assets		
Land	$70,000	
Buildings	320,000	
Equipment	<u>60,000</u>	
Total Fixed Assets		*<u>$450,000</u>*
Total Assets		**$712,000**

LIABILITIES AND OWNER'S EQUITY

Current Liabilities		
Accounts Payable	$120,000	
Total Current Liabilities		*$120,000*
Long-Term Liabilities		
Notes Payable	$120,000	
Total Long-Term Liabilities		*<u>$120,000</u>*
Total Liabilities		**$240,000**
Owner's Equity		
Common Shares	$80,000	
(40,000 shares @ $2)		
Retained Earnings	<u>$392,000</u>	
Total Owner's Equity		*<u>$472,000</u>*
Total Liabilities and Owner's Equity		**$712,000**

Chapter 18

Banking and Financial Management

LEARNING OBJECTIVES

After studying this chapter, you should be able to:

1. Identify the responsibilities of a financial manager. (542)
2. Name the five main steps involved in the financial planning process. (542-543)
3. Cite three things financial managers must consider when selecting an appropriate funding vehicle. (545-549)
4. List the three major types of short-term debt and the three major types of long-term debt. (549-551)
5. Identify the main advantages and disadvantages of public equity financing. (552-553)
6. Name the three functions and four characteristics of money. (553-554)
7. Cite the four ways the Federal Reserve System influences the money supply. (558-559)
8. Explain how the internet is influencing the U.S. banking and monetary systems. (566)

TRUE-FALSE

Indicate whether the statement is generally true or false by placing a "T" or "F" in the space provided. If it is a false statement, correct it so that it becomes a true statement.

_____ 1. Financial management is the effective acquisition and use of money.

_____ 2. A financial plan is a forecast of financial requirements and the financing sources to be used.

_____ 3. Financial control is the process for evaluating proposed investments in select projects that provide the best long-term financial return.

_____ 4. The prime interest is the lowest rate of interest charged by banks for short-term loans to their most credit-worthy customers.

_____ 5. The discount rate is the interest rate the Fed charges banks whenever banks borrow from the Federal Reserve.

_____ 6. The three major types of short-term debt are loans, leases, and bonds.

_____ 7. The three major types of long-term debt are trade credit, loans, and commercial paper.

_____ 8. Leverage is a technique of increasing the rate of return on an investment by financing it with borrowed funds.

_____   9. Marketable securities are stocks, bonds, and other investments that can be turned into cash quickly.

_____   10. Capital structure is the financing mix of a firm.

_____   11. A company cannot get into trouble by taking on too much debt.

_____   12. Stocks are certificates of indebtedness that are sold to raise long-term funds for a corporation.

_____   13. A leveraged buyout (LBO) is a situation in which individuals or groups of investors purchase companies primarily with debt secured by the company's assets.

_____   14. Venture capitalists are investment specialists who provide money to finance new businesses or turnarounds in exchange for a portion of the ownership, with the objective of making a considerable profit on the investment; also called VCs.

_____   15. Selling your stock to the public does not have many disadvantages.

_____   16. Money is anything generally acceptable as a medium of exchange.

_____   17. Debit cards are plastic cards that allow the customer to buy now and pay back the loaned amount at a future date.

_____   18. The euro is a planned unified currency to be used by European nations who meet certain requirements.

_____   19. The Federal Reserve, created in 1913 and commonly referred to as the Fed, is America's central bank which is charged with the responsibility of controlling the nation's money supply.

_____   20. The Fed determines the reserve requirement which impacts how much banks can loan out.

_____   21. If the Fed buys U.S. government bonds, this will decrease the money supply.

_____   22. The internet is a new channel of distribution that allows customers to shop for banking services anywhere in the world.

MULTIPLE CHOICE

Circle the one best answer for each of the following questions.

1. The responsibilities of a finance manger include
    a.   forecasting and planning for the future, and developing a financial plan.
    b.   managing the company's cash flow and coordinating and controlling the efficiency of operations.
    c.   deciding on specific investments and how to finance them, and raising capital to support growth, as well as interacting with banks and capital markets.
    d.   all of the above.

2. When developing a financial plan, the financial manager:
    a.   estimates the flow of money into and out of the business, and determines whether cash flow is negative or positive and how to use or create excess funds.
    b.   chooses which capital investments should be made.
    c.   selects the best way to finance investments, and compares actual results to projections to discover variances and takes corrective action.
    d.   does all of the above.

3. Finance managers must
    a.   determine whether the financing is for the short term or the long term.
    b.   analyze the advantages and disadvantages of internal versus external financing.
    c.   evaluate the merits of debt versus equity financing in light of their own needs.
    d.   do all of the above.

4. Which of the following statements is true?
    a.   Cash flow management is the task of ensuring that all bills are paid and there is enough money left over to improve the business.
    b.   Corporations can obtain funds to finance the purchase of new plant and equipment through retained earnings (undistributed profits), by borrowing or by selling more shares of stock.
    c.   The cost of capital depends on the risk associated with the company, the prevailing interest rates, and management's selection of funding vehicles.
    d.   All of the above are true.

5. Which of the following statements is true?
    a.   One of the first things a company must decide is whether the company's financing needs are for the short term or the long term.
    b.   Internal financing can result in leveraging the company.
    c.   Most funds are raised by companies selling more shares of stock.
    d.   All of the above are true.

6. Which of the following is a disadvantage of public equity financing?
    a.   It improves the liquidity of the company.
    b.   It increases financing.
    c.   It increases filing requirements.
    d.   It establishes a market value for the company.

7. Which of the following is an advantage of public equity financing?
    a.   There is a loss of ownership control.
    b.   There are voluntary dividend payments.
    c.   It is expensive.
    d.   There is increased public visibility.

8. An IOU, backed by the corporation's reputation, issued to raise short-term capital is
   a. commercial paper.
   b. trade credit.
   c. a secured loan.
   d. collateral.

9. Which of the following statements is true?
   a. Long-term debt is borrowed funds used to cover current expenses (generally repaid within one year).
   b. A bond is a document that proves stock ownership.
   c. Trade credit is obtained by the purchases directly from the supplier.
   d. All of the above are true.

10. Money functions as
    a. a medium of exchange.
    b. a measure of value.
    c. a store of value.
    d. all of the above.

11. Money must be
    a. divisible.
    b. portable.
    c. durable and secure.
    d. all of the above.

12. The Fed can change the money supply by
    a. setting selective credit controls.
    b. changing the discount rate or by changing reserve requirements.
    c. carrying out open market operations.
    d. doing all of the above.

13. To increase the money supply, the Fed should
    a. increase the discount rate.
    b. increase reserve requirements.
    c. buy U.S. government bonds.
    d. do any of the above.

14. Which of the following statements is true?
    b. Demand deposits are money in a checking account that can be used by the customer at any time.
    a. M1 is that portion of the money supply consisting of currency, demand deposits, and small time deposits.
    c. Time deposits are bills and coins that make up the cash money of a society.
    d. Open market operations refers to the Fed setting the interest rate on loans banks receive from the Fed.

15. The internet is a new channel of distribution that
    a. allows customers to shop for banking services anywhere in the world.
    b. has made the banking environment highly competitive.
    c. has redefined the types off services banks offer.
    d. has done all of the above.

JEOPARDY

You have 5 seconds to complete the question to each of the following answers.

	Financial Management	**Money**	**The Federal Reserve**
$100	Effective acquisition and use of money. (542) What is_____ _____?	The three functions of money. (553-554) What is_____ _____?	The major function of the Fed. (555) What is_____ _____?
$200	A forecast of financial requirements and the financing sources to be used. (542) What is_____ _____?	The four things money must do to be an effective medium of exchange. (554) What is_____ _____?	The percentage of a bank's deposit that must be set aside. (558) What is_____ _____?
$300	The three major types of short-term debt. (549) What is_____ _____?	Money in a checking account that can be used by the customer at any time. (556) What is_____ _____?	Activity of the Fed in buying and selling government bonds on the open market. (559) What is_____ _____?
$400	The three major types of long-term debt. (550-552) What is_____ _____?	Bank accounts that pay interest and require advance notice before money can be withdrawn. (556) What is_____ _____?	Federal Reserve' power to set credit terms on various types of loans. (559) What is_____ _____?
$500	This type of financing involves selling ownership rights in the company. (551) What is_____ _____?	That portion of the money supply consisting of currency and demand deposits. (557) What is_____ _____?	What the Fed should do to increase the money supply. (558-559) What is_____ _____?

MATCH THE TERMS AND CONCEPTS TO THEIR DEFINITIONS

a. automated teller machines (ATMs) (563)
b. bonds (551)
c. capital budgeting (543)
d. capital investments (543)
e. capital structure (548)
f. checks (556)
g. collateral (549)
h. commercial paper (549)
i. compensating balance (549)
j. cost of capital (544)
k. credit cards (554)
l. currency (556)
m. debit cards (554)
n. demand deposit (556)
o. discount rate (545)

p. electronic funds transfer system (EFTS) (563)
q. euro (555)
r. Eurodollars (558)
s. financial control (543)
t. financial management (542)
u. financial plan (542)
v. lease (550)
w. leverage (547)
x. leveraged buyout (LBO) (551)
y. line of credit (549)
z. long-term debt (545)
aa. M1 (557)
bb. M2 (557)
cc. M3 (558)
dd. marketable securities (547)

ee. money (553)
ff. open-market operations (559)
gg. prime interest rate (prime) (544)
hh. reserve requirement (558)
ii. secured loans (549)
jj. selective credit controls (559)
kk. short-term debt (545)
ll. smart cards (554)
nn. stock certificate (548)
oo. time deposits (556)
pp. trade credit (549)
qq. unsecured loan (549)
rr. venture capitalists (552)

_____ 1. Plastic cards that allow the customer to buy now and pay back the loaned amount at a future date.

_____ 2. Average rate of interest a firm pays on its combination of debt and equity.

_____ 3. Tangible asset a lender can claim if a borrower defaults on a loan.

_____ 4. Stocks, bonds, and other investments that can be turned into cash quickly.

_____ 5. Bills and coins that make up the cash money of a society.

_____ 6. Certificates of indebtedness that are sold to raise long-term funds for a corporation or government agency.

_____ 7. Loan requiring no collateral but a good credit rating.

_____ 8. Electronic terminals that permit people with plastic cards to perform simple banking transactions 24 hours a day without the aid of a human teller.

_____ 9. Plastic cards that allow the bank to take money from the user's demand-deposit account and transfer it to a retailer's account.

_____ 10. A planned unified currency to be used by European nations who meet certain strict requirements.

_____ 11. Effective acquisition and use of money.

_____ 12. That portion of the money supply consisting of M1 and M2 plus large time deposits and other restrictive deposits.

_____ 13. Technique of increasing the rate of return on an investment by financing it with borrowed funds.

_____ 14. Loans backed up with something of value that the lender can claim in case of default, such as a piece of property.

_____ 15. Portion of an unsecured loan that is kept on deposit at the lending institution to protect the lender and increase the lender's return.

_____ 16. Lowest rate of interest charged by banks for short-term loans to their most credit-worthy customers.

_____ 17. Legal agreement that obligates the user of an asset to make payments to the owner of the asset in exchange for using it.

_____ 18. Written orders that tell the customer's bank to pay a specific amount to a particular individual or business.

_____ 19. An IOU, backed by the corporation's reputation, issued to raise short-term capital.

_____ 20. Plastic cards that include an embedded chip to store money drawn from the user's demand-deposit account and information that can be used for purchases.

_____ 21. A forecast of financial requirements and the financing sources to be used.

_____ 22. Anything generally accepted as a means of paying for goods and services.

_____ 23. Credit obtained by the purchaser directly from the supplier.

_____ 24. Investment specialists who provide money to finance new businesses or turnarounds in exchange for a portion of the ownership, with the objective of making a considerable profit on the investment; also called VCs.

_____ 25. Financing mix of a firm.

_____ 26. Arrangement in which the financial institution makes money available for use at any time after the loan has been approved.

_____ 27. Interest rate charged by the Federal Reserve on loans to commercial banks and other financial institutions.

_____ 28. That portion of the money supply consisting of currency, demand deposits, and small time deposits.

_____ 29. Computerized systems for performing financial transactions.

_____ 30. The process of analyzing and adjusting the basic financial plan to correct for forecasted events that do not materialize.

_____ 31. Situation in which individuals or groups of investors purchase companies primarily with debt secured by the company's assets.

_____ 32. Document that proves stock ownership.

_____ 33. Activity of the Federal Reserve in buying and selling government bonds on the open market.

_____ 34. Borrowed funds used to cover current expenses (generally repaid within a year).

_____ 35. That portion of the money supply consisting of currency and demand deposits.

_____ 36. Bank accounts that pay interest and require advance notice before money can be withdrawn.

_____ 37. Process for evaluating proposed investments in select projects that provide the best long-term financial return.

_____ 38. Percentage of a bank's deposit that must be set aside.

_____ 39. Federal Reserve's power to set credit terms on various types of loans.

_____ 40. Money in a checking account that can be used by the customer at any time.

_____ 41. Dollars deposited in banks outside the United States.

_____ 42. Money paid to acquire something of permanent value in a business.

_____ 43. Borrowed funds used to cover long-term expenses (generally repaid over a period of more than one year).

WORD SCRAMBLE

1. _____   2. _____   3. _____
    cryrcuen   snodb   nyome

LEARNING OBJECTIVES--POTENTIAL SHORT ANSWER OR ESSAY QUESTIONS

Learning Objective #1: "Identify the responsibilities of a financial manager." (542)

Learning Objective #2: "Name the five main steps involved in the financial planning process." (542-543)

Learning Objective #3: "Cite three things financial managers must consider when selecting an appropriate funding vehicle." (545-549)

Learning Objective #4: "**List the three major types of short-term debt and the three major types of long-term debt.**" (549-551)

Learning Objective #5: "**Identify the main advantages and disadvantages of public equity financing.**" (552-553)

Learning Objective #6: "**Name the three functions and four characteristics of money.**" (553-554)

Learning Objective #7: "**Cite the four ways the Federal Reserve System influences the money supply.**" (558-559)

Learning Objective #8: "**Explain how the internet is influencing the U.S. banking and monetary systems.**" (566)

CRITICAL THINKING QUESTIONS

1. What is the potential problem with leveraging your company?

2. How can the Federal Reserve decrease the money?

BRAIN TEASER

1. How can an increase in the money supply stimulate the economy?

ANSWERS

True-False--*Answers*

1. True
2. True
3. False: *Capital budgeting* is the process for evaluating proposed investments in select projects that provide the best long-term financial return.
4. True
5. True
6. False: The three major types of *long*-term debt are loans, leases, and bonds.
7. False: The three major types of *short*-term debt are trade credit, loans, and commercial paper.
8. True
9. True
10. True
11. False: *Sometimes companies* get into trouble by taking on too much debt.
12. False: *Bonds* are certificates of indebtedness that are sold to raise long-term funds for a corporation *or government agency*
13. True
14. True
15. False: Selling your stock to the public *has* many disadvantages: *one of which is that ownership control is lost.*
16. True
17. False: *Credit* cards are plastic cards that allow the customer to buy now and pay back the loaned amount at a future date.
18. True
19. True
20. True
21. False: If the Fed buys U.S. government bonds, this will *increase* the money supply.
22. True

Multiple Choice--*Answers*

1. d	5. a	9. c	13. c
2. d	6. c	10. d	14. a
3. d	7. b	11. d	15. d
4. d	8. a	12. d	

Jeopardy—*Answers*

	Financial Management	**Money**	**The Federal Reserve**
$100	financial management	it must be generally acceptable as a medium of exchange, a measure of value, and a store of value	to control the money supply
$200	a financial plan	divisible, portable, durable, and secure (or difficult to counterfeit)	a reserve requirement
$300	trade credit, loans, and commercial paper	demand deposits	open market operations.
$400	loans, leases, and bonds	time deposits	selective credit controls

$500	equity financing	M1	decrease the discount rate, decrease reserve requirements, buy bonds on the open market, and loosen up on credit controls

Match the Terms and Concepts to their Definitions--*Answers*

1. k	7. qq	13. w	19. h	25. e	31. x	37. c	43. z
2. j	8. a	14. ii	20. ll	26. y	32. nn	38. hh	
3. g	9. m	15. i	21. u	27. o	33. ff	39. jj	
4. dd	10. q	16. gg	22. ee	28. bb	34. kk	40. n	
5. l	11. t	17. v	23. pp	29. p	35. aa	41. r	
6. b	12. cc	18. f	24. rr	30. s	36. oo	42. d	

Word Scramble--*Answers*

1. currency   2. bonds   3. money

Learning Objectives--Potential Short Answer or Essay Questions--*Answers*

Learning Objective #1:

The responsibilities of a financial manager include forecasting and planning for the future, developing a financial plan, managing the company's cash flow, coordinating and controlling the efficiency of operations, deciding on specific investments and how to finance them, raising capital to support growth, and interacting with banks and capital markets.

Learning Objective #2:

When developing a financial plan, the financial manager estimates the flow of money into and out of the business; determines whether cash flow is negative or positive and how to use or create excess funds; chooses which capital investments should be made; selects the best way to finance these investments; and compares actual results to projections to discover variances and take corrective action.

Learning Objective #3:

Finance managers must determine whether the financing is for the short term or the long term. They must analyze the advantages and disadvantages of internal versus external financing, and they must evaluate the merits of debt versus equity financing in light of their own needs.

Learning Objective #4:

The three major types of short-term debt are trade credit, loans, and commercial paper. The three major types of long-term debt are loans, leases, and bonds.

Learning Objective #5:

The main advantages are the increased financing, improved liquidity, voluntary dividend payments, and enhanced visibility; it also establishes a market value for the company. The main disadvantages are high costs, loss of ownership control, increased filing requirements, and increased public visibility.

Learning Objective #6:

Money functions as a medium of exchange, a measure of value, and a store of value. It must be divisible, portable, durable, and secure (or difficult to counterfeit).

Learning Objective #7:

The Fed regulates the money supply by changing reserve requirements, changing the discount rate, carrying out open-market operations, and setting selective credit controls.

Learning Objective #8:

The internet is a new channel of distribution that allows customers to shop for banking services anywhere in the world. It has made the banking environment highly competitive, redefined the types of services banks offer, and has made it more difficult for governments to regulate and control their money supply.

Critical Thinking Questions--*Answers*

1. It may burden your company with debt it might find impossible to repay.

2. The Fed could decrease the money supply by increasing the discount rate, increasing reserve requirements, selling government bonds, or tightening up on select credit controls.

Brain Teaser--*Answer*

1. An increase in the money supply will decrease interest rates which will stimulate borrowing and, therefore spending. An increase in spending means more sales. More sales will stimulate production which will increase employment and national income. A portion of the additional income earned will be spent, creating a further expansion in national employment, income and production (GDP). The Fed should increase the money supply to fight a recession (and decrease the money supply to fight inflation which is typically experienced during a rapidly expanding economy).

Chapter 19

Securities Markets

LEARNING OBJECTIVES

After studying this chapter, you should be able to:

1. Explain the differences between common stock, preferred stock, and bonds from an investor's perspective. (574-578)
2. Explain the safety and tax advantages of investing in U.S. government securities. (578)
3. Name five criteria to be considered when making investment decisions. (581-584)
4. Explain what mutual funds are, and describe their main benefits. (583-584)
5. Describe the two types of security marketplaces and the challenges they are facing. (584-590)
6. Explain how the internet is redefining the investment industry. (590)
7. Identify the two major broad market indexes, and explain their differences. (590-597)
8. Explain how government regulation of securities trading tries to protect investors. (597-599)

TRUE-FALSE

Indicate whether the statement is generally true or false by placing a "T" or "F" in the space provided. If it is a false statement, correct it so that it becomes a true statement.

_____ 1. Bonds are ownership shares investors buy in a corporation.

_____ 2. Preferred stockholders can vote and share in the company's profits and losses through dividends and capital gains or losses, whereas common stockholders get a fixed claim on assets after creditors.

_____ 3. Bondholders get a fixed return and do not vote or share in profits or losses.

_____ 4. U.S. government securities, including those backed by the U.S. Treasury and those backed by agencies of the government, are relatively safe because the government and its agencies are unlikely to default on interest payments.

_____ 5. Investors should consider the income, growth, safety, liquidity, and tax consequences of alternative investments.

_____ 6. Bonds that can be exchanged at the owner's discretion into common stock of the issuing company are called secured bonds.

_____ 7. U.S. Treasury bonds are federal government debt securities that mature within 1 to 10 years.

_____   8. Municipal bonds are debt issued by a state or local government agency, and the interest earned is exempt from federal income tax and from taxes in the issuing jurisdiction.

_____   9. A stock option is a legally binding agreement to buy or sell a financial instrument at a future date.

_____   10. Two types of investors buy and sell marketable securities (investments that can be easily be converted into cash): institutions and individuals.

_____   11. There is a tradeoff between the risk, liquidity, and yield associated with a financial instrument.

_____   12. Mutual funds are pools of money drawn from many investors to buy diversified portfolios of stocks, bonds, and other marketable securities.

_____   13. A primary market is a market where subsequent owners trade previously issued shares of stocks and bonds.

_____   14. Auction exchanges are decentralized marketplaces in which dealers are connected electronically.

_____   15. The over-the-counter (OTC) market is a network of dealers who trade securities that are not listed on an exchange.

_____   16. The Dow Jones Industrial Average tracks the prices of 30 blue-chip stocks and is a barometer, not a predictor of performance.

_____   17. The Standard and Poor's 500 includes the prices of stocks in 500 large and small companies, which are selected to represent the performance of all U.S. corporations.

_____   18. A bull market is a falling stock market.

_____   19. A price-earnings ratio (p/e ratio) is a stock's current market price divided by the issuer's annual earnings per share; also known as the price-earnings multiple.

_____   20. Even though almost every state has its own laws governing securities trading, the federal government has the leading role in investment regulation.

MULTIPLE CHOICE
Circle the one best answer for each of the following questions.

1. Shares of ownership in a company that give their owners first claim on a company's dividends and assets after paying all debts are
   a. common stock.
   b. preferred stock.
   c. a corporate bond.
   d. a convertible bond.

2. Which of the following statements is true?
   a. The par value of a stock is an arbitrary value assigned to the stock that is shown on the stock certificate.
   b. Bonds imply ownership, whereas stocks do not.
   c. A mortgage bond is a corporate bond backed only by the reputation of the company.
   d. Junk bonds are bonds that guarantee a fixed rate of return.

3. Which of the following statements is true?
   a. As ratings decline, investors take on more risk, so interest rates on those investments decline.
   b. Capital gains is an account into which a company makes annual payments for use in redeeming its bonds in the future.
   c. Standard & Poor's Corporation and Moody's Investors Service are the two primary companies that rate the safety of corporate bonds.
   d. Debentures are corporate bonds that can be exchanged at the owner's discretion into common stock of the issuing company.

4. Short-term debt issued by the federal government are
   a. Treasury notes
   b. Treasury bills.
   c. Treasury bonds.
   d. municipal bonds.

5. General obligation bonds are
   a. municipal bonds backed by the issuing agency's general taxing authority.
   b. municipal bonds backed by revenue generated from the projects financed with the bonds.
   c. not tax-exempt from federal taxes.
   d. issued only by states; they are not issued by county or city governments.

6. Which of the following statements is true?
   a. A stock option is a contract allowing the holder to buy or sell a given number of shares or a particular stock at a given price by a certain date.
   b. To hedge is to make an investment that protects the investor from suffering loss on another investment.
   c. Financial futures are legally binding agreements to buy or sell financial instruments at a future date.
   d. All of the above are true.

7. Which of the following statements is *false*?
   a. Stock options and financial futures contracts are derivative investments, which means their price at any given time is derived from or linked to the performance of an underlying asset (like a stock), the performance of a financial market, or current interest rates.

   b. Derivatives have become increasingly popular in recent years as corporations look for new and better ways to manage financial and operating risks.

   c. Government bonds and U.S. Treasury bills have returned far more over time than stocks.

   d. All options fall into two broad categories: puts and calls.

8. Which of the following is statements is true?

   a. Yield is the income received from securities, calculated by dividing dividend or interest income by market price.

   b. Blue-chip stocks are equities issued by large, well-known established companies with consistent records of stock price increases and dividend payments.

   c. Growth stocks are equities issued by small companies with unproven products or services.

   d. All of the above are true.

9. Which of the following statements is true?

   a. Money market funds are mutual funds that invest in the stock market.

   b. Diversification is assembling investment portfolios in such a way that a loss in one investment won't cripple the value of the entire portfolio.

   c. The secondary market is the market where newly issued securities are traded.

   d. All of the above are true.

10. Which of the following statements is true?

   a. A broker is an individual registered to sell securities.

   b. Margin trading is borrowing money from brokers to buy stock, paying interest on the borrowed money, and leaving the stock with the broker as collateral.

   c. Discount brokerages are financial services companies that sell securities but give no advice.

   d. All of the above are true.

11. The internet:

   a. allows investors to get an abundance of securities information that was previously available only to brokers.

   b. is changing the function of brokers and in many cases restructuring the business in that it is paving the way for a virtual stock exchange in the future where brokers and exchanges will not be needed.

   c. has spurred the growth of on-line brokers and lowered the commission costs to investors.

   d. does all of the above.

12. Which of the following statements is true?

   a. Market indexes are measures of security markets calculated from the prices of a selection of securities.

   b. A bull market is a falling stock market.

   c. Virtually all institutional investors compare their performance with the DOW, and not the Standard & Poor's 500 Stock Average (S&P 500).

   d. All of the above are true.

13. Government regulation tries to protect investors by

   a. reducing fraud when it requires companies to file periodic information reports so that investors receive accurate information.

   b. trying to monitor insider trading.

   c. policing fraudulent manipulation of securities.

   d. doing all of the above.

JEOPARDY

You have 5 seconds to complete the question to each of the following answers.

	Investors and Their Choices	Security Marketplaces	Analysis of the Financial News
$100	Shares whose owners have voting rights and have the last claim on distributed profits and assets. (575) What is_____ _____?	Individual registered to sell securities. (587) What is_____ _____?	A rising stock market is characterized by this term. (591) What is_____ _____?
$200	Corporate bonds backed only by the reputation of the issuer. (576) What is_____ _____?	Market where subsequent owners trade previously issued shares of stocks and bonds. (585) What is_____ _____?	Measures of security markets calculated from the prices of a selection of securities. (591) What is_____ _____?
$300	Debt securities issued by the federal government that mature in 10 to 30 years. (578) What is_____ _____?	Decentralized marketplaces where securities are bought and sold by dealers out of their own inventories. (585) What is_____ _____?	The most widely used indicator of stock prices. (591-595) What is_____ _____?
$400	Legally binding agreements to buy or sell financial instruments at a future date. (579) What is_____ _____?	Automated securities transactions using computer programs to buy or sell large numbers of securities in response to price changes exceeding predetermined amounts. (585) What is_____ _____?	The most widely used index of market performance by institutional investors. (595) What is_____ _____?
$500	The five criteria to be considered when making investment decisions. (581-584) What is_____ _____?	Financial-service companies with a full range of services, including investment advice, securities research, and investment products. (589) What is_____ _____?	A stock's current market price divided by the issuer's annual earnings per share. (597) What is_____ _____?

MATCH THE TERMS AND CONCEPTS TO THEIR DEFINITIONS

a. arbitrage (585)
b. asset allocation (583)
c. auction exchange (585)
d. authorized stock (574)
e. bear market (591)
f. blue-chip stocks (582)
g. broker (587)
h. bull market (591)

x. institutional investors (581)
y. investment portfolios (583)
z. issued stock (574)
aa. junk bonds (577)
bb. limit order (587)
cc. margin trading (587)
dd. market indexes (591)
ee. market makers (585)

rr. primary market (585)
ss. principal (576)
tt. program trading (585)
uu. rate of return (583)
vv. revenue bonds (578)
xx. secondary market (585)
yy. secured bonds (576)
zz. short selling (588)

i.   capital gains (578)
j.   commodities (580)
k.   common stock (575)
l.   convertible bonds (576)
m.   dealer exchanges (585)
n.   debentures (576)
o.   denomination (576)
p.   discount brokerages (589)
q.   discretionary order (587)
r.   diversification (583)
s.   financial futures (579)
t.   full-service brokerages (589)
u.   general obligation bonds (578)
v.   growth stocks (581)
w.   hedge (579)

ff. market order (587)
gg. money-market funds (583)
hh. mortgage bonds (576)
ii. municipal bonds (578)
jj. mutual funds (583)
kk. NASDAQ (National Association of Securities Dealers Automated Quotations) (587)
ll. open order (587)
nn. over-the-counter (OTC) market (586)
oo. par value (574)
pp. preferred stock (574)
qq. price-earnings ratio (p/e ratio) (597)

a1. sinking fund (578)
a2. speculators (582)
a3. stock exchanges (585)
a4. stock option (579)
a5. stock specialist (585)
a6. stock split (576)
a7. transaction costs (589)
a8. Treasury bills (578)
a9. Treasury bonds (578)
b1. Treasury notes (578)
b2. unissued stock (574)
b3. U.S. savings bonds (578)
b4. yield (581)

_____ 1. Assortment of investment instruments.

_____ 2. Corporate bonds that can be exchanged at the owner's discretion into common stock of the issuing company.

_____ 3. Market where subsequent owners trade previously issued shares of stocks and bonds.

_____ 4. Account into which a company makes annual payments for use in redeeming its bonds in the future.

_____ 5. Individual registered to sell securities.

_____ 6. Arbitrary value assigned to a stock that is shown on the stock certificate.

_____ 7. Contract allowing the holder to buy or sell a given number of shares of a particular stock at a given price by a certain date.

_____ 8. Bonds that pay high interest because they are below investment grade.

_____ 9. Debt instruments sold by the federal government in small denominations.

_____ 10. Location where traders buy and sell stocks and bonds.

_____ 11. To make an investment that protects the investor from suffering loss on another investment.

_____ 12. Difference between the price at which a financial asset is sold and its original cost (assuming the price has gone up).

_____ 13. Equities issued by large, well-established companies with consistent records of stock price increases and dividend payments.

_____ 14. Percentage increase in the value of an investment.

_____ 15. Shares that a corporation's board of directors has decided to sell eventually.

_____ 16. Assembling investment portfolios in such a way that a loss in one investment won't cripple the value of the entire portfolio.

_____ 17. Amount of a debt, excluding any interest.

_____ 18. Stock's current market price divided by issuer's annual earnings per share; also known as the price-earnings multiple.

_____ 19. Authorization for a broker to buy or sell securities at the best price that can be negotiated at the moment.

_____ 20. Short-term debt issued by the federal-government; also referred to as *T-bills*.

_____ 21. Investors who purchase securities in anticipation of making large profits quickly.

_____ 22. Authorized shares that have been released to the market.

_____ 23. Legally binding agreements to buy or sell financial instruments at a future date.

_____ 24. Debt issued by a state or a local agency; interest earned on municipal bonds is exempt from federal income tax and from taxes in the issuing jurisdiction.

_____ 25. Municipal bonds backed by revenue generated from the projects financed with the bonds.

_____ 26. Centralized marketplace where securities are traded by specialists on behalf of investors.

_____ 27. Market order that stipulates the highest or lowest price at which the customer is willing to trade securities.

_____ 28. Method of shifting investments within a portfolio to adapt them to the current investment environment.

_____ 29. Debt securities issued by the federal government that mature within 1 to 10 years.

_____ 30. Market order that allows the broker to decide when to trade a security.

_____ 31. Authorized shares that are to be released in the future.

_____ 32. National over-the-counter securities trading network.

_____ 33. Raw materials used in producing other goods.

_____ 34. Intermediary who trades in a particular security on the floor of an auction exchange; "buyer of last resort."

_____ 35. Bonds backed by specific assets.

_____ 36. Limit order that does not expire at the end of a trading day.

_____ 37. Pools of money raised by investment companies and invested in stocks, bonds, or other marketable securities.

_____ 38. Municipal bonds backed by the issuing agency's general taxing authority.

_____ 39. Companies that invest money entrusted to them by others.

_____ 40. Financial-services companies with a full-range of services, including investment advice, securities research, and investment products.

_____ 41. Shares that give their owners first claim on a company's dividends and assets after paying all debts.

_____ 42. Measures of security markets calculated from the prices of a selection of securities.

_____ 43. Network of dealers who trade securities that are not listed on an exchange.

_____ 44. Decentralized marketplaces where securities are bought and sold by dealers out of their own inventories.

_____ 45. Debt securities issued by the federal government that mature in 10 to 30 years.

_____ 46. Selling stock borrowed from a broker with the intention of buying it back later at a lower price, repaying the broker, and pocketing the profit.

_____ 47. Corporate bonds backed only by the reputation of the issuer.

_____ 48. Face value of a single bond.

_____ 49. Mutual funds that invest in short-term securities.

_____ 50. Income received from securities, calculated by dividing a dividend or interest income by market price.

_____ 51. Dealers in dealer exchanges who sell securities out of their own inventories so that a market is always available for buyers and sellers.

_____ 52. Borrowing money from brokers to buy stock, paying interest on the borrowed money, and leaving the stock with the broker as collateral.

_____ 53. Shares whose owners have voting rights and have the last claim on distributed profits and assets.

_____ 54. Falling stock market.

_____ 55. Corporate bonds backed by real property.

_____ 56. Simultaneous purchase in one market and sale in a different market with a profitable price or yield differential.

_____ 57. Financial-services companies that sell securities but give no advice.

_____ 58. Market where firms sell new securities issued publicly for the first time.

_____ 59. Equities issued by small companies with unproven products or services.

_____ 60. Increase in the number of shares of ownership that each stock certificate represents.

_____ 61. Costs of trading securities, including broker's commission and taxes.

_____ 62. Rising stock market.

_____ 63. Automated securities transactions using computer programs to buy or sell large numbers of securities in response to price changes exceeding predetermined amounts.

WORD SCRAMBLE

1. _____   2. _____   3. _____ _____
   afiictiondivers   deghe   mocmon   kotsc

LEARNING OBJECTIVES--POTENTIAL SHORT ANSWER OR ESSAY QUESTIONS

Learning Objective #1: **"Explain the differences between common stock, preferred stock, and bonds from an investor's perspective."** (574-578)

Learning Objective #2: **"Explain the safety and tax advantages of investing in U.S. government securities."** (578)

Learning Objective #3: "Name five criteria to be considered when making investment decisions." (581-584)

Learning Objective #4: "Explain what mutual funds are, and describe their main benefits." (583-584)

Learning Objective #5: "Describe the two types of security marketplaces and the challenges they are facing." (584-590)

Learning Objective #6: "Explain how the internet is redefining the investment industry." (590)

Learning Objective #7: **"Identify the two major broad market indexes, and explain their differences."** (590-597)

Learning Objective #8: **"Explain how government regulation of securities trading tries to protect investors."** (597-599)

CRITICAL THINKING QUESTIONS

1. What is the tradeoff for investors between the yield, risk, and liquidity?

2. Why might it be better for an investor to buy stock in a company that does not pay dividends as opposed to a company that does pay dividends?

BRAIN TEASER

1. What is the relationship between a bond's price and its yield?

ANSWERS

True-False--*Answers*
1. False: *Stocks* are ownership shares investors buy in a corporation.
2. False: *Common* stockholders can vote and share in the company's profits and losses through dividends and capital gains or losses, whereas *preferred* stockholders get a fixed claim on assets after creditors.
3. True
4. True
5. True
6. False: Bonds that can be exchanged at the owner's discretion into common stock of the issuing company are called *convertible* bonds.
7. False: U.S. Treasury *notes* are federal government debt securities that mature within 1 to 10 years.
8. True
9. False: A *financial future* is a legally binding agreement to buy or sell a financial instrument at a future date.
10. True
11. True
12. True
13. False: A *secondary* market is a market where subsequent owners trade previously issued shares of stocks and bonds.
14. False: *Dealer* exchanges are decentralized marketplaces in which dealers are connected electronically.
15. True
16. True
17. True
18. False: A *bear* market is a falling stock market.
19. True
20. True

Multiple Choice--*Answers*

1. b	5. a	9. b	13. d
2. a	6. d	10. d	
3. c	7. c	11. d	
4. b	8. d	12. a	

Jeopardy—*Answers*

	Investors and Their Choices	**Security Marketplaces**	**Analysis of the Financial News**
$100	common stock	a broker	a bull market
$200	debentures	a secondary market	market indexes
$300	Treasury bonds	dealer exchanges	the Dow Jones Industrial Average
$400	financial futures	program trading	the Standard & Poor's 500 Stock Average (S&P 500)
$500	the income, growth, safety, liquidity, and tax consequences	full-service brokerages	the price-earnings ratio (p/e ratio)

Match the Terms and Concepts to Their Definitions--*Answers*

1. y	9. b3	17. ss	25. vv	33. j	41. pp	49. gg	57. p
2. l	10. a3	18. qq	26. c	34. a5	42. dd	50. b4	58. rr
3. xx	11. w	19. ff	27. bb	35. yy	43. nn	51. ee	59. v
4. al	12. i	20. a8	28. b	36. ll	44. m	52. cc	60. a6
5. g	13. f	21. a2	29. b1	37. jj	45. a9	53. k	61. a7
6. oo	14. uu	22. z	30. q	38. u	46. zz	54. e	62. h
7. a4	15. d	23. s	31. b2	39. x	47. n	55. hh	63. tt
8. aa	16. r	24. ii	32. kk	40. t	48. o	56. a	

Word Scramble---*Answers*

1. diversification   2. hedge   3. common stock

Learning Objectives--Potential Short Answer or Essay Questions--*Answers*

Learning Objective #1:
    Stocks are ownership shares investors buy in a corporation. Bonds are loans investors make to corporations and governments. Common stockholders can vote and share in the company's profits and losses through dividends and capital gains or losses whereas preferred shareholders get a fixed return on their investment and a priority claim on assets after creditors. Bondholders get a fixed a return. They do not vote or share in profits or losses.

Learning Objective #2:
    U.S. government securities, including those backed by the U.S. Treasury and those backed by agencies of the government, are relatively safe because the government and its agencies are unlikely to default on interest payments. Interest from Treasury notes and Treasury bonds is exempt from state and local income taxes.

Learning Objective #3:

Investors should consider the income, growth, safety, liquidity, and tax consequences of alternative investments.

Learning Objective #4:

Mutual funds are pools of money drawn from many investors to buy diversified portfolios of stocks, bonds, and other marketable securities. The primary benefit is that investors gain greater diversification from buying a share in a mutual fund than from investing the same money in the stock of one company.

Learning Objective #5:

Auction exchanges funnel all buy and sell orders into one centralized location. This process is rapidly becoming antiquated, and specialists are finding it difficult to serve as "buyers of last resort" --especially with higher volume trades. Dealer exchanges are decentralized marketplaces in which dealers are connected electronically. They are under attack from investors who no longer want to pay the spread--the fees dealers earn on the trade.

Learning Objective #6:

The internet allows investors to get an abundance of securities information that was previously available only to brokers. As a result, it is changing the function of brokers and, in many cases, restructuring their business. It has spurred the growth of online brokers and lowered the commission costs to investors. And some think it is paving the way for a virtual stock exchange in the future where brokers and exchanges will not be needed.

Learning Objective #7:

The Dow Jones Industrial Average tracks the prices of 30 blue-chip stocks. It is a barometer, not a predictor of performance. It gives more weight to higher priced shares. The Standard & Poor's 500 includes the prices of stocks in 500 large and small companies, which are selected to represent the performance of all U.S. corporations. The index is weighted by market value, giving bigger companies more weight in the formula.

Learning Objective #8:

It tries to prevent fraud in the securities markets by requiring companies to file registration papers, fulfill certain requirements, and file periodic information reports so that investors receive accurate information. Regulations also try to monitor the use of insider information and police fraudulent manipulation of securities.

Critical Thinking Questions--*Answers*

1. Typically, the greater the liquidity (the ability to turn into cash), the lower the risk and the lower the yield (rate of return measured as a percentage). Likewise, the less liquid an investment, the riskier it is and the greater the yield. Note that the riskier an investment becomes, the greater the yield must be to compensate an investor for their risk incurred.

2. If you buy stock in a company that does not pay dividends, then that company will have more undistributed profits to re-invest in the company. That investment in new plant and equipment will likely enhance the company's competitive position. If the company is more competitive, then its profits will likely rise. As the profits rise, the company's stock prices will rise. It is very possible that, as an investor, the higher price for your stock (realizing a capital gain) could be greater than any dividends which could have been earned.

Brain Teaser--*Answer*

1. There is an inverse relationship between a bond's price and its yield. That is, whatever happens to the price of the bond, its yield will do the opposite. Suppose a $1,000 bond pays an interest rate of 10% or $100 annually. If you paid $1,000 for the bond, the yield would be 10% ($100/$1,000). Now, suppose the market price increases to $1,100 (possibly because the current market interest rate went down and the 10% guaranteed annual payment associated with this bond now looks very attractive). You sell the bond to someone else. This person will now realize that the yield has gone down to 9.09% ($100/$1,100). As the price of a bond goes up, its yield goes down, and vice versa.

Component Chapter A

Government Regulation, Taxation, and Business Law

TRUE-FALSE

Indicate whether the statement is generally true or false by placing a "T" or "F" in the space provided. If it is a false statement, correct it so that it becomes a true statement.

_____ 1. Although the United States is philosophically committed to the free-enterprise system, and even though its economy is shaped primarily by market force, the government has often stepped in to solve specific problems.

_____ 2. Although it often seems that business and government are adversaries, the opposite is true.

_____ 3. By setting ground rules and establishing basic standards of proper business behavior, government helps prevent conflicts and facilitates the workings of the economic system.

_____ 4. The Clayton Act restricted interlocking directorates.

_____ 5. Tying contracts attempt to force buyers to purchase unwanted goods along with goods actually desired.

_____ 6. Government regulations do not impact very many industries.

_____ 7. Businesses universally dislike regulation.

_____ 8. A tax credit is a reduction in the amount of income on which tax must be paid.

_____ 9. One of the most pervasive ways in which government affects business is through the legal system.

_____ 10. A tort is a noncriminal act that results in injury to a person or to property.

_____ 11. A punitive damage award is designed to punish the wrongdoer.

_____   12. A breach of contract exists when one party to the contract fails to live up to the terms.

_____   13. Property is actually the relationship between the person having the rights to any tangible or intangible object and all other persons.

_____   14. A patent protects the invention or discovery of a new and useful process, an article of manufacture, a machine, a chemical substance, or an improvement on any of these.

_____   15. Trademarks protect the creators of literary, dramatic, musical, artistic, scientific, and other intellectual property.

MULTIPLE CHOICE
Circle the one best answer for each of the following questions.

1. Government support for business takes the form of
    a.   promoting economic growth and foreign trade.
    b.   supporting and subsidizing business.
    c.   maintaining the infrastructure and buying industry's products.
    d.   all of the above.

2. Which of the following are examples of legislation designed to promote competition?
    a.   The Sherman Antitrust Act.
    b.   The Clayton Act.
    c.   The Federal Trade Commission Act
    d.   All of the above are.

3. Which of the following created a watchdog group to monitor activities that might be unfair?
    a.   The Sherman Antitrust Act.
    b.   The Clayton Act.
    c.   The Federal Trade Commission Act.
    d.   All of the above did.

4. Government acts as
    a.   watchdog.
    b.   regulator.
    c.   tax collector.
    d.   all of the above.

5. Business tries to influence government through
    a.   lobbying.
    b.   political action committees.
    c.   both of the above.
    d.   none of the above.

6. Law written by legislative bodies is
    a.   administrative law.
    b.   statutory law.
    c.   a consent order.
    d.   business law.

7. Which of the following statements is true?
    a.   Common law is the type of law that comes out of courtrooms and judges' decisions.
    b.   A consent order does allow companies to promise to stop doing something without actually admitting to any illegal behavior.
    c.   Business law includes those elements of law that directly affect business activities.
    d.   All of the above are true.

8. Strict product liability is possible if it has been established that
    a.   the company is in the business of selling the product and the product reached the consumer or user without change in its condition.
    b.   the product was defective.
    c.   the defective product was unreasonably dangerous and it caused injury.
    d.   all of the above apply.

9. In a breach of contract situation the afflicted party can
    a.   be discharged from the contract.
    b.   sue in court.
    c.   force the other party to live up to the contract if money damages would not be adequate.
    d.   do all of the above.

10. Which of the following statements is true?
    a.   A deed is a legal document by which an owner transfers to a new owner the title, or rights of ownership, to real property.
    b.   Bankruptcy is the legal means of relief for debtors who are no longer able to meet their financial obligations.
    c.   A negotiable instrument is a transferable document that represents a promise to pay a specified amount.
    d.   All of the above are true.

ANSWERS

True-False--*Answers*

1. True
2. True
3. True
4. False: The *Sherman Antitrust Act* restricted interlocking directorates.
5. True
6. False: Government regulations *affects almost every aspect of every industry.*
7. False: Businesses *do not* universally dislike regulation.
8. False: A tax *deduction* is a reduction in the amount of income on which tax must be paid.
9. True
10. True
11. True
12. True
13. True
14. True
15. False: *Copyrights* protect the creators of literary, dramatic, musical, artisitic, scientific, and other intellectual property.

Multiple Choice--*Answers*

1. d	5. c	9. d
2. d	6. b	10. d
3. c	7. d	
4. d	8. d	

Component Chapter B

Risk Management and Insurance

TRUE-FALSE
Indicate whether the statement is generally true or false by placing a "T" or "F" in the space provided. If it is a false statement, correct it so that it becomes a true statement.

_____ 1. Insurance is a contractual arrangement whereby one party agrees to compensate another party for losses.

_____ 2. The process of reducing the threat of loss from uncontrollable events and funding potential losses is called risk management.

_____ 3. Once you have assessed your potential risk, the next step is to try to control it.

_____ 4. Actuaries review the insurance applications and either accept them at an appropriate rate or reject them.

_____ 5. Not all private insurance companies are regulated by state law.

_____ 6. A fidelity bond attempts to address the possibility of dishonest people outside the company.

_____ 7. A surety bond is a three-party contract where the surety (insurance company) is required to pay a second party (the obligee) if a third party (the principal) fails to fulfill an obligation to the obligee.

_____ 8. Liability losses are financial losses suffered by firms or individuals held responsible for property damage or injuries suffered by others.

_____ 9. Disability income insurance pays the medical bills of employees who are hurt or become ill as a result of their work.

_____ 10. One way companies have tried to contain the high cost of health insurance is to join health maintenance organizations.

_____ 11. Term life insurance provides a combination of insurance and savings.

MULTIPLE CHOICE

Circle the one best answer for each of the following questions.

1. The threat of loss without the possibility of gain is
   a. speculative risk.
   b. pure risk.
   c. insurable risk.
   d. uninsurable risk.

2. Which of the following statements is true?
   a. By purchasing insurance, companies contractually transfer the risk of loss to an insurance firm.
   b. An insurable risk is one that an insurance company will not cover.
   c. The only requirement for a risk to be insurable is if someone is willing to pay for the insurance.
   d. All of the above are true.

3. Which of the following statements is true?
   a. A stock insurance company is similar to all other profit-making corporations; they try to make a profit.
   b. A mutual insurance company is a nonprofit cooperative.
   c. Self insurance is becoming an increasingly popular method of insuring against risk.
   d. All of the above are true.

4. The different types of business insurance include all but the following:
   a. Loss of property.
   b. Loss due to dishonesty.
   c. Loss due to a lack of profits.
   d. Loss due to nonperformance.

5. Which of the following are types of liability insurance?
   a. Commercial general liability
   b. Product liability
   c. Automobile liability
   d. All of the above are.

6. Which of the following is a type of employee insurance?
   a. Health insurance
   b. Worker's compensation
   c. Life insurance
   d. All of the above are.

7. Insurance which replaces income not earned because of illness or accident is called
   a. disability insurance.
   b. long-term care insurance.
   c. no-fault insurance.
   d. managed care insurance.

8. Life insurance which covers a person for a specified period of time is called
   a. whole life insurance.
   b. term life insurance.
   c. universal life insurance.
   d. all of the above.

ANSWERS

True-False--*Answers*

1. True
2. True
3. True
4. False: *Underwriters* review the insurance applications and either accept them at an appropriate rate or reject them.
5. False: *All* private insurance companies are regulated by state law.
6. True
7. True
8. True
9. False: *Worker's compensation* insurance pays the medical bills of employees who are hurt or become ill as a result of their work.
10. True
11. False: *Whole* life insurance provides a combination of insurance and savings.

Multiple Choice--*Answers*

1. b   5. d
2. a   6. d
3. d   7. a
4. c   8. b

Component Chapter C
The Internet and Business Success

TRUE-FALSE
Indicate whether the statement is generally true or false by placing a "T" or "F" in the space provided. If it is a false statement, correct it so that it becomes a true statement.

_____ 1. Hypertext are words or phrases that are colored or underlined and that enable you with a click of your mouse to jump to another document within the World Wide Web.

_____ 2. Downloading is transferring data from your computer to the internet.

_____ 3. Telnet is a class of internet application program that allows you to connect with a remote host computer even though your computer is not a permanent part of the network that the host supports.

_____ 4. The intranet uses the same technologies as the internet and the World Wide Web, but the information provided and the access allowed are restricted to the boundaries of a company-wide computer network.

_____ 5. A firewall is a special type of gateway that controls access to the company's network.

_____ 6. The telephone line-modem combinations are much faster at transmitting information than the coaxial cable, fiber optic systems.

_____ 7. One can get hooked up to the internet either through an internet service provider or through an online service.

_____ 8. A uniform resource locator will enable you to access a site on the Web by simply typing in the address.

MULTIPLE CHOICE

Circle the one best answer for each of the following questions.

1. People can communicate on the internet by
    a. sending e-mail.
    b. a telnet
    c. internet telephony
    d. all of the above.

2. Which of the following statements is true?
    a. One of the most common uses of the internet is to search for information.
    b. Usenet groups are the same as mailing lists.
    c. Telnets are no longer in use.
    d. All of the above are true.

3. The Internet allows one to:
    a. transfer files between computers.
    b. participate in discussion groups.
    c. search for information.
    d. do all of the above.

4. Businesses use the internet to
    a. communicate and to collaborate.
    b. market their products.
    c. to participate in the global economy
    d. do all of the above.

5. Business use their intranets to
    a. place their policy manuals for everyone to read.
    b. publish employee benefits information and job openings.
    c. present marketing information and record-keeping information.
    d. do all of the above.

6. Which of the following statements is true?
    a. Gopher is a text-based internet-browsing program that allows you to locate information through a huge menu tree from which you select items as you narrow down to a specific topic.
    b. For searchers, well-known, commercially backed search engines mean more dependable results.
    c. Computerized search mechanisms are based on Boolean logic, which uses the priamry operators AND, OR, and NOT.
    d. All of the above are true.

ANSWERS

True-False--*Answers*

1. True
2. False: Downloading is transferring data from *the internet* to *your computer.*
3. True
4. True
5. True
6. False: The telephone line-modem combinations are much *slower* at transmitting information than the coaxial cable, fiber optic systems.
7. True
8. True

Multiple Choice--*Answers*

1. d   5. d
2. a   6. d
3. d
4. d